Llewellyn's 2021

Sabbats
ALMANAC

Samhain 2020
to
Mabon 2021

Llewellyn's Sabbats Almanac
Samhain 2020 to Mabon 2021

Cover art © Carolyn Vibbert
Cover design by Shira Atakpu
Editing by Hanna Grimson
Interior Art: © Carolyn Vibbert, excluding illustrations on pages 38, 75, 111, 114, 150, 183, 221, 256, 294, which are © Wen Hsu

You can order annuals and books from *New Worlds*, Llewellyn's catalog. To request a free copy, call 1-877-NEW WRLD toll-free or order online by visiting our website at http://subscriptions.llewellyn.com.

ISBN: 978-0-7387-5485-7

Llewellyn Worldwide Ltd.
2143 Wooddale Drive
Woodbury, MN 55125-2989
www.llewellyn.com

Printed in the United States of America

2020

JANUARY
S	M	T	W	T	F	S
			1	2	3	4
5	6	7	8	9	10	11
12	13	14	15	16	17	18
19	20	21	22	23	24	25
26	27	28	29	30	31	

FEBRUARY
S	M	T	W	T	F	S
						1
2	3	4	5	6	7	8
9	10	11	12	13	14	
15	16	17	18	19	20	21
22	23	24	25	26	27	28
29						

MARCH
S	M	T	W	T	F	S
1	2	3	4	5	6	7
8	9	10	11	12	13	14
15	16	17	18	19	20	21
22	23	24	25	26	27	28
29	30	31				

APRIL
S	M	T	W	T	F	S
			1	2	3	4
5	6	7	8	9	10	11
12	13	14	15	16	17	18
19	20	21	22	23	24	25
26	27	28	29	30		

MAY
S	M	T	W	T	F	S
					1	2
3	4	5	6	7	8	9
10	11	12	13	14	15	16
17	18	19	20	21	22	23
24	25	26	27	28	29	30
31						

JUNE
S	M	T	W	T	F	S
	1	2	3	4	5	6
7	8	9	10	11	12	13
14	15	16	17	18	19	20
21	22	23	24	25	26	27
28	29	30				

JULY
S	M	T	W	T	F	S
			1	2	3	4
5	6	7	8	9	10	11
12	13	14	15	16	17	18
19	20	21	22	23	24	25
26	27	28	29	30	31	

AUGUST
S	M	T	W	T	F	S
						1
2	3	4	5	6	7	8
9	10	11	12	13	14	15
16	17	18	19	20	21	22
23	24	25	26	27	28	29
30	31					

SEPTEMBER
S	M	T	W	T	F	S
		1	2	3	4	5
6	7	8	9	10	11	12
13	14	15	16	17	18	19
20	21	22	23	24	25	26
27	28	29	30			

OCTOBER
S	M	T	W	T	F	S
				1	2	3
4	5	6	7	8	9	10
11	12	13	14	15	16	17
18	19	20	21	22	23	24
25	26	27	28	29	30	
31						

NOVEMBER
S	M	T	W	T	F	S
1	2	3	4	5	6	7
8	9	10	11	12	13	14
15	16	17	18	19	20	21
22	23	24	25	26	27	28
29	30					

DECEMBER
S	M	T	W	T	F	S
		1	2	3	4	5
6	7	8	9	10	11	12
13	14	15	16	17	18	19
20	21	22	23	24	25	26
27	28	29	30	31		

2021

JANUARY
S	M	T	W	T	F	S
					1	2
3	4	5	6	7	8	9
10	11	12	13	14	15	16
17	18	19	20	21	22	23
24	25	26	27	28	29	30
31						

FEBRUARY
S	M	T	W	T	F	S
	1	2	3	4	5	6
7	8	9	10	11	12	13
14	15	16	17	18	19	20
21	22	23	24	25	26	27
28						

MARCH
S	M	T	W	T	F	S
	1	2	3	4	5	6
7	8	9	10	11	12	13
14	15	16	17	18	19	20
21	22	23	24	25	26	27
28	29	30	31			

APRIL
S	M	T	W	T	F	S
				1	2	3
4	5	6	7	8	9	10
11	12	13	14	15	16	17
18	19	20	21	22	23	24
25	26	27	28	29	30	

MAY
S	M	T	W	T	F	S
						1
2	3	4	5	6	7	8
9	10	11	12	13	14	15
16	17	18	19	20	21	22
23	24	25	26	27	28	29
30	31					

JUNE
S	M	T	W	T	F	S
		1	2	3	4	5
6	7	8	9	10	11	12
13	14	15	16	17	18	19
20	21	22	23	24	25	26
27	28	29	30			

JULY
S	M	T	W	T	F	S
				1	2	3
4	5	6	7	8	9	10
11	12	13	14	15	16	17
18	19	20	21	22	23	24
25	26	27	28	29	30	31

AUGUST
S	M	T	W	T	F	S
1	2	3	4	5	6	7
8	9	10	11	12	13	14
15	16	17	18	19	20	21
22	23	24	25	26	27	28
29	30	31				

SEPTEMBER
S	M	T	W	T	F	S
			1	2	3	4
5	6	7	8	9	10	11
12	13	14	15	16	17	18
19	20	21	22	23	24	25
26	27	28	29	30		

OCTOBER
S	M	T	W	T	F	S
					1	2
3	4	5	6	7	8	9
10	11	12	13	14	15	16
17	18	19	20	21	22	23
24	25	26	27	28	29	30
31						

NOVEMBER
S	M	T	W	T	F	S
	1	2	3	4	5	6
7	8	9	10	11	12	13
14	15	16	17	18	19	20
21	22	23	24	25	26	27
28	29	30				

DECEMBER
S	M	T	W	T	F	S
			1	2	3	4
5	6	7	8	9	10	11
12	13	14	15	16	17	18
19	20	21	22	23	24	25
26	27	28	29	30	31	

Contents

Lammas

Mabon

Introduction

NEARLY EVERYONE HAS A favorite sabbat. There are numerous ways to observe any tradition. This edition of the *Sabbats Almanac* provides a wealth of lore, celebrations, creative projects, and recipes to enhance your holiday.

For this edition, a mix of writers—Mickie Mueller, Kate Freuler, Melissa Tipton, Kerri Connor, Blake Octavian Blair, and more—share their ideas and wisdom. These include a variety of paths as well as the authors' personal approaches to each sabbat. Each chapter closes with an extended ritual, which may be adapted for both solitary practitioners and covens.

In addition to these insights and rituals, specialists in astrology, history, cooking, crafts, and spells impart their expertise throughout.

Ivo Dominguez Jr. gives an overview of planetary influences most relevant for each sabbat season and provides details about the New and Full Moons, retrograde motion, planetary positions, and more.

Charlie Rainbow Wolf explores festivals and beliefs from around the world and how they connect to, and sometimes influence, each sabbat. From Guy Fawkes Night to the Chinese Mooncake Festival, this section is the place for celebration.

Sue Pesznecker conjures up a feast for each festival that includes an appetizer, entrée, dessert, and beverage.

Tess Whitehurst offers instructions on DIY crafts that will leave your home full of color and personality for each and every sabbat.

Michael Furie provides spells to celebrate and utilize the unique forces in each season.

About the Authors

Blake Octavian Blair is a shamanic practitioner, ordained minister, writer, Usui Reiki Master-Teacher, tarot reader, and musical artist. Blake incorporates mystical traditions from both the East and West, with a reverence for the natural world, into his own brand of spirituality. Blake holds a degree in English and religion from the University of Florida. He is an avid reader, knitter, crafter, pescatarian, and member of the Order of Bards, Ovates and Druids (OBOD). He loves communing with nature and exploring its beauty whether it is within the city or hiking in the woods. Blake lives in the New England region of the US with his beloved husband. Visit him on the web at www.blakeoctavianblair.com or write him at blake@blake octavianblair.com.

Kate Freuler lives in Ontario, Canada and is the author of *Of Blood and Bones: Working with Shadow Magick & the Dark Moon*. She has owned and operated the witchcraft shop www.whitemoon witchcraft.com for ten years. When she's not writing or crafting items for clients, she is busy being creative with art or reading a huge stack of books.

Michael Furie (Northern California) is the author of *Supermarket Sabbats*, *Spellcasting for Beginners*, *Supermarket Magic*, *Spellcasting: Beyond the Basics*, and more, all from Llewellyn Worldwide. A practicing Witch for more than twenty years, he is a priest of the Cailleach. He can be found online at www.michaelfurie.com.

Jason Mankey is a Wiccan-Witch who lives in Northern California with his wife, Ari, and two cats. He's the author of *Transformative*

Witchcraft: The Greater Mysteries, Witch's Wheel of the Year: Rituals for Circles, Solitaries & Covens, and several books in The Witch's Tools Series. He writes online at the blog Raise the Horns.

Mickie Mueller explores magic and spirituality through art and the written word at her home studio and workshop in Missouri. She is the author/illustrator of *The Voice of the Trees,* the illustrator of *The Mystical Cats Tarot* and *The Magical Dogs Tarot,* author of *The Witch's Mirror* and *Llewellyn's Little Book of Halloween.* Since 2007, Mickie has been a regular article and illustration contributor to Llewellyn's almanacs and annuals and many Llewellyn books. Her art has been seen as set dressing on SyFy's *The Magicians* and Bravo's *Girlfriend's Guide to Divorce.* Visit her online at MickieMuellerStudio.etsy.com

Suzanne Ress has been practicing Wicca for about twelve years as the leader of a small coven, but she has been aware of having a special connection to nature and animal spirits since she was a young child. She has been writing creatively most of her life—short stories, novels, and nonfiction articles for a variety of publications—and finds it to be an important outlet for her considerable creative powers. Other outlets she regularly makes use of are metalsmithing, mosaic works, painting, and all kinds of dance. She is also a professional aromatic herb grower and beekeeper. Although she is an American of Welsh ancestry by birth, she has lived in northern Italy for nearly twenty years. She recently discovered that the small mountain in the pre-alpine hills that she inhabits with her family and animals was once the site of an ancient Insubrian Celtic sacred place. Not surprisingly, the top of the mountain has remained a fulcrum of sacredness throughout the millennia, and this grounding in blessedness makes Suzanne's everyday life especially magical.

Charlie Rainbow Wolf is happiest when she is creating something, especially if it's made from items that others have discarded. Pottery, writing, knitting, astrology, and tarot ignite her passion, but she happily confesses she's easily distracted; life offers such wonderful things to explore! A recorded singer-songwriter and published author, she champions holistic living and lives in the Midwest with her husband and special needs Great Danes. Visit her at www.charlierainbow.com.

Laura Tempest Zakroff is a professional artist, author, dancer, designer, and Modern Traditional Witch. She is the author of *Weave the Liminal, Sigil Witchery*, and *The Witch's Cauldron*, and the co-author of *The Witch's Altar*. Laura blogs for Patheos and Witches & Pagans, contributes to *The Witches' Almanac*, and edited *The New Aradia: A Witch's Handbook to Magical Resistance*. Visit her at www.LauraTempestZakroff.com.

Tess Whitehurst is a co-host of the *Magic Monday* podcast as well as the founder and facilitator of The Good Vibe Tribe Online School of Magical Arts. She has written nine books that have been translated into eighteen languages, including *Unicorn Magic: Awaken to Mystical Energy & Embrace Your Personal Power*. She's also the author of the *Magic of Flowers Oracle* and *The Cosmic Dancer Oracle*. She lives in the Rocky Mountains of Colorado.

Melissa Tipton is a Structural Integrator, Reiki master, and tarot reader who helps people live more magically through her healing practice, Life Alchemy Massage Therapy. She's the author of *Living Reiki: Heal Yourself and Transform Your Life* and *Llewellyn's Complete Book of Reiki*. Take online classes and learn more at getmomassage.com and yogiwitch.com.

Ivo Dominguez Jr. has been active in Wicca and the Pagan community since 1978. He is an Elder of the Assembly of the Sacred Wheel, a Wiccan syncretic tradition, and is one of its founders. He is a part of the core group that started and manages the New Alexandrian

Library. Ivo is the author of *Keys To Perception, Practical Astrology for Witches and Pagans, Casting Sacred Space, Spirit Speak, Beneath the Skins,* and numerous shorter works. Ivo is also a professional astrologer who has studied astrology since 1980 and has been offering consultations and readings since 1988. Ivo lives in Delaware in the woods of Seelie Court. www.ivodominguezjr.com.

Kerri Connor has been practicing her craft for thirty years and runs an eclectic family group called The Gathering Grove. She is a frequent contributor to Llewellyn annuals and the author of *Spells for Tough Times, Wake, Bake & Meditate: Take Your Spiritual Practice to a Higher Level with Cannabis,* and the forthcoming book *420 Meditations.* Kerri resides in northern Illinois.

Susan (Sue) Pesznecker is a mother, writer, nurse, and college English professor living in the beautiful Pacific Northwest with her poodles. An initiated Druid, green magick devotee, and amateur herbalist, Sue loves reading, writing, cooking, travel, and anything having to do with the outdoors. Previous works include *Crafting Magick with Pen and Ink, The Magickal Retreat,* and *Yule: Rituals, Recipes & Lore for the Winter Solstice.* She's a regular contributor to the Llewellyn annuals; follow her on Instagram as Susan Pesznecker.

Samhain

Samhain 2020

Suzanne Ress

IN POPULAR CULTURE FOR at least the last five or six hundred years, the night of October 31 has been, of all the Pagan sabbats, the one most closely identified with witches and witchcraft. The most prevalent symbol of modern-day Halloween (Samhain) is a witch with a black pointy hat and a cauldron. This image comes directly from Elizabethan times, just before the Pilgrims came over to the "New World" on their ship, the Mayflower, when wide-brimmed pointy hats were all the rage.

Even people who claim not to believe in magic and the powers available to human beings via natural phenomena usually do acknowledge that unusual things are more likely to happen when there is a full moon. Samhain 2020 is an exceptionally powerful time for magic, because not only will the moon be full on October 31, but this will also be a blue moon, an infrequent occurrence that every witch or practitioner of magic should try to make the most of.

The Blue Moon: Is It Really Blue?

No, blue moons aren't blue. The name *blue moon* is a distortion of the medieval English "belewe moon," where *belewe* meant "betrayer."

In the western Christian religion, the date of Easter Sunday, which does not have a fixed date like Christmas, is calculated to be the first Sunday after the full moon that occurs on or after the Spring Equinox, March 21. Hence, Easter Sunday could be as early as March 22, but no later than April 25. This full moon is also supposed to be the third of three full winter moons, and is also called the Lenten moon, as it occurs during the forty-day fasting period that precedes Easter Sunday, called Lent. (Talk about a mix-up of Pagan and Christian beliefs!) But, because a lunar phase lasts twenty-nine and a half solar days, every two or three years there will be thirteen full moons in a year rather than twelve, and one of these thirteen full moons will have to share its month with another one. These are the blue moons. In a year with only twelve full moons, there are three full moons per season. Once upon a time, for farmers and for Pagans, it was the duration of these three lunar cycles that determined the dates of the four seasons, rather than set calendar dates. But if, in a third year, the first full moon of the winter season arrived early, then there would be a fourth, a blue moon, before the Spring Equinox, which would interfere with the Christian church's Easter (the symbol of rebirth and spring) dating. So, in this case, the fourth moon of the winter season was disregarded, because, like Judas, it was a betrayer, a belewe moon. Nowadays, any thirteenth moon, or the fourth full moon in any season, can be called a blue moon.

An even more modern way of deciding that a moon is blue is when it is the second full moon in a single month, regardless of how many full moons come in that season. On October 1, 2020, there will be a full moon, and on October 31, there will be a full blue moon. It is counted as the thirteenth, or the extra moon of 2020.

The number thirteen has long been feared as unlucky. The tarot card thirteen is the card of Death. Friday the thirteenth is believed by many to be unlucky. In the religion of the Mayflower Pilgrims, the number thirteen was considered unlucky because, according to the Christian Bible, Judas, the betrayer of Jesus, was the thirteenth disciple to be seated at the "Last Supper."

The moon and sun have different rotation times, and our human -invented measurements reflect this. The sun, considered "masculine," takes precedence, but the moon is not ignored. A solar year is divided into twelve (not a random ten) months because of the twelve moons, and hence there are twelve inches to a foot, thirty-six (three times twelve) inches to a yard, twelve signs of the zodiac, twelve, or twenty-four (two times twelve) hours to a day, sixty (five times twelve) seconds to a minute, sixty minutes to an hour, and so on.

But a fertile woman has thirteen menstrual cycles in a year, and witchcraft, being a strongly feminine-influenced craft, embraces this lunar number. Thirteen is considered the ideal number of witches for a coven, and is also the number that best represents mysticism and spiritual unity.

The moon is the ruler of femininity, and its various phases are always important in magic and spellwork. In general, spells seeking any kind of increase or initiation are cast at the new moon, so that the power of the spell will increase for two weeks as the visible size of the moon increases. The opposite is true when casting spells for decrease or finality—these should be worked shortly after the full moon for a two-week waning of power.

The full moon is considered a perfect time to charge magical tools, mirrors, and water for future spellwork, and the most powerful time to "draw down the moon" and use her power, especially for female-inspired spellwork. Magical tools charged under the blue moon of Samhain will absorb powerful spellcasting moonlight that can be used throughout the rest of the Pagan year.

Samhain

Samhain marks the new year in the Pagan calendar, and also the beginning of the dark half of the year, which continues until Beltane. These two sabbats are considered thresholds between the spiritual world and the living natural world, and it is at these thresholds that the passage of spirits and otherworldly beings between the lightness (known) and the darkness (unknown) is most likely. Therefore, Samhain is considered the best time of the entire Pagan year for contacting spirits from the Otherworld. These could be loved ones who have died, and they may have dwelt in the Otherworld for a very long time indeed—even those who are your own distant ancestors.

The Christian church has tried to transform Samhain into All Hallows' Eve, aka All Souls' Day, or All Saints' Day, or Day of the Dead—Catholic holidays on October 31, November 1, and November 2 when living Christian people trudge to the cemetery to pay homage to, or to celebrate with, their dead relatives and friends. This festival of the dead, or darker side, has been with us for thousands of years.

The year 2020 marks the four-hundredth anniversary of the landing of the Pilgrim ship, the Mayflower, at Plymouth, Massachusetts. After sixty-six days at sea, at dawn on November 9, the Pilgrims first caught sight of land. This must have been a tremendous relief, as the passage had been rough, and living conditions onboard the ship were crowded and uncomfortable. The Mayflower sailed closer to land and the crew realized that they were further north than they had intended to be, so, staying just offshore, they attempted to sail southward. November 9 passed, and on November 10 there was a full moon and the ocean grew very rough. The rough sea, combined with the challenge of navigating Cape Cod's notoriously difficult bars, made the captain decide to turn the Mayflower back northward and anchor in what is now Provincetown harbor. The first Pilgrims went on land there on November 11, 1620.

As someone with multiple Mayflower passenger ancestors, I am especially interested in the Pilgrims' personal stories, and I like to imagine what it would have been like. It would take incredible courage to leave one's homeland and family and head out for a lengthy sea voyage to an unknown place. Their belief in what they were setting out to do together was so strong that, as a group, they were able to overcome personal fears and uncertainties.

Without going into too much detail, their reason for leaving England at that time was because, as a Puritan Protestant minority, they were being persecuted for their religious beliefs and actions. The only way they could attain the freedom to believe and to worship as they desired was to leave England. At the time, North America must have seemed a relatively safe place, as far as freedom of religion went.

After several weeks anchored at Provincetown, the Mayflower sailed along the inner coast of Cape Cod to what they named Plymouth, after the place they had left behind in England. It was there that they built their little village. Although they arrived at Plymouth shortly before Christmas, they did not celebrate Christmas (nor Yule). Onboard the ship they had not celebrated All Hallows' Eve (nor Samhain). Part of the Puritan belief was that holiday celebrations had become corrupt. They viewed partying as a waste of time that would be better spent in productive, God-honoring activities. They observed only the sabbath day, Sunday, by quietly reading their holy book. Back in England at that time, All Hallows' was celebrated with gambols, ale drinking, and the ringing of the church bells all day until midnight.

Although the Pilgrims' way of life may seem severe to us now, I think what they believed and what they were doing at that time was a radical departure from the accepted cultural norm. They were outcasts from society. They marched to a different drummer. And because of this, I think we Pagans and witches can relate to them and to their plight.

It is significant to me that the Mayflower first anchored at Provincetown, which, for many decades now, has been a well-known haven for individuals of unusual sexual orientation and for artists and writers of all kinds—in short, for people who seek a place where they are free to be the individuals they believe they were meant to be, without societal disapproval and persecution.

The White Lady

Years ago, around Samhain, I had a vision of a pretty, long-haired woman dressed in old-fashioned white clothes. She came to me at night as I lay in bed and sat at my bedside, urging me to come with her, to cross over into her world. The apparition was clear, not a dream, and after I declined to follow her, she disappeared. Over the years I have thought about her frequently.

Although I was not aware of it at the time, the appearance of a White Lady is usually associated with a local tragedy involving violent death, suicide, or death in childbirth. Some legends make out the White Lady to be a vengeful ghost who frightens her victims and causes them to have fatal accidents. In other legends, the White Lady appears to someone to show them the location of a hidden treasure. In other traditions, the White Lady represents an ancestral ghost.

Vila, or Veles, are white lady fairy folk who guard animals and the forest, and are friends of women, but punish men who betray women. Punishment consists of making the man dance himself to death. Sometimes, it is said, Veles or Vila invite mortal women to come with them to the forest to be given lessons in the magical arts.

The apparition appeared to me in our house in Ohio, which had been built over previous farmlands, and which, years before that, had been Shawnee Indian territory. Had it previously been forested land, and were the Shawnee (or later the Mingo) villages located near there? Hundreds and even thousands of years ago, native people built elaborate underground tombs, known as burial mounds, in central Ohio. Many, if not most of them were destroyed when the white settlers from the east came and took the lands. Could the White Lady have been one of the Native Americans whose grave was disturbed, inviting me to return to the underworld with her?

Or was she the Pilgrim Susanna Jackson White, who gave birth to the Mayflower group's first baby in the new world? She had spent the last trimester of her pregnancy aboard a stuffy, smelly, roiling wooden ship—how uncomfortable that must have been! Or was she Priscilla Mullins, only seventeen years old, accompanied by her father, William, and who, soon after the voyage, lost her parents and brother to the Great Sickness and about two years later married fellow passenger John Alden?

I like to think that the White Lady who appeared to me that Samhain was an ancestor stepping through the threshold into my world, trying to make friendly contact with me, her descendant. At Samhain, such things are possible!

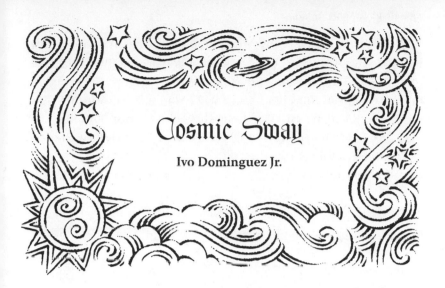

Cosmic Sway

Ivo Dominguez Jr.

SAMHAIN CAN BE CELEBRATED on the calendar date of October 31 or when the Sun is at the 15th degree of Scorpio on November 6. Or it can be celebrated on both days depending upon your ritual needs. All of the sabbats can be celebrated over the course of several days, but the cross-quarter sabbats have a longer period of influence, especially Samhain. So many people work their magic on or near October 31 that the powers are summoned, the spirits are stirred, and the veils are parted, but the qualities associated with Samhain continue to rise until November 6. It is easier to access subtle energies and open the way between the worlds on all the sabbats, but at Samhain this is felt more intensely.

On October 31 the Moon will be full in Taurus and conjunct a retrograde Uranus. It is also a blue moon. Mercury, Mars, Neptune, and the asteroid Chiron are also retrograde, with Mercury squaring Saturn. The Sun is moving toward an opposition with Uranus that peaks on November 4. There is also a stellium of Jupiter, Saturn, and Pluto that is building to a Jupiter-Pluto conjunction the middle of November. If you are fluent in the language of astrology you may be taking a moment to contemplate the challenges these imply. However, challenges are often the keys to opening the way to opportunities, and this Samhain season can do just that.

Let's start with how to work with all those retrogrades as you plan your rituals, celebrations, and workings. For many, Samhain is a time to work with the ancestors, the lessons of the past, and the bringing in of the harvest. Retrogrades are an invitation to move slowly, to dig deeply, and enter into the reverie of remembrance. They are not the best time to begin new things, but they are an excellent time to review, refine, and release what has already been in progress.

When Neptune is retrograde, it facilitates your ability to experience what lies beyond the physical. It is also easier to release whatever illusions and delusions you may be harboring. Neptune retrogrades will often challenge you by stripping away layers of fantasy and leaving you with the task of seeing things as they are. If you can still find the will and desire to move forward with a realistic perspective, you win.

When Uranus is retrograde, its swift, transformative power is slowed down enough so we can see how its lightning flash branches and grounds into the Earth. This is particularly true while Uranus is in the slow and robust sign of Taurus. The urge to quickly change the material conditions of your life will be strong; instead, use this time to reconnoiter and make a plan of action. Profound change is achievable if you find the balance between Uranus's drive for action and Taurus's drive for durability.

When Chiron is retrograde, our old psychological and spiritual wounds become more evident. Chiron is also the bridge between the outer and the inner places, as well as the network that unites the various parts that make up our whole, and when retrograde it is possible to trace those connections and find the breaks in your integrity. While the healing may happen after Chiron goes direct, the insight that starts this process is easier to find during the retrograde.

When Mars is retrograde, physical energy and power to assert your will in the world turns inward. You may feel frustrated, but pushing yourself and forcing outcomes probably won't serve you well. It is a good time for self-care and recharging. This is also a time to examine your wants, needs, and priorities. If you evaluate your methods in life for reaching your goals during a Mars retrograde, it will be easier to see what does and doesn't work.

When Mercury is retrograde, it is important to be very careful in how you listen and how you speak. Of all the retrogrades, people seem to be the most concerned about Mercury's. However, if you work with, rather than against, its natural tendencies, it can serve you well. It is an excellent time to edit and review what you have written, as well as your unwritten inner dialogue. If you adjust your pace, you will find that you will notice subtleties and details that would've been missed when moving at your normal speed.

Mercury is also squaring Saturn at Halloween. This does have a tendency to encourage sharp conversation and conflict. But it does not have to be the case. It can also allow you to find the details that cause conflict so that they can be adjusted or negotiated. If the desired outcome is an ending of a connection, then use this aspect mindfully for that purpose. With the Moon being conjunct Uranus, there will be a pressure to act up and act out. This sense of urgency can be redirected to raise energy in your rituals and workings. Feel it for what it is and turn it into power instead of agitation or anxiety.

For November 6, when the Sun is at the 15th degree of Scorpio, astrological Samhain, the retrogrades are still in effect with the exception of Mercury, which will have gone direct on November 3. The conjunction between Jupiter and Pluto continues to tighten and will be exact on November 12. This conjunction will be the third and last in a series. The stellium of Saturn, Jupiter, and Pluto is the strongest influence during this period. These aspects arouse a desire for profound change from the smallest details of your life to the largest structures in society. The key to good choices is to focus on what you hold to be the most personally meaningful. When Jupiter and Saturn reach an exact conjunction at the Winter Solstice, the influences peak, but start working with them at Samhain. This conjunction is much like the pouring of a foundation or the planting of a perennial garden; the decisions that are made will have a lasting impact. This Samhain is truly a crossroads, a threshold, filled with endings and beginnings that will reverberate for years to come. Empower your choices.

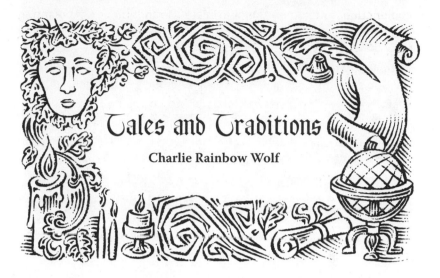

Tales and Traditions

Charlie Rainbow Wolf

MANY TRADITIONS BELIEVE SAMHAIN is the end of the old year and the beginning of the next.

New Beginnings

TO THE CHEROKEES of North America, this was also the case. The Great New Moon Festival was held in October between Mabon and Samhain, and it marked the beginning of the new Cherokee year. Their mythology suggests that many Cherokees believed the world was created during the fall season.

As with many festivals, food was one of the focal points. Several years ago I regularly spent time with my Cherokee friends at their festivals. I observed it was customary to see the men providing the food and the women preparing it. The usual harvest foods like pumpkin pie, pecan pie, roasted ears of corn, and venison were on offer as well as dishes made from beans and squash.

When the time for feasting arrived, the children went first, preparing plates and giving them to the elders. The young ones then got back in line and filled their own plates last. This is done not just to respect the elders, but also to teach the young ones to recognize the position that the older ones have earned among their people.

The Great New Moon Festival was just one of the autumnal festivals held by the Cherokee. The second one came just a few days later, and it was called the Friends Made Ceremony. It was at this time that you made amends with anyone that you'd fallen out with over the last year, to strengthen existing bonds and to make new friends. Gifts were exchanged, and it was a time of feasting, rejoicing, and purifying. As the Great New Moon Festival was seen as the start to a new year, the Friends Made Ceremony was seen as a time to ensure the new start was positive and uplifting.

Everyone who participated was given a specific task to do, from helping to prepare the ritual space, to leading songs or dances, cleaning, preparing food, looking after the little ones, or anything else the elders requested so that everyone could enjoy the day. When I went, there was always sage and tobacco burning outside the council house, and the Going to Water Ceremony was a big part of this gathering.

Going to Water

The Going to Water Ceremony is an act of purification. The elders explained to me that, back in the day, this was a ritual cleansing done as the men came in from a hunt or a battle. They would fully bathe in running water before they returned to their homelands, washing all their clothing and their weapons and tools as well, so none of the death was brought back to their loved ones (even a Cherokee woman used two knives—one to harvest herbs and vegetables and another one to prepare them). Nowadays, Going to Water is frequently more symbolic than anything else. Water is poured by an elder and participants wash themselves in it before entering into the sacred ceremonial space. The intention to cleanse and purify remains the same.

The sacred fire is important to many—if not all—Cherokee ceremonies. It is the fire keeper's job to tend to the fires in the sacred space. During the Friends Made Ceremony, it is time to renew the fire. The fire keeper takes a cinder he has saved from the fire of the last Friends Made Ceremony and adds it when lighting the new fire, so that the old feeds the new. It is his responsibility to ensure that this fire never goes out during the festival, which traditionally lasts for four days. At the end of the gathering, he takes a cinder from this fire and keeps it safe until the next Friends Made Ceremony next year.

Guy Fawkes and Mischief Night

In England, Mischief Night falls near Samhain, usually between the thirtieth of October and the fourth of November. In both Lincolnshire and Lancashire I recall it being the night before Bonfire Night. This is when the local youths would get up to harmless pranks, such as throwing eggs at windows and cars or playing "knock-a-door-run," which is just what it sounds like: knock on the door then run away and hide before it is answered!

The fifth of November is Guy Fawkes Night, also called Bonfire Night and Fireworks Night. It's one of the few times in history that someone's failure, not their success, is celebrated! This all started when the Catholics wanted to end the Protestant government's persecution of them, replacing the Protestant heads with those of the Catholic faith. They made plans to blow up the House of Lords, and Guy Fawkes—a member of the Gunpowder Plot—was arrested for guarding the explosives. You may be familiar with some of this from the 2005 film *V for Vendetta*.

It's not uncommon for children to make a large scarecrow-type doll and carry or drag it from door to door, or gather with it in popular spots, asking for "a Penny for the Guy." Effigies of Guy Fawkes are often burned on the fires during Bonfire Night. Today the firework displays are organized by communities or put on by private promoters, much like the Fourth of July celebrations held in the US. Jacket (baked) potatoes, roasted chestnuts, and the seasonal bonfire toffee and parkin—a sticky cake made with treacle—are the usual refreshments.

Honoring the Ways

Many of the above traditions exist in harmony with the usual Samhain festivities. As well as Halloween decorations and costumes, perhaps you could add in your own Guy Fawkes. One year we cast our ritual circle with sparklers and then fed them to the fire, adding bursts of color and flash.

Perhaps as part of your preparation you might find inspiration in the Going to Water ceremony. Just as we did as part of the Friends Made Festival, you could have an elder with jugs of purified water to symbolically purify yourself prior to starting your ritual activities. Simply have your High Priest or High Priestess pour some water into the hands of those participating, and then use that water to splash the face and clothing to signify that cleansing has taken place.

As Samhain ends the old year and begins the new in many traditions, you could incorporate the idea of saving the cinders from the fire—once they've cooled, of course—and use them to light your next ritual fire. Similar to the duty of the fire keeper, you could appoint someone as the keeper of the fire and ask them to take a cooled cinder and keep it safe for the next year, guaranteeing that the fires would again burn at the next Samhain gathering. The person appointed might also be given the responsibility of keeping this year's fire burning for the duration of your gathering.

For your feast, consider adding bonfire toffee or cinder toffee to your menu. There are many good recipes online for these. Bonfire toffee is a very old sweet treat, going back centuries. It's a good way to honor the ancestors at this time of year, as well as adding something different and a bit decadent to your proceedings.

References

Fraser, Antonia. *Faith and Treason: The Story of the Gunpowder Plot*. New York: Anchor Books, 1997.

Mooney, James. *Myths of the Cherokee and Sacred Formulas of the Cherokees*. Nashville, TN: C Elder-Bookseller, 1982.

Feasts and Treats

Sue Pesznecker

SAMHAIN MEANS "DEEP AUTUMN" to some and the start of the Celtic winter to others. Regardless, it's a season of wild weather and growing chill, and our focus here will be on humble, nurturing recipes that warm heart and soul. First, we'll simmer up a kettle of soup from scratch, serving that with a piece of herbed homemade bread. For dessert? A pear clafouti—fancy looking but deceptively simple. And we'll get started on a cranberry cordial that'll be ready to use at Yule time.

Chicken Stock and Chicken Soup

Start your stock in the morning and be eating soup for dinner. Even better, let it simmer into a second day. Once you know how to make stock, you can apply the same techniques to make an array of different types.

Prep time: 15 minutes for the stock; 15 minutes for the soup
Cooking time: 6 hours–2 days (stock); 1 hour (soup)
Cooling time: a couple of hours or overnight (stock)
Servings: about 4

Stock

1 whole chicken (or 8 or more chicken parts), excess fat removed*
1 small carrot, root end removed
½ yellow onion
2 ribs celery
Handful of fresh parsley
2 garlic cloves, halved
1 teaspoon salt
10–12 black peppercorns
½ teaspoon thyme
¼ teaspoon red pepper flakes
¼ teaspoon ground allspice
1 bay leaf

*Vegetarian option: Substitute 3–4 sliced portabella mushrooms for the chicken. Sauté the mushrooms in 1–2 tablespoons of olive oil until they begin to brown, then proceed with the recipe. Simmer for 4–6 hours, and then finish the stock.

Place all ingredients into a large, deep kettle. Cover with enough cold water to fully submerge the ingredients. Place kettle over medium heat. Bringing the stock to a slow boil is essential to getting the most flavor.

Once the mixture boils, lower the heat so it's barely bubbling. Skim foam from the stock as it forms. Allow the stock to boil gently over medium-low heat for 6 or more hours, adding water as needed to keep the contents submerged. If possible, make a two-day stock the way the French do: at the end of day one turn the stove off, put a lid on the kettle, and let it sit in the fridge overnight. In the morning, turn the stove back on, and once the stock boils again, remove the lid, letting the contents cook for another 4–6 hours.

After the stock has cooked for the first hour, pull out a couple of meaty portions, shred or chop the meat, and put it in the refrigerator for later use in the soup. Don't be afraid to take as much meat as you want; the stock's real flavor is coming from the soup bones.

Strain the stock, discarding the solids. If you have time, chill the stock overnight, and remove the solidified fat layer before using. Otherwise, let the stock sit in the fridge and cool for a couple of hours, and hand-skim fat from the surface.

Soup

2 tablespoons olive oil
2 carrots, peeled and diced
2 ribs celery, sliced
¼ yellow onion, diced
Chicken stock (from stock recipe)
1 garlic clove, minced
Pinch of turmeric
Chicken left from making stock
2 cups cooked egg noodles
Handful of fresh parsley, roughly chopped
Salt and pepper to taste

Place a large, clean kettle over medium heat. Add the olive oil. Once it's hot, add the carrots, celery, and onion, and sauté just until they begin to soften (avoid browning). Add the stock, garlic, and turmeric. Bring to a gentle boil, then reduce the heat and simmer for about 15 minutes.

Add the chicken, noodles, and parsley. Allow to simmer for 10 more minutes, then taste and add salt and pepper as needed.

Serve and enjoy! I like to tuck a container of soup into the freezer—it comes in handy when cold and flu season arrives.

White Bread

Breadmaking is one of the most basic cooking skills around; after all, people have been baking bread for thousands of years. The trick is to use gently warmed liquids—too hot liquids can kill the yeast. Follow this dictum and don't be afraid to pound the heck out of... er, *knead* your dough, and you'll end up with something pretty wonderful.

Prep time: 10 minutes for mixing; 5–10 minutes for kneading, punching, and shaping
Rising time: 90 minutes–2 hours
Baking time: 30 minutes
Serves: many!

½ package active dry yeast (about 1 teaspoon)
¼ cup warm water (no hotter than 110° F*)
2 tablespoons sugar
1 cup cool water
2 teaspoons salt
2 tablespoons unsalted butter, softened
3 ½ cups all-purpose flour
Additional flour as needed
2 tablespoons butter or vegetable oil
1 tablespoon melted butter (optional)
Optional: Add olive oil, crumbled fresh or dry herbs (rosemary, thyme, basil, oregano), and seeds (fennel, cumin, caraway, pumpkin) as desired.
*If the water is too hot, it will kill the yeast.

In a large bowl, combine the yeast, warm water, and sugar. Allow to sit for a few minutes until the yeast begins to bubble up and expand. This is good—it tells you the yeast is alive and ready to go to work. (If this doesn't happen, start over with a new package of yeast.)

Pro tip: When buying yeast, always check the date on the package to make sure it isn't expired. For best results, keep unused yeast in the fridge.

Once the yeast has bubbled up, stir in the cool water, salt, butter, and 1 cup of the flour. Stir this until mixed, then add and stir in 2 cups more flour. When it becomes too difficult to stir, scatter ¼ cup of flour on a clean countertop and plop the dough onto the counter.

Now comes the fun part: kneading. This is the part people are afraid of—but truly, there's nothing to it. Plus, it's great exercise and a nice way to get rid of tensions and frustrations (a secret our grandparents knew). One "kneading motion" consists of three parts: First, plant the heel of your hand in the front third of the dough blob and, at the same time, push the dough down and away from you. Second, lift and rotate the dough blob one quarter turn. Third, pick up the edge of the dough furthest from you and fold it over, toward you, creating a shape like a taco shell. Now repeat all three steps. You're kneading.

As you knead, pull in loose flour and bits of dough from the countertop. Pay attention to the way the dough feels at the beginning, and be aware of how the texture and elasticity begin to change. The kneading develops the gluten in the flour, creating a dough that's smooth and springy. If the dough sticks, use a table knife or bench scraper to release it from the counter, then add a small amount of additional flour. Don't add any more flour than you need to—it's okay for the dough to be a little sticky as long as you can handle it. Keep kneading for 4–5 minutes until the dough is springy and elastic.

Oil a medium bowl with 1 tablespoon of butter or cooking oil. Plop the dough into the bowl and turn the dough all around, coating it on all sides. Cover the bowl with a clean tea towel, place in a warm room, and allow to rise for 45 (or more) minutes. During this time, the dough will double in size. Test for "doubling" by poking two fingers into the dough: if deep finger-holes remain, it's doubled. Rising time will vary depending on the room temperature.

While rising, grease a 9-inch loaf pan with 1 tablespoon of butter or vegetable oil. Once the dough has doubled, punch fists into it, punching out all the air. Shape it into a loaf, with any irregular spots or seams tucked under. Set it in the loaf pan, put the towel over it again, and let rise for 30–45 minutes, until double again. But don't poke your fingers in it this time! Just eyeball it.

Preheat your oven to 425° F. When the dough has doubled, put it into the oven and immediately reduce heat to 375° F. If you want a soft, buttery crust, brush with melted butter before putting it into the oven.

Bake for about 30 minutes until it's risen even more, nicely browned, and has filled the house with an incredible fragrance. Remove immediately from the pan and cool on a cooling rack. Do your best to not cut it until it's cool, as doing so tends to dry the loaf. (But I won't blame you if you can't resist!)

Pro tip: A perfectly baked loaf of bread will sound hollow when thumped on the bottom.

Note: If you aren't able to knead the bread yourself, using the bread hook on a stand mixer or the kneading function in a bread machine works too.

Pear Custard Clafouti

Pronounced "clah-FOO-tee," this versatile dish looks special but is easy to make and will bring a lovely finish to your autumn meal. The leftovers make a delicious breakfast or snack as well.

Prep time: 15 minutes
Cooking time: 45 minutes
Cooling time: 10–15 minutes
Servings: 6–8

Cooking spray
4 ripe pears, peeled and thinly sliced
¼ cup unsalted butter, melted
3 eggs
¾ cup whole milk
¼ teaspoon salt
⅓ cup sugar
⅓ cup flour
2 teaspoons vanilla extract
Confectioner's sugar, as desired

Preheat the oven to 350° F. Spray cooking spray on a 9-inch round pan.

Arrange the pear slices on the bottom of the pan any way you wish. I usually do a spoke and wheel pattern.

Place the butter, eggs, milk, salt, sugar, flour, and vanilla in a blender and process until smooth (or use an immersion blender).

Pour the batter over the pears. Bake 40–45 minutes until the custard is lightly browned and just barely firm to the touch.

Cool 10–15 minutes. Sprinkle with confectioner's sugar before serving.

Note: This recipe works with any fruit; it's a lovely way to use up the "here and there" straggly bits of produce.

Sparkling Sugared Cranberries

Use these little jewels as holiday garnishes or just enjoy munching on them.

Prep time: 20 minutes, plus a few hours drying time
Cooking time: 10 minutes
Inactive: several hours to overnight
Servings: varies

½ cup water
½ cup sugar
12 ounces fresh cranberries
1 cup sugar

Bring the water and ½ cup of sugar to a boil in a small saucepan. Remove from heat; add cranberries and stir until they're all coated. Allow them to sit in the hot liquid for about 10 minutes, stirring occasionally. Use a slotted spoon to move them to a wire rack. Let dry for about an hour until they're tacky but not wet.

Place 1 cup of sugar on a rimmed cookie sheet. Add the cranberries and shake the sheet to roll them and coat them with sugar. When all are coated, allow to dry on the sugary sheet for several hours or even overnight. They'll keep at room temperature in a sealed container for a week.

Cranberry Cordial

Start this brilliantly red, sweet-tart cordial now, and it'll be ready for Yule celebrations in six weeks.

Prep time: 10 minutes
Inactive: 6 weeks
Servings: varies

1 quart glass canning jar with lid
12 ounces fresh cranberries
1½ cups sugar
2–3 cups good quality vodka (unflavored)

Rinse the berries and drain on a towel. Crush or chop coarsely— the more finely chopped, the better. You should have about 2 cups of chopped fruit, but a little more or less is fine.

Place the berries in the canning jar and add the sugar. Fill slowly with vodka. As the sugar dissolves over the next 1–2 days, you may need to add more vodka to fill the jar.

When full, screw on the lid and set on your kitchen counter out of direct light. Let sit for 5–6 weeks, shaking once or twice a day. It may take the sugar 2–3 days to dissolve; top off with more vodka if needed.

Finishing: In six weeks, the cordial will be done. Strain through a fine sieve or cheesecloth and pour your brilliant scarlet concoction into a decorative bottle or decanter. Store in the refrigerator. The Yule recipe section will give you ideas for using your cordial.

Crafty Crafts

Tess Whitehurst

FOR MOST OF THE YEAR, we have both feet planted firmly in the realm of the living. But at Samhain, it seems the whole world has the impulse to lift the veil and sidle up to the realm of the dead. That's because, as portals go, Samhain is a big one. It literally translates to "summer's end," and it is the moment in time when the golden light of the summery harvest finally gives way to the wintery darkness. In many parts of the world, the autumn leaves dwindle and we bid farewell to the expansive months of growth as we burrow into our homes for the coldest and darkest months of the year.

As the Wheel of the Year turns, the colors fade, and visibly burgeoning life disappears from the landscape. We are reminded of our own mortality, and of the blessed and beloved souls who have already transitioned out of their physical form. While our mainstream culture often depicts death as frightening and even horrific, it is actually a natural and necessary phase in the unending cycle of existence, which of course doesn't stop with death but endlessly spirals through its adjacent cycles. In other words, after death there is always rebirth: the time when another cycle of life begins.

Some Buddhists find comfort, inspiration, and liberation in meditating on, and visualizing in detail, their body's eventual death and decay. In South American countries, the Día de los Muertos

(Day of the Dead) celebrations at the end of October and earliest days of November include elaborate altars featuring decorative skeletons and skulls. And, of course, many modern Pagans like to work with a human or animal skull as a focal point for connecting with their beloved dead.

This craft calls upon a similar impulse: by decorating a realistic looking plaster skull, you make friends with the eventual demise of your current human form while remembering that you are more than your body; you are a soul. By creating beauty out of a symbol of death, you celebrate your eternal nature and transform fear into power.

Decorative Skull

Depending on your aesthetic sensibility, you may enjoy keeping your uniquely beautiful skull on your altar or in your magical workspace year-round.

Consider making a tradition out of this craft by decorating a new skull every Samhain. You could even make it a yearly family ritual: many kids (of a certain age— you can decide what that is) will love to participate, and to add a new skull to their collection every October.

You may like to set an intention for your skull. What are you connecting with, or whom are you invoking? Perhaps you'd like to create a skull that represents someone you love or admire who has transitioned, or perhaps it can represent you and your eventual mortality. You can create a skull that celebrates the spirit of rebirth, or one that symbolizes all the things you'd like to let go.

Materials

A realistic-looking, ready-to-paint plaster skull (you can find them
    on Etsy.com)
Craft paint in any color or colors (I used metallic purple)
A paintbrush
Sticky jewels and/or glue-able rhinestones
Glue (I used Elmer's)
Newspaper to line your workspace
Optional: sparkles, scrapbooking decorations (paper cutouts of
    symbols and images), faux flowers, faux butterflies, feathers,
    smaller paintbrushes for detail, essential oils for anointing, and
    really anything you'd like to use to decorate your skull
Cost: $20–$30
Time spent: 20–60 minutes plus dry time

Paint your skull with the craft paint and allow it to dry for 10 minutes or so. Then decorate it with additional paint, jewels, and whatever else you'd like to use to adorn your skull. I glued jewels around the eye sockets and put a large jewel at the skull's brow chakra to symbolize intuition and gazing beyond the veil. You might like to paint a spiral, pentacle, or mandala on the scalp; paint one of the teeth gold; perch a tiny faux butterfly on the crown; or hot glue a silk flower near the ear area. You could even adorn your skull with a hat, a headband, eyeglasses, or a flower crown. (But don't feel limited by these suggestions!)

Of course, allow any glue or additional paint to dry.

If you're doing this craft with others, encourage everyone to discuss their artistic choices and to share their thoughts and intentions with the group.

Easy Candy Corn Candles

Even if you don't love eating candy corn, its vibrant yellow and orange hues can add a cheerful pop of color to your Samhain decorating scheme. According to "The History of Candy Corn: A Halloween Candy Favorite" on the *Better Homes & Gardens* website, candy corn originated in the 1880s, and it was initially called "Chicken Feed" (Broek 2018).

Symbolically, candy corn represents two things that magically correlate with the Samhain season: corn and sweetness.

According to Judika Illes in *The Element Encyclopedia of Witchcraft*, "Grain…is harvested in autumn, often in late October, corresponding to what is now Samhain/Halloween. Corn, sacrificed so that people can live, was traditionally cut with a scythe or sickle, harvest tools still associated with the Grim Reaper… [Eventually, a] complex system of agricultural magic developed" (Illes 2005).

In *Cunningham's Encyclopedia of Magical Herbs*, Scott Cunningham writes, "The Corn Mother, or Goddess, is a deity of plenty and of fertility, long worshipped throughout the East and North America" (Cunningham 1985).

Of course, candy and sugar also abound at this time of year, from Halloween treats to the skulls made out of sugar in Día de los Muertos celebrations. As we explore the topic of death, the taste of sweetness reminds us of the endless and expansive love we feel for those who have transitioned to the other side, and of the sweet quality of being an eternal soul that transcends this physical existence.

Materials

A bag of candy corn

Mason jars and/or glass jar-like candleholders

Tea lights (electric or traditional)

Cost: $5–$10

Time spent: 5–10 minutes

I meant it when I called this craft "easy." All you do is fill the bottom quarter or half of the jar/holder with candy corn and then nestle a tea light in each one. Then, when you're ready to set the room aglow, take a moment to feel gratitude to the earth for the sustenance of the harvest. Invoke the sweetness of the season. Then light your candles.

Oh, and I hope you left some candy corn in the bag! Because you'll probably want to snack on one or two (or twenty). As a matter of fact, maybe you should just eat some before you start the craft.

References

Brock, Sara. 5 October 2018. "The History of Candy Corn: A Halloween Candy Favorite." *Better Homes and Gardens.* Meredith Home Group. bhg.com/Halloween/recipes/the-history-of-candy-corn.

Cunningham, Scott. *Cunningham's Encyclopedia of Magical Herbs.* St. Paul, MN: Llewellyn Publications, 1985.

Illes, Judika. *The Element Encyclopedia of Witchcraft: The Complete A-Z for the Entire Magical World.* London: HarperElement, 2005.

Spells

Michael Furie

WHETHER REVELING IN THE modern traditions of Halloween, focusing exclusively on the spiritual and magical significance of Samhain, or choosing to include elements of both in your celebrations, this sabbat can be a time of immense magic and joy. In the past, there was a much stronger focus on the fearsome elements of this time of year and the magical protections that could be used to safeguard yourself, loved ones, and your home. In these modern times, it is still wise to have a few solid methods of magical protection for home and family, as well as magic that taps into the full potential of this most powerful time.

Pumpkin Protection Spell

Pumpkins are considered magically aligned with the earth element and the moon, making them attuned to prosperity, protection, healing, and moon magic. Folklore tells that jack-o'-lanterns have been used in the past to frighten away evil, first carved from turnips (also aligned to earth and moon) and later from pumpkins.

Materials

1 carved pumpkin
1 candle
Banishing powder (recipe follows)
Tip: The carving on the pumpkin can be any design you prefer, as long
    as it feels correct to you. The candle should be a white or black tea
    light or votive, but if safety is a concern, a battery-powered candle
    or pumpkin light can be used.

Banishing Powder

1 teaspoon chamomile (2 tea bags)
1 teaspoon cinnamon
1 teaspoon black pepper
1 teaspoon rosemary
1 teaspoon sage
½ teaspoon garlic powder
1 teaspoon salt

Cut open two chamomile tea bags and pour into a bowl, this
should make about a teaspoon. Add the remaining ingredients into
the bowl, mixing them with your hands while focusing on the intention that the powder neutralizes and repels all harm.

To cast the spell, open the jack-o'-lantern, sprinkling in some of
the powder while saying:

*Moon above and earth beneath, upon my home protection be-
queath; magical lantern and banishing powder, safeguard this space
hour by hour; throughout the night this candle shall shine, as a shield
of power, defending what's mine.*

Light the candle and set it in the pumpkin, placing the now
completed jack-o'-lantern in a visible area either inside or outside
your home.

Magical Masks

This sabbat not only marks a single point in time, but also stands as a threshold into an uncharted world. Wearing a costume on Halloween can actually be a powerful magical act that serves to clarify and unleash your intentions out into the universe. The easiest way to do this is through the use of a symbolic mask. Ideally, the mask should be one that doesn't cover your mouth or restrict your eyesight. Another plus would be if it were the type of mask that could be adorned in some way to personalize it.

The first step is to determine what you'd like to accomplish in the new year and what best symbolizes that goal to you personally. After this, gather the costume and mask essentials. Once these have been obtained, the spell can begin. If the costume has many pieces to it, place them all together on your altar or working table so that the mask can be placed at the top. Decorate the mask in such a way that it will easily call to mind your goal. For example, if your goal is prosperity-related you could sprinkle the mask with gold glitter or glue on some sparkly, simulated gemstones or coins; whatever makes you feel prosperous. Allow the mask to fully dry (if needed) before setting it on the altar.

Materials
1 pin
1 black candle
Matches
Optional: cinnamon oil

Using the pin, scratch your desire into the candle, being as specific as possible. Next, anoint the candle from the top down to the bottom with a bit of your saliva to further bond the magic to you. You can also anoint it with cinnamon oil (a wonderful multipurpose magical spice attuned to Samhain), if desired. Pick up the candle, hold it in your strong hand (the hand you write with), and squeeze it firmly while visualizing your goal. Once you feel your hand pulsing with energy, you can set the candle down into a holder placed on the altar table directly behind the costume. Hold both hands over the mask and mentally send energy into it while saying:

Magic of Samhain, witches' night, empower this spell to achieve my aim; when mask is donned with purpose in sight, the power unleashed, my goals I claim; so mote it be.

Allow the candle to burn out if safe to do so. The mask (and costume) is now charged with the power of the spell and is further activated as you wear it.

Trick or Treat Safety Spell

With the popularity of trick or treating comes the necessary issue of security for our children. Though safety has always been an important concern during Samhain, and indeed through the entire season with the dread of dangerous otherworldly forces, modern times have brought the added dimension of automobile traffic and fears of tainted candy. While it is sensible to take all of the usual precautions, as magically minded people we have additional safety options at our disposal. My preferred method of magical personal protection is to enchant a favorite piece of clothing and/or accessory to act as a magical shield. For children, a good method is to magically charge the shoes that they will be wearing so that they will be protected as they make their rounds.

Materials
Item to be enchanted (shoes)
Rosemary incense
Censer and incense charcoal
Large plate or cloth
1 cup salt, in a bowl
1 cup water
1 orange candle
Cinnamon oil

The plate or cloth must be large enough to set the shoes upon but not so large that the rest of the tools cannot be placed around it on the working table. When you are ready, place the incense behind the large plate or cloth. Place the bowl of salt to the front right side of the plate and the cup of water to the front left side. The orange candle should be placed on the back right side, forming a triangle of incense (air), salt (earth), and water with the candle representing both the element of fire and the power of the autumn sun. The shoes are set in the center of the plate, and some of the salt should be sprinkled carefully in a clockwise circle around them. Anoint the candle with the cinnamon oil then light the wick. Use the flame of the candle to light the incense.

Hold both hands over the shoes while visualizing the child being encircled in an impenetrable orb of dazzling white light. Mentally pour this energy into the shoes so that they will emanate this power for as long as they exist and will be renewed every time sunlight shines upon them; in this way their protective power will last long after this night. To seal the charge place a drop of cinnamon oil inside each shoe, then sprinkle a few drops of water over them and a small amount of salt from the bowl. Next, pick up the shoes and pass them through the smoke of the incense and over the flame of the candle, saying:

Blessed by earth, water, and air, charged by the flame of the autumn sun; to keep from harm, wrapped in loving care, magical shoes for my little one. For good of all, safe and free, as I will, so shall it be.

Snuff out the candle and the spell is complete.

Samhain Ritual

Suzanne Ress

A TRADITIONAL WICCAN WAY to honor one's ancestors is to set up an ancestor altar. This could be a side table or a mantelpiece in your home, which would not give your identity as a witch away to judgmental guests. It requires photographs or drawings of the ancestors, as well as objects and various knickknacks you associate with them. Additionally, one or more white candles can be placed on the altar, in addition to a small crucible, fireproof dish, or ashtray for burning paper items and incense.

Honoring My Ancestors at Samhain

This is a ritual for solitary witches. It can be modified slightly for groups.

Items needed:

A small table or other surface somewhere in your home or workplace that you see several times daily, to be used as an ancestor altar

Photographs or artwork that represent your ancestors

One white candle for each ancestor

Any mementos or items that remind you of your ancestors, or things
that belonged to them

A fireproof dish, crucible, or ashtray

Dried elder leaves

Dried sage

Any items to be moon-charged, and a dish of spring water

At least a week before Samhain, you should set up your altar with
all of its paraphernalia, excluding the items to be moon-charged
and/or the dish of spring water, which should not be placed there
until darkness falls on October 31. Your altar can be a small table, a
mantelpiece, a wall shadowbox, or anything else you already have or
that you can fit naturally in with your existing furnishings.

Arrange your pictures, candles, and other items attractively, and
place the dried leaves in a small muslin bag near the ashtray or crucible. Save a little space for the dish of water and other items.

Every time you pass by this altar, take a moment to remember
your ancestors and imagine what their lives must have been like.
The more you are able to think about them during the time leading
up to the full blue moon on Samhain, the more intense your connection with them will be.

In my Samhain approach to my Mayflower ancestors, I must be
sensitive to their ingrained fear of witchcraft, which was prevalent at
the time. I shall concentrate instead on the things I have in common
with them—my independent spirit, my respect of other peoples'
freedoms, and my willingness to overcome difficult obstacles with
endurance and a positive outlook.

On my altar, a thick section of oak log (to represent strength
and longevity), I place my Mayflower Society certificates. I place
five kernels of dried corn from the crop my husband and I grew the
previous year (a symbol used by the Pilgrims to remember the hard
times but look forward to the easier times). I prepare my altar at the
full moon in September, which falls on the second, four days and
four hundred years before the Pilgrims set off from England. Each
time I see my altar I am reminded of my ancestors and of their voy-

age, and I try to cast myself back to that time and be with them on the crowded ship, if only for a few minutes each day.

Be creative when you make your own ancestor altar, and tailor it to your personal heritage as much as possible.

On Samhain, night of the full blue moon, turn off your house-lights, lock your doors, and arrange a blue, white, or silver platter of blue lunar foods for yourself and your ancestors. These could be blue cheeses, blue crabs, blueberries, a round cake with blue frosting, blue bubbly cocktails, or others, as you see fit.

Wash your body in a bath with a few drops of lavender or night-blooming lily oil, and dress in clean white clothes. If you choose to wear jewelry it should be previously moon-charged silver or crystal, or, best of all, something that was actually worn by the ancestor you are contacting.

Place the items you wish to charge, as well as a small dish of spring water, on your altar. Light the candles and sit comfortably before your altar. Breathe deeply and stare at the candle flame, concentrating on your ancestor and everything you know about them. Visualize yourself together with your ancestor. Feel the power of the full moon above you in the sky. Perhaps its beams are visible through a skylight or a window. Feel how you are connected to your ancestor by being under the same moon they lived (and are still) under.

Say these words:

Oh, well done! I commend your pains;
Because of you I share in the gains.
And now about the altar I sing
Like elves and fairies in a ring,
Drawing forth all that linger near,
The ancestral spirits from the other realm
Join me under this blue moon clear.

Sing, hum, whistle, or chant to raise energy and attract your spirit. Go on doing this for as long as you feel it is necessary. You may know how long because you will begin to feel the presence of a spirit that has entered your realm. Embrace this. Do not fear it.

Whether or not you feel a distinct presence, you should now light the dried leaves in the ashtray or crucible and continue to meditate on your ancestor until the leaves have burned down completely to ash.

I will light my ancestor candle and go back in time to be on board the Mayflower. There is a waxing moon overhead, and in another nine days we will see land. Our hopes rise steadily as the moon's size increases. It is All Hallows' Eve, the old Pagan Samhain, but out here at sea no church bells ring, for we have freed ourselves from the ways of England and our ship sails onward, rocking and rolling on the rough autumnal Atlantic, toward a new land and a new life, a freer and happier life for those of us on this ship who will survive the first year. I stand beside the heavily pregnant Susanna White and her young son, Resolved, and I hold her hand and offer her steadiness and courage. I know that her husband William will die before a year passes, but that she will remarry to fellow passenger Edward Winslow two months later. Spring will come again, and the crops we planted, following the Wampanoags' generous instruction, will grow and eventually flourish, as will her children and their many descendants. I have come to reassure her of that and to thank her for her courage.

Now, close your eyes for a few moments in thankfulness for your ancestors' efforts. Realize how much they did for you and how they have contributed to the person you are now.

When you open your eyes, you can bring your platter of lunar foods close to the altar to share with your ancestor. Savor these slowly, as you watch the candles burn down.

Notes

Notes

Yule

Yule: Joy at the Winter Solstice

Jason Mankey

HUMAN BEINGS HAVE BEEN observing the Winter Solstice for over ten thousand years, making it one of the oldest "holidays" in recorded history. Ancient monuments across the world are aligned with the sun's rise on the year's shortest day, and by the time of the Roman Empire, celebrations of the early winter season had turned joyous and festive. The Roman holidays of Saturnalia (celebrated December 17–23) and the January Kalends (the first days of January) were so revered that many of the customs associated with those days are still with us, and the Western world as a whole, today.

Saturnalia celebrations were primarily about joy. They were a time for heavy drinking and disrupting the social order. Men wore women's clothes, and women returned the favor. Masters waited upon their slaves, everyone ate fine food, and both homes and government buildings were decorated with evergreen branches and holly. This behavior continued during the January Kalends, and in early January people also exchanged presents. All of these customs were later absorbed by the Christian Christmas.

The term *Yule* (sometimes spelled *Jul*) comes to us from the Germanic people of Northern Europe. Yule most likely referred to both a specific holiday (the Winter Solstice) and an extended season. Ancient

Yule most likely lasted from the middle of November until the middle of January. With their world far too cold for agriculture, the Vikings would have sat in their long halls and drank copious amounts of beer and mead in observance of the holiday.

In addition to the heavy drinking, the Norse Yule was similar to the holidays of ancient Rome in other ways too. People decorated with evergreen branches, ate fine food (especially pork), and exchanged gifts. The Norse also decorated with mistletoe at Yule and were probably the first people to center their winter celebrations around the Yule Log.

Yuletide was so popular among the Norse that when Christianity took over Yule was used as a synonym for Christmas. Amongst modern day Witches and Pagans "Yule" is generally used to signify the Winter Solstice. Less popular, but still common in some places, is the term *Midwinter* for the Winter Solstice. Though the solstice marks the start of winter from a celestial perspective, the Celts started their winter season at Samhain (October 31) and marked the beginning of spring at Imbolc (February 2). From that perspective, the Winter Solstice is truly the middle of winter.

In addition to what's been mentioned above, it's likely that other Pagan traditions once associated with the Winter Solstice were absorbed into the Christmas holiday. I use the word *likely* here since it's nearly impossible to tell where Pagan traditions ended and Christian ones began. What's most important when celebrating Yule is using the trappings that speak most to you, regardless of origin.

Amongst the most Pagan of holiday traditions are the gift-givers who visit every Yuletide. Santa Claus is undoubtedly based on the figure of the Christian Saint Nicholas, but Nicholas as a historical figure is rather dubious, and some people think many of his myths were borrowed from Pagan sources. On the road to becoming Santa Claus, Saint Nicholas also borrowed several attributes from the Norse god Odin, including the idea of jumping down the chimney and riding a magickal flying horse (a horse that was later converted into eight or nine reindeer, depending on your feelings about Rudolph).

Northern Europe is full of other Yuletide gift givers who most likely pre-date Christianity. The Yule Goat found in many Scandinavian countries is probably related to the goats who pulled Thor's chariot (they don't tell you that in the Marvel movies!). Iceland's Yule Lads (or goblins and also known as *Jólasveinar* in Icelandic) are thirteen brothers who visit the houses of children over the thirteen nights leading up to Christmas. Originally more pranksters than gift givers, stories about the Yule Lads were banned in Iceland near the end of the eighteenth century for being too scary! The mother of the Yule Lads is the ogress Gryla, who is mentioned in the *Prose Edda* from the early 1200s BCE.

With his horns and cloven hooves, the most Pagan of all Yuletide figures is the Krampus. Native to Germany, but feared as far south as Croatia, the Krampus has been experiencing a serious resurgence over the last two decades. Once an afterthought for many during Yule, the Krampus is now acknowledged throughout Europe and North America, bringing both joy and fear depending on how one feels about him. The Krampus gets his name from the German word *krampen* which translates to "claw" in English. It's also believed that he might be an ancient Pagan figure and has been linked to several Norse deities, though no one is absolutely certain how he originated.

Up until the middle of the nineteenth century, early winter celebrations focused heavily on "misrule." Misrule generally refers to "naughty behavior" such as heavy drinking, gluttony, and fornication, but it has a more sinister side too. In the early 1800s, misrule was increasingly linked to petty vandalism, which is why the practice has largely disappeared in many urban areas. During the winter holidays it was common in many places for those with lower incomes to visit the homes of the rich and exchange songs or small performances for money, gifts, and strong drink. When the rich chose not to comply, they were often the victims of misrule and could potentially end up with a broken window or egg on their house.

Certain parts of misrule have lasted until the present day. The tradition known as *wassailing*, which often revolves around singing in exchange for alcoholic wassail (made from apple cider), became the far more mundane (and benign) custom we now call *caroling*. Misrule eventually became a part of another popular late year holiday, Halloween, and we honor this ancient custom every time we say "Trick or treat."

Celebrating Yule

The celebrations at most sabbats are dictated by the earth's fertility. We celebrate the return of life in the spring and the decline of life in the autumn, but Yule is different. Its celebrations can be joyous or somber, silly or highly meaningful. It's a time for ghost stories and kisses under the mistletoe. Yule can be used to celebrate whatever most resonates with you at the start of winter.

For many Witches, Yule is about the return of the light. The Winter Solstice marks the beginning of the sun's "waxing" phase. From Yule until the Summer Solstice the days will only grow longer. It's common in many Witch circles to hear that the sun has been "reborn" at Yule. Often this rebirth is linked to a Mother Goddess giving birth to the Lord of the Sun who will age throughout the coming year, die at Samhain, and then be reborn once more.

The waxing and waning halves of the year are often depicted as the Oak and Holly Kings by many Witches. The tale of the Oak and Holly Kings involves two brothers in a battle for eternal dominance. At the Summer Solstice the Oak King rises to prominence and vanquishes his brother, the Holly King. The Oak King then rules over the waning half of the year. But at the Winter Solstice the Holly King returns, reborn, and dispatches his brother; he then rules over the waxing half of the year until the story repeats itself again.

Because of the sun's rebirth at Yule some Witches and Pagans celebrate the start of a New Year on the Winter Solstice. While never the most popular "starting point" for the year amongst Witches (that honor goes to Samhain), it does make a certain degree of sense.

Besides, what's wrong with celebrating as many "New Years" as possible?

Many Witches honor Yule with a solstice vigil. They invite friends and family over in the late evening hours on the day of the solstice and then stay up all night playing games, drinking hot chocolate, performing rituals, and doing various magickal activities. As night gives way to day, they watch the sunrise and celebrate the returning light. Solstice vigils can be "drop by" affairs with some people staying just for a few hours and others staying until dawn.

The darkness of Yule provides a wonderful opportunity to look inward and celebrate our shadow selves. Our shadow sides are generally the parts of our subconscious that we don't share with the world at large. Often thought of as negative, our shadow selves are worthy of acknowledgement and respect. By integrating our shadow with our day-to-day self we become better adjusted and more well-rounded Witches. The short days and dark nights of Yuletide are well suited to exploring this side of ourselves.

Divination has been a part of the winter holidays for thousands of years. Yule is a great time of year to get a tarot reading or divine the future by dripping some candle wax into a bowl of cold water and interpreting what shows up. (Melted lead is more traditional here but far messier and more dangerous; candle wax works just fine!)

For the last three thousand years, celebrations on Yule and in late December have been filled with joy. For many people, the period around the Winter Solstice was a time of leisure. In Northern Europe agricultural work was at a minimum, and the grain harvested in September and October had been turned into fine beer (along with the fall's grapes and apples turned into wine and cider respectively). With alcohol and time both plentiful, Yule was an opportunity to be free from the yoke of work and sobriety.

Feasting has been a part of Midwinter celebrations since the Roman Empire and is still with us today. Feasting was popular in the ancient Pagan world and medieval Europe because it marked a time of year when fresh meat was abundant. Animal herds were culled in the late autumn, and the meat was easily stored in the snow and cold to be enjoyed throughout the winter season. Feasting is still a part of December traditions and why my grandmother always served a large Christmas dinner. In Victorian England it was common to celebrate the season with a strong glass of wassail and wishes for continued good health, a practice which makes for a fun and satisfying Witch ritual.

Christmas and Hanukkah are not the only December holidays set aside for gift giving; Yule is the perfect time for exchanging presents. One of Italy's traditional gift givers is Befana, a winter Witch who visits the houses of good children (and Witches!) on her broom. In my coven there's no "Secret Santa," only "Secret Befana!" Gifts don't have to be material things either; cleaning up the natural spaces where we live is a wonderful present to the Earth we love so much.

Nearly all the celebrations associated with Christmas today are either secular or have roots in pre-Christian societies. Because of this it's certainly acceptable to embrace as much of the "Christmas spirit" as you want at Yuletide. Decorate a tree, hang some mistletoe, and put up as many lights as you want! Those traditions belong to Witches and Pagans just as much as they belong to Christians or anyone else.

Many of us who are solitaries or find ourselves away from our chosen magickal families at Yule end up celebrating Christmas by default, and there's nothing wrong with that. When I was forced to miss out on the Solstice due to being with my parents, I simply celebrated Christmas with them and was comforted by the overlap between the two holidays. No matter where you are or who you are with, it's easy to celebrate Yule.

Cosmic Sway

Ivo Dominguez Jr.

BEFORE YULE THERE IS a total solar eclipse on December 14 in the sign of Sagittarius. This is also the New Moon before Yule. The Winter Solstice is symbolically the equivalent to the New Moon in the solar cycle of seasons. You may wish to begin your preparations for Yule by aligning your work and observances with this eclipse. Use this celestial event to move deep within yourself rather than doing active or outwardly-directed work. Clear away the old, release what no longer serves you, and be open to what will come rather than gripping tightly to what was. Listen closely to your lower and your higher nature for guidance. This eclipse occurs midway during Hanukkah and may have special meaning for those that are observant.

There is irony, whimsy, and wisdom in celebrating the light when the dark of the night is longest. With the Winter Solstice the promise of growth is proven with each minute of daylight that increases with the turning of the season. This year the aspects are harmony, with themes of facing the dark and beginning anew. On December 21, the Sun is conjunct Mercury in Capricorn, Jupiter is conjunct Saturn in Aquarius, and a first quarter Moon is conjunct Neptune in Pisces at the Winter Solstice. There are some especially interesting things about the Jupiter and Saturn conjunction that can be used for rituals or working for long-term change.

The Sun conjunct Mercury favors short trips, interaction, and communication. You may wish to have an open house or check in on friends, neighbors, and family. One of the ways that the light returns is in the sharing that comes from seeing the light in each other's eyes. This means face-to-face contact. In your rituals and celebrations include words and deeds where people exchange blessings and affirm their connection to one another. You are passing along a spark of the Sun to each other, and all have the rekindled light. The full manifestation of what you do on the Solstice will come in February at Imbolc.

The first quarter Moon conjunct Neptune in Pisces brings forth the power of your imagination and your psychic senses. The drawback to this aspect is that it is easy to drift off into dreaming and forget to anchor your visions back to things that are tangible here. If you emphasize the waxing of the moon, then its forward thrust will help you bring visions into reality. This aspect also makes you more sensitive to your feelings and to the feelings of others, which can be put to good use or can become overwhelming. But you have a choice in how this plays out. In planning any ritual observances, it will be helpful if you make symbolic linkages either by words or actions between the growing of the light of the solar cycle and the waxing of the Moon. Take advantage of the fact that both energetic tides are moving in the same direction.

Jupiter, among other things, is the power of hope and inherent understanding of growth and development, philosophies of life, and more. Saturn, among other things, is the knowledge of how things work in the physical world, it is limits and form, it is the soul of pragmatism. Whenever a conjunction occurs between Jupiter and Saturn, it is the beginning of a new cycle of development that sets the tone for the following twenty years. In and of itself this would be significant, but it is also the beginning of a new two-hundred-year cycle. These conjunctions between Jupiter and Saturn slowly move through the four elements of the signs. For the last two-hundred years, the conjunctions have been in earth signs and, beginning with the Winter Solstice, they will be in air signs for the next two-hundred years.

This Yule, it is particularly important to focus on what is needed to fulfill your long-term goals. If you are uncertain about your goals, then take time to explore your thoughts and feelings to clarify them. It would be prudent to include plans related to fostering safety, stability, and comfort in your life. The transition from one element to another also means the ending of the status quo of the last two-hundred years and dramatic changes as the new pattern for the next two centuries takes hold. This conjunction takes place in Aquarius, which is ruled by Saturn and Uranus, and is also one of the markers for the slow and steady shift into the Age of Aquarius. This means that the conjunction will lean more towards far-reaching change at all levels of society; be prepared. Consider what part you have to play in making the world better. This is one of the deepest lessons of Yule: bring the light back to the world starting with the bright spark that dwells within you.

For those that may be attending Christmas festivities, Mercury is trine to Uranus after the Moon is conjunct Uranus on Christmas Eve. These aspects have the potential to facilitate good communication and hopeful attitudes, so long as there is an awareness that it takes time to mend or improve relationships. The December holidays can be stressful, but they can also renew your connections to people. If you expect immediate change you may be disappointed. If you choose to value the sparks of possibilities that can, with tending, grow brighter, then you will feel the warmth of the holidays.

The morning of New Year's Eve may start with you feeling ungrounded and unmotivated with the Moon void-of-course in Cancer. There is also the lingering influence of Venus square Neptune from the previous day. This aspect can encourage procrastination and excuses for neglecting your to-do list. The Moon moves into Leo in time for evening revelries. With the Moon in Leo, the time is right for dressing up and having fun. If you love parties, this is the Moon for a spectacular party. If you prefer a night at home, this is a great time for pampering yourself and indulging in whatever you like.

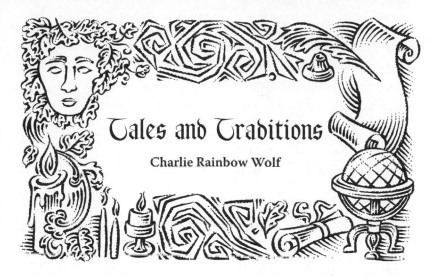

Tales and Traditions

Charlie Rainbow Wolf

YOU'VE NO DOUBT HEARD of the song "The Twelve Days of Christmas." Many people believe this is about the twelve days running up to Christmas Day, but it's actually about the twelve days *after* Christmas, leading up to Twelfth Night. This was celebrated on either the fifth or sixth of January and was a time for feasting and parties.

Twelfth Night Celebrations

In medieval England and later, Twelfth Night signified the end of winter, which started at Samhain. Twelfth Night cake—a very rich fruit cake made with nuts and spices—was eaten, and it was not uncommon for the servants to take up the role as master and mistress of the household, with their rich employers acting as their servants. Some Twelfth Night cakes would include a pea or a bean or other such marker. Whoever got that slice was appointed the head of the house for the evening and given the title of Lord (or Lady) of Misrule, echoing the old Roman celebrations of Saturnalia.

In our household, Twelfth Night was the time that all the Christmas and Yule decorations came down. My mother always believed it was bad luck to take them down before Twelfth Night.

Anything left up after the sixth of January needed to stay up for the rest of the year until the next Yule festivities. Even now, I still have a string of blue fairy lights around one of my doors because they got overlooked when packing things away!

Holly and Mistletoe

Other beliefs, or some might even say superstitions, surrounded the seasonal decorations of holly and mistletoe. Mistletoe is steeped in folklore and was used in order to bring happiness and prosperity to the household. Some traditions thought it was bad luck to bring mistletoe into the home before New Year's Day, and to do so was inviting trouble for the coming year. Others said it was bad luck to take it down immediately after Yule, and that it should be left in place until the following Yuletide celebrations and only then replaced with a fresh sprig. Kissing under the mistletoe is still popular. It is said that to have a long and happy marriage you must kiss your partner under the mistletoe, and refusing to do this would bring bad luck to your relationship. An unwed woman should place sprigs of mistletoe under her pillow so that she might dream about her future husband.

Holly is another seasonal decoration, and like mistletoe it has a lot of—sometimes contradictory—folklore behind it. In some areas it is bad luck to burn holly when finished with it, yet in other places this is the only way to dispose of it to ensure bad luck does not follow! Holly boughs were often hung with garlands of ivy, representing the divine male and female energies. In some traditions these were kept up until Shrove Tuesday and then burned in the fire that cooked the pancakes.

Wassailing

Twelfth Night was also known for wassailing. The word wassail comes from an old Saxon phrase, *waes hael*, meaning "good health to you." You may have heard of this in the Christmas song "Here We Come a-Wassailing," an established English carol also sung at Yule and composed in the mid-nineteenth century.

Wassail is an alcoholic beverage made from hot mulled cider. At this time of year, when the "Christmas spirit" often made people more generous than usual, the poorer class would go caroling and sing this song, hoping to get a sip from the wassail bowl, a coin, something to eat, or even just to stand in the warmth briefly. Wassail was sometimes known as lamb's wool because of its frothy appearance.

Honoring the Ways

You can host your own Twelfth Night celebrations. Make the fruitcake and put a token in it, and let that person be the Lord or Lady of Misrule for the evening. Turn taking down the seasonal decorations into an event that is just as festive as when they went up, full of laughter and merriment and optimism for what the new year has to bring. Enjoying each other's company is a wonderful tonic for the lull in energy that often follows Yule and the New Year.

Games were traditionally a big part of the Twelfth Night events, so why not include them in your own gathering? One popular game was to give each person a spoon and pass an egg from spoon to spoon; drop the egg, and you're out! A new egg was introduced, and the game continued until there was a winner. Another game had two people toss an egg back and forth, moving farther apart after each toss, until one person dropped it and was out. (For a vegan alternative, plastic Easter eggs filled with some kind of weight such as sand or clay will work just as well.)

You might also want to make your own wassail. The ingredients can be as simple or as complex as you wish to make them. Traditionally wassail was alcoholic, but you could use soft cider to get a similar beverage. This is the recipe I have used in the past:

6 small, tart apples
2 ounces of demerara sugar
4 pints of hard cider (or apple juice)
2 lemons, halved and with 4 cloves stuck into the skin of each half

6 ounces of granulated sugar
½ ounce fresh ginger, grated finely
Assorted seasonal spices, such as nutmeg, cinnamon, and cardamom

Core the apples and put a spoonful of the demerara sugar in the holes. Place them on a baking tray (one that has sides) lined with parchment paper and bake them in a moderate-temperature oven until soft. At the same time, bring the liquid ingredient to a simmer and add the lemons, granulated sugar, ginger, and the spices. When it is simmering, remove the apples from the oven and add them to the mixture. Serve hot. (Please note that some traditional wassail recipes include egg yolks; we do not add them to ours and never have.)

References

Reed, Simon. *Wassailing: The British Midwinter Blessing Custom.* London: Troy Books, 2013.

"'Wassail', 'Yule', and More: The Stories Behind 8 Holiday Words." Merriam-Webster, n.d. https://www.merriam-webster.com /words-at-play/wassail-yule-holiday-word-origins/wassail.

Struthers, Jane. *The Book of Christmas: Everything We Once Knew and Loved About Christmastime.* Ebury Press, 2012.

Feasts and Treats

Sue Pesznecker

Yule marks the arrival of the Winter Solstice and its deep darkness. It's a traditional time to gather with family and friends, share gifts and feasts, and celebrate the return of the light. Our main dish of lemon chicken features bright, citrusy flavors to welcome the sun's return and a round cake of crispy golden rice to emulate the sun itself. For dessert? A Brandy Alexander pie, because everyone likes a little celebratory libation, right?

Auntie Donna's Lemon Chicken

This recipe came to me from my sister-in-law, and I've modified it and made it my own. She had a favorite Chinese restaurant and eventually talked the chef into sharing the base recipe. My variation has become my son's most-requested birthday dinner. He's forty now, and I'm still making it!

Prep time: 1 hour
Inactive: 2–3 hours to overnight
Cooking time: 30–45 minutes
Servings: 4–8

Marinade

Chicken thighs or breasts (with bones and skin; allow 2 pieces per
person)
2 tablespoons vegetable oil
4 teaspoons soy sauce
1 teaspoon sherry
½ teaspoon black pepper

Several hours (or the day before) dinner:
Bone the chicken,* leaving the skin on. (Leaving the skin on is
very important!)
Combine the boned breasts, vegetable oil, soy sauce, sherry, and
black pepper. Stir well. Cover and refrigerate for at least 2–3 hours
or as long as overnight.
*Freeze the bones for your next pot of soup stock (see Samhain
recipes).

Lemon Sauce

1½ cups water
6 tablespoons sugar
¼ cup ketchup
Juice of 2 large lemons
1 teaspoon vegetable oil
Dash of salt
1 tablespoon cornstarch
3 tablespoons cold water

About 90 minutes before dinner:
Prepare the lemon sauce. Combine the water with the sugar,
ketchup, lemon juice, oil, and salt. Bring to a very light boil over
medium heat. Combine the cornstarch and cold water in a custard
cup, stirring to dissolve. When the lemon sauce mixture comes to a
boil, slowly add the cornstarch and water mixture. Simmer the mixture until it thickens slightly. Cover and keep warm.

For frying
1 box cornstarch
½–¾ cup vegetable oil

About an hour before dinner:
Drain the chicken. Dredge the chicken pieces in cornstarch and set in a single layer on a clean wire rack. The dredging should set up and dry slightly, and the chicken will warm up a little.

About 30 minutes before dinner:
Preheat the oven to 170° F. Heat the vegetable oil over medium heat in a deep frying pan or large, broad-bottomed kettle. When it is quite hot (about 350°; it will look shimmery), add the chicken pieces, frying 2–3 at a time. Don't crowd the pan by adding too many at once as this will drop the oil temperature.

Turn the pieces once as they brown. Total cooking time is 8–9 minutes. If using breasts and thighs, cook all the thighs first (they'll cook more quickly than the white meat) and then all the breasts.

Drain the fried pieces on paper towels for a few minutes, then arrange on a serving platter and place in the preheated oven to keep warm while the rest cook.

Garnish
Fresh lemon, thinly sliced
Shreds of green onion, sliced the long way

To serve, slice each piece of chicken into 1-inch slices and arrange on a platter. Drizzle with a small amount of warm lemon sauce. Garnish with lemon slices and long shreds of green onion. Serve additional lemon sauce on the side.

Crispy Rice Cake

This variation of a Persian recipe is a perfect foil for the lemon chicken. The end result is a plate-sized buttery rice cake with a crispy golden top.

Prep time: 20 minutes
Cooking time: 15 minutes to make the rice; 25–30 minutes to cook the cake
Inactive: 2–3 hours
Servings: 4–8

2 cups white rice (jasmine works too)
1 tablespoon salt
6–8 tablespoons unsalted butter
Slivered green onions or parsley sprigs for garnish

Early in the day, or at least three hours before dinner:
Cook the rice in 2 quarts of water with the salt until the rice is done and has a soft bite. Note: All the water will not be absorbed!

Immediately rinse the rice in a strainer, flushing with cold water to stop the cooking. Allow the rice to drain and dry somewhat. Set aside, covered, at room temperature until time to use.

About 30 minutes before dinner:
Heat a wide, deep frying pan over medium heat.

Add 3 tablespoons of the unsalted butter and swirl to coat the pan. Immediately add the rice to the frying pan, packing it in to form a solid cake. Drizzle with another 3–5 tablespoons of melted butter (depending on how much decadence you're looking for). Lay a paper towel* over the rice, add a tight lid, and allow to cook on stove top for 20–30 minutes.

Use a table knife to pry back an edge of the cake—you should see a golden crispy layer. To serve, remove the pan from the heat, loosen the edges with a table knife, place a large platter over the frying pan, and (using two pot holders) flip them over to release the rice cake onto the platter. Garnish with parsley or more green onions.

*The paper towel helps absorb moisture from steam.

Brandy Alexander Pie

This is a spin-off of the famous grasshopper pie, only with flavors of chocolate and brandy instead of chocolate and mint.

Prep time: 30 minutes
Cooking time: 10 minutes
Freezing time: several hours
Servings: 8

1⅓ cups chocolate cookie crumbs, finely ground, or a premade chocolate cookie crust
5–6 tablespoons unsalted butter, melted
30 large marshmallows
⅔ cup whole milk
1½ ounces white creme de cacao
1½ ounces good quality brandy
1 cup heavy cream
Optional:
½ cup heavy cream
½ teaspoon vanilla
1 teaspoon sugar

Nine or more hours before serving:
Preheat oven to 325° F.

Make the crust. Place the cookie crumbs in a pie plate. Drizzle 5 tablespoons of the melted butter over the crumbs, then mix them and press into the pie pan. (If the crumbs don't come together, add the additional 1 tablespoon of melted butter.)

Bake the crust for 10 minutes. Cool completely on a wire rack.

Seven or more hours before serving:
In a double boiler over simmering water, melt the marshmallows in the milk. When completely melted and smooth, remove from heat and cool. When just barely warm, stir in the liquors.

Whip the cream to stiff peaks and *gently* fold into the cooled marshmallow mixture. Pile this into the cooled crust. Cover and freeze until solid, at least 4–6 hours.

Ten to fifteen minutes before serving:

Remove pie from freezer.

If desired, prepare sweetened whipped cream. Beat heavy cream in a chilled bowl with the vanilla and sugar until peaks form.

Slice pie and serve with dollops of the whipped cream.

Yuletini

Remember the cranberry cordial you made in the Samhain recipes section? It's time to put it to work.

Prep time: 5 minutes

Servings: varies

1 tablespoon whole cranberry sauce (homemade is best!)

3 tablespoons cranberry cordial (from the Samhain recipes section),
    finished according to the recipe

Juice of ½ mandarin or satsuma orange, freshly squeezed

Bubbly: champagne, Prosecco, lemon-lime soda, ginger ale, or sparkling water

Orange peel

Ice a martini glass.

Muddle the cranberry sauce in a cocktail shaker or glass canning jar. Add the cordial, juice, and several ice cubes; shake to blend and chill. Strain into the chilled martini class. Top with your choice of bubbly to fill the glass, and garnish with a piece of orange peel.

Crafty Crafts

Tess Whitehurst

ALMOST EVERYTHING WE DO to celebrate Yuletide is about one thing: bringing light and warmth to our hearts during this cold, dark time of year. While the bright sun and long days of the summer months naturally promote energy and vitality, we often feel the need to generate our own excitement and enthusiasm during the winter season. Many ancient people believed that our own actions, behaviors, and beliefs assisted the sun in being reborn at the Winter Solstice. Psychologically this still feels true to us today. At the Winter Solstice, we feel that our hearts contain and protect the seed form of the bright potentiality of the sun's full flowering. By celebrating sweetness and joy during these darker months that are often bitterly cold, we sense that we are supporting the turning of the wheel and the rebirth of the sun.

This craft is a fun way to bolster our anticipation and festive spirits as we approach Yule, the year's darkest day, which contains the promise of the light's return.

Chocolate contains theobromine, an alkaloid that gets its name from chocolate's scientific name, *Theobroma cacao*, which literally translates to "food of the gods" (Singh and Cook 2018). In addition to boosting your mood, some studies indicate that theobromine is good for your heart, boosts energy, reduces inflammation, and supports throat and respiratory health (Martínez-Pinilla et al. 2015). The Aztecs credited their wise and powerful deity Quetzalcoatl with gifting the world with cacao beans (the definitive ingredient in chocolate). Aztecs and Mayans valued cacao beans so highly they used them as currency. Magically, chocolate draws and enhances romantic love and helps us resonate at the frequency of luxurious wealth. And, of course, it's always nice to have a bit of sweetness to look forward to during these bitterly dark and cold winter days.

Yule Countdown Bunting

In feng shui, triangles (such as the triangle shapes featured in this decoration) symbolize and hold the energy of the fire element. In addition to its other magical and mood-boosting benefits, you'll find this bunting brings a burst of cheerful warmth to your space, just as any Yule decoration should.

Materials

Wrapping paper scraps (this is a good opportunity to use up the ends of rolls and even old gift bags you no longer want to use)

Construction or copy paper (you could even use old scratch paper)

An iron

Scissors

A hole punch

Glue (I used Elmer's)

Hemp twine

Small chocolates (I used Ghirardelli minis)

21 small paper squares or gift tags

Optional: a Yule season journal (any notebook or journal will do, but consider finding a festive one that you love) and pen

Cost: $10–$12

Time spent: 1–1½ hours, plus dry time

Using the wrapping paper, cut 21 triangles for the bunting. I made mine about 8 inches long and about 5–6 inches wide at the top.

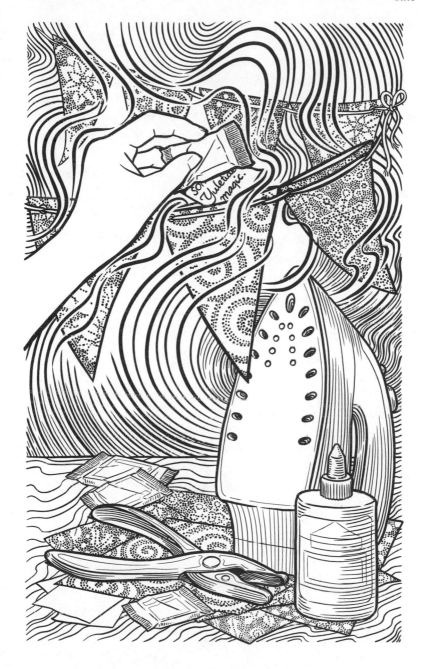

Next, set the iron on low heat and use it to flatten any curling or bent pieces.

For each triangle, cut one triangle at equal size using the construction, copy, or notepaper. Line the bottom edges of the wrapping paper with glue and affix it to the construction or copy paper. Repeat with each triangle until all 21 are glued along the bottom edges so each one forms a triangular pouch that is open on top. Allow to dry for 4 hours or overnight.

While the glue is drying, on each of the 21 paper squares or gift tags, write one of the following instructions:

Savor the scents of Yuletide.

Seek out the beauty of colored lights.

Eat a delicious treat.

Laugh as much as you can.

Spread joy wherever you go.

Receive gifts and compliments graciously.

Give with joy.

Make a Yuletide wish.

Listen to a Yuletide song.

Make someone smile.

Dance.

Relax your mind and go within.

Tell someone something you love about them.

Sing a Yule carol.

Perform a random act of kindness.

Wear something festive.

Work some Yuletide magic.

Establish a new tradition.

Expect a miracle.

Connect with the light within.

Celebrate.

When you've written each of these instructions (or other ones—feel free to dream up your own) on one tag, turn them upside down and shuffle them around.

Once the glue is dry, use the hole punch to create a hole at the upper corners of each triangle. You may need to use the iron on a low setting again if any of the triangles have curled or warped.

Use a long piece of hemp twine to string each triangle together. Thread it from back to front and then from front to back so the hemp twine is visible at the top of each triangle. Tie another piece to the original piece if necessary to make sure you have enough twine. Leave plenty of twine on either end so you can hang it. Now, take one instruction tag (without looking at what it says) and one piece of chocolate and tuck them into one of the triangles. Repeat until every triangle contains one chocolate and one instruction.

On November 30 or December 1, hang the bunting somewhere that looks right. Anywhere indoors will do: on your mantel, near your altar, in your kitchen, in your entryway, or along the side of your staircase. In addition to being a festive addition to your Yuletide décor, these delightful paper flags will help you count down the days to the Solstice while keeping your spirits bright in the process. Starting on the far left on December 1, remove the contents from the first triangle. Sometime throughout the day, savor the chocolate and follow the instruction.

If you'd like, you can take some time at the end of each day to write in your Yuletide journal about how you followed the daily instruction, how it went for you, and what you learned about Yule. For example, perhaps you received the instruction to "Celebrate." Throughout the day, you looked for reasons to celebrate: the parking spot you found, the cake someone brought to work, the discount you unexpectedly received. Instead of simply saying, "Thank you," you instead exclaimed, "Yay!" "Awesome," or "Woohoo!" This not only brought a smile to your face, it also in some cases sparked smiles and laughter from those around you, which lifted your spirits even further. When recording all this in your journal, you may discover that spreading joy at Yuletide can be much simpler than you thought.

Here are some questions to help you integrate the magic and deepen your relationship with this profoundly powerful time of year.

Answer the following questions at the end of each day:

- What was your instruction for the day?
- How did you follow it?
- What happened when you followed it?
- How did it feel?
- What Yule wisdom did you learn or observe today?

References

Martínez-Pinilla, Eva, Ainhoa Oñatibia-Astibia, and Rafael Franco. 2015. "The Relevance of Theobromine for the Beneficial Effects of Cocoa Consumption." *Frontiers in Pharmacology* 6, no. 30. https://doi.org/10.3389/fphar.2015.00030.

Singh, R. Paul, and L. Russell Cook. 2018. "Cacao: Tree." Encyclopedia Britannica. Encyclopedia Britannica, Inc. https://www.britannica.com/plant/cacao.

Spells

Michael Furie

THE WINTER SOLSTICE IS truly an enchanted time filled with the promise of new light, and yet it also marks the official beginning of winter when the cold weather and early sunsets may feel a bit bleak. In order to keep the festivities properly focused and attuned to the comfort and hope that underlies this season, it is good practice to have some extra little magical touches in place that will energize the atmosphere with holiday joy and give a bit of magic to those in need.

Yuletide Witch Ball Spell

Witch balls are an old magical device most often used as a protection against malevolent magic, but they can be used for any purpose. This time of year they are quite easily made, as their primary component is a hollow glass (or plastic) ball. Ideally it will have a loop or hook for hanging, like a Christmas tree ornament. An effective, seasonally appropriate witch ball to bring vitality and ward off illness can be made from just a few ingredients. Craft stores are the most likely places to find clear or translucent round ornaments that can be opened.

Materials

1 round ornament that can be opened at the top
Sea salt
A few small sprigs of fresh rosemary
1 small culinary funnel
1 red candle
1 green candle
1 stick pine incense and a holder
Cup of water

If you have a Yule or Christmas tree set up in your home, this witch ball can certainly be placed upon it. To begin, gather all of the needed items on a work table, placing the green candle at the rear left and the red candle at the rear right with the incense in between them. The cup of water can be set on the middle left while the salt is placed on the middle right with the rest of the materials in between them. Light the green candle, which represents continued life and greenery, and then light the red candle, which represents the life force and the power of the sun. The incense is lit next, which not only represents the season but also healing and vitality. Once the atmosphere is prepared, the witch ball can be made.

Using the funnel, pour some of the salt into the witch ball, filling it about halfway. Pick up two or three of the rosemary sprigs, trim them if needed so that they'll fit into the witch ball, and stick them through the hole into the salt. This is intended to look like a winter scene with evergreen trees in the snow. Once you have added the desired amount of rosemary, but before you put the lid back on, hold the witch ball in both hands and visualize a snow-covered field with a few evergreen trees. See the winter sunlight shining down upon the trees, filling them with strength and energy. Mentally send this power through your hands into the witch ball. When you feel like the ball is fully charged, end the visualization and screw the top back on while saying:

Orb of power and vitality, gathered, captured, held within; witch ball now a magical battery, to fuel my strength, my vigor and vim; boost to health each winter day, the waxing sun shall light my way.

Once the witch ball is sealed, it can either be hung on a string in a window, on a mantle, or directly on a Yule tree.

Cranberry Garland for Protection and a Loving Home

For many, one of the most cherished aspects of the winter holidays is the time spent in "old fashioned" activities like making home-made gifts or decorations. Witches and other magical folk can take this to a heightened level and infuse energy and intent into all of our creations, which can be a delightful aid to our celebrations. This spell will empower a traditional Yule tree garland—a string of cran-berries—and energize it with protective and harmonizing qualities to help ensure a happy home.

Materials

Large sewing needle
Heavy thread or dental floss
Fresh cranberries

The amount of cranberries that will be needed varies according to how long you wish the garland to be, but a couple of pounds should make a decent-sized string. Before you begin, make certain to wear old clothes, and cover your work space with newspaper or a drop cloth because the cranberry juice could stain. First, measure out the desired length of thread or dental floss plus an extra two feet, and thread it through the needle. Tie a knot about one foot from the end. String the cranberries one or two at a time until the thread is full, then tie a knot in the needle end of the cord, again leaving about one foot of extra length. Remove the needle and coil the finished garland up small enough that you can hold it in both hands. While holding it, close your eyes and visualize a cheerful, happy environment as strongly as possible. Try to feel all warm and fuzzy, and as you mentally send this energy into the cranberry garland, say:

Bright red berries of winter's delight, bringing warmth and happiness into this place; protect and nurture the love and the light, of yuletide cheer and comfort and grace; gift all those who gaze on thee with holiday joy and blessed be.

Place the garland on the Yule tree or wherever you have chosen to hang it. The spell is now complete.

Spreading Good Cheer

Most spells that are cast are centered on our own lives and sometimes around our loved ones, but this spell differs in that it is designed to give a bit of luck and blessings to unknown strangers who may be struggling during the holiday season.

Materials
1 roll of coins (quarters or dimes)
1 bowl of saltwater
1 clean bowl
1 towel
1 white candle
1 bottle frankincense or cinnamon oil
1 small bag, pouch, or coin purse

Break open the roll of coins and place all of the coins into the saltwater, leaving them there overnight. This will cleanse the coins as well as remove any random energy from them. The next morning, rinse the coins in fresh water and dry them. After they have dried, gather the coins into the clean bowl and take them to your working table. Anoint the white candle with the oil (either frankincense or cinnamon, as they are both high-vibration oils) from the wick end to the base and set it behind the bowl of coins. Also anoint your hands and forehead (on the third eye area) lightly with the oil. Light the candle. Holding both hands over the bowl of coins, concentrate on feelings of blessing and happiness; visualize white light streaming out of your hands into the bowl, imbuing each of the coins with magical power.

As you visualize, say:

Blessings be on every token, each one touched with universal light; gentle spell of blessing spoken, these special gifts, left in plain sight; upon the bearer good fortune bestowed, and from hand to hand the magic shall grow; for good of all with harm to none, so I say, this spell is done.

Snuff out the candle and pour the coins from the bowl into the coin purse for storage until you are ready to distribute them. When you are ready, take some or all of the coins with you when you run errands, leaving a coin or two in random places as your intuition guides. You can leave them on store shelves, on the ground, at payphones (the few that still exist), or anywhere that seems safe to do so.

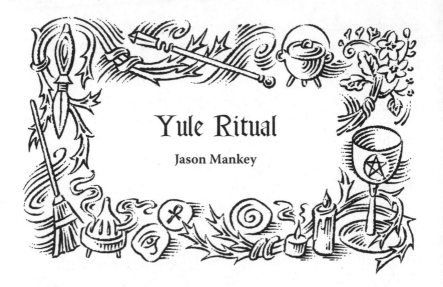

Yule Ritual

Jason Mankey

MANY YULE RITUALS FOCUS on the returning sun and the increasing sunlight that comes after the Winter Solstice. But Midwinter is also a time to look into the darkness, to gaze upon our deficiencies and do something about them.

Into Winter's Darkness

This ritual focuses on changing ourselves through getting rid of the emotions and tendencies that hold us back and stop us from reaching our full potential.

For this ritual, you'll need:
Flash paper
Sturdy ceramic bowl or small iron cauldron
Lighter
Pencil or pen
Pitcher of water to keep nearby (just in case)

This ritual can be performed any time of day, though I think it works better if started in the darkness of night (or evening). Unlike many sabbat rituals, this rite continues on in small ways past

Yule, so it requires a bit of an investment in time. But the results are worth it. This ritual is designed for solitary practitioners but can be adapted for group ritual.

Start by setting up your ritual space in whatever way is most comfortable for you. Call the powers of the four elements (earth, air, fire, and water), light a few candles, and cast a magick circle if that calls to you. Once your container is set up to your liking, invoke the higher powers to bless your rite and lend their energies to it.

This night of Yule I call to the Lord and Lady and all that lies in between. Great God of the Sun, be with me in this sacred space. Lend me your cleansing and purifying energies as I seek to vanquish that which is negative in myself. Eternal Lord, join me as the Horned One, he who finds joy in all that is pleasurable and good and guards the wild spaces.

Loving Mother, Goddess of the Earth, bless this rite and this space tonight. Help me to grow as your world does, strong and vibrant, with deep roots and healthy branches. Watch over me as I purge from myself all that is unneeded in this life. Lovely Lady, impart your wisdom to me as the Crone, she who knows all and shares all secrets with those who love her.

To the Lord and Lady and all that lies in between, I say, hail and welcome!

Sit for a moment in the candlelight and take a couple of deep, purifying, breaths. Focus upon being in a magickal place, surrounded by the changing energy of the Earth as she approaches her rebirth at Yule. Feel her power shift and pulse as we prepare to move into the waxing half of the year.

Now look inward and reflect on the habits and attitudes that hold you back in life. This could be an addiction or a harmful lifestyle choice, or it might be something far more subtle. It could be an unhealthy anger that you can't let go of, or a tendency towards sloth and inaction. Think deeply upon the things that hold you back in this life and that which you most wish to change.

When you've decided upon what it is that you wish to get rid of, write those things down on the flash paper. You don't have to choose just one thing. When I perform this ritual, I usually pick three or four aspects of myself that need improvement. As you write down the behaviors that are holding you back, reflect upon them and how they impact your life in negative and harmful ways.

Using either a lighter, a match, or a lit candle, set your first piece of flash paper to light, immediately dropping it into your cauldron or ceramic bowl. As you drop the burning paper, imagine what is written upon it burning away inside of yourself, and visualize overcoming its harmful influence. As it burns, say:

With the power of the newborn sun, I burn away all that no longer serves me. I rid myself of all that stops me from being the person I know that I can be. May the returning light cleanse and guide me in the coming year, allowing me to rise up and seize the life I am meant to have! In the names of the Lord and Lady, so mote it be!

Repeat this step as many times as needed until all of your pieces of flash paper are burnt. I suggest letting each piece of flash paper burn down completely before lighting another one. This will help keep your magickal area safe and prevent the chance of an unwanted bigger fire. (Unlikely with flash paper, but it doesn't hurt to be careful.)

After all the pieces of paper have been burned, finish your spell by thanking the goddess and god:

Lord and Lady, take me from that which holds me back in this life. Let your magick and energies wash over me tonight and in the days going forward, as I celebrate the waxing half of the year. By the power of the cleansing sun, so mote it be!

Your magickal work having ended, thank the higher powers you've called to, and release the energy and powers you've summoned forth. Be sure to extinguish the candles you've lit and that the flash paper you've burned has been completely extinguished. (I usually take my bowl or cauldron to my kitchen sink when I'm done with this ritual and pour water into it, just in case.) As you head off to sleep, think of the negative things inside of you burning away and moving out of your life.

The next morning, as you first step outside, raise your face up to the sun. Even if it's cold, feel its rays upon your skin. Think for a moment about the things from last night that you are trying to remove from your life, and imagine the sun's energy moving through you, cleansing you, and burning away all that doesn't serve you. As the sun shines down upon you (or its energy pierces the December clouds), say:

As the sun grows in the sky, so too shall I grow! May the power of the reborn sun drive away that which holds me back and keep it from returning! Hail the sun!

Repeat the above for the first couple of days after your Yule ritual and notice the sun's growing power. Continually feel that energy moving through you and keeping your worst impulses in check. Throughout the year if your bad behaviors and/or tendencies try and re-emerge, stand in the light of the sun and use its energy to burn away those feelings. Happy Yule!

Notes

Imbolc

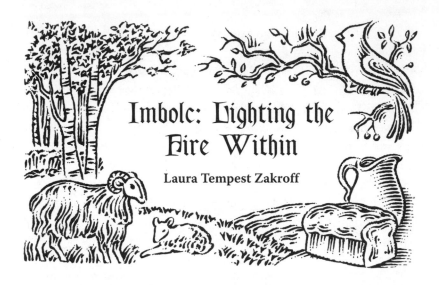

Imbolc: Lighting the Fire Within

Laura Tempest Zakroff

WHEN WE CELEBRATE THE Winter Solstice, we simultaneously mark the shortest day and the longest night. With seasonal traditions focusing on the lighting of candles and the making of bonfires, our spirits are warmed to know that the light shall be returning, and with it, spring. But there are still a fair amount of dark days ahead of us before we truly feel that the light is back. With blankets of snow and dried leaves often covering the ground, the earth may still look very much asleep to our eyes. But there is life stirring below.

Settled in the space between the Winter Solstice and the Spring Equinox is Imbolc. On the calendar in the Northern Hemisphere, we find that the middle point rests traditionally on the dates between January 31 and February 2. Imbolc rests in a liminal space between the end of winter and the beginning of spring. This threshold timing is ideal for refreshing our spaces and to remind ourselves that the promise of spring is almost upon us.

The word Imbolc, also spelled Imbolg, is commonly believed to have originated from Old Irish and means "in the belly." This phrase likely refers to the swollen bellies of pregnant livestock—in particular the ewes, who will be giving birth soon. Another popular translation is "to wash/cleanse oneself," which could connect to ritual baths, cleansing the home, or the tending of wells to clear away winter debris, etc.

Imbolc is also known as Saint Brigid's Day (in Scottish Gaelic, *Là Fhèill Brìghde;* and in Irish, *Lá Fhéile Bríde*), or as most Pagans and Witches know her—the goddess Brigid. She is known to preside over many things including the hearth, springs and wells, animals and fertility, healing, poetry, and fire and smith working. It is through Brigid that we see how both of the Imbolc meanings of "in the belly" and "to wash/cleanse" make perfect sense historically. As a protector of animals and bringer of fertility, she would be asked to bless the flocks and fields. The cleaning of the home in preparation for spring, as well as tending to wells and springs, was done in her honor and with her blessing for good health. Her fire illuminates the darkness and inspires the spirit in song and poetry. By the way, if you're curious as to why a Pagan goddess is also known as a saint, many believe that she was such a popular and beloved goddess that the Catholic Church had to transform her into a saint to bring her followers into the fold. (For more information on this multifaceted deity, I highly recommend *Brigid: History, Mystery, and Magick of the Celtic Goddess* by Courtney Weber.)

Another name for this day is Candlemas, which is the Feast of the Purification of the Blessed Virgin Mary in the Catholic Church. Yuletide decorations in both the church and home were to be cleared out and disposed of on this day, and parishioners could bring their candles in to be blessed for the year. It's also interesting to note that February 3 is the feast day of Saint Blaise of Sebaste. The observation of his day involves the Blessing of the Throats, which is done with a pair of crossed white candles adorned with a red ribbon. Note the connection and old associations with cleansing, healing, light, and fire that carry through on these feast days.

Navel-Gazing for Good

You might be thinking, "Hmmm…but what if I don't have any livestock that need blessing, no wells to clear, and I'm not big on smith work or the bardic arts?" Or perhaps you don't feel aligned with a Celtic goddess and the related traditions at this point in your path. That's fine. Imbolc can still play an important role in helping you center yourself.

Modern culture is very result-oriented, prizing benchmarks of progress, awards and certificates, and letters at the end of a name. We ask ourselves, "What's the next major deadline, the big goal on the horizon? Where do I need to get to?" It's even true in Witchcraft. How often do we ask, "What degree or level of training are you at? What are you doing for the *big* sabbat? What's the next thing?"

Yet it's the journey between where we are in the present moment and those high-priority, important destinations that makes everything worthwhile. Imbolc is an ideal opportunity to take stock of the moment, to reflect upon our paths right here, right now. We can use this time to heal and clear away mental and emotional debris, make room for new growth, and illuminate our paths for the next step.

If you crafted a sigil at the beginning of the year to set the tone, or made a resolution for yourself, this is a wonderful time to check in and see how you are doing. Are there old habits that are impeding your progress that you wish to curb or eliminate? Now's the time to do some cleansing work to help release you from what's holding you back. Are there opportunities and new patterns you wish to implement? This is a great time to do some drawing spellcraft to give fertility to those possibilities.

But what if you feel you're making good progress all around? You feel on top of what you need to get rid of and what you need to manifest. Then perhaps consider giving yourself a little break and take this opportunity to do some self-care, because once things get moving, it may be a while before you get another chance to rest. That may seem counterintuitive, but you can clearly see in nature that it's necessary. In many of the places I have lived, at Imbolc you can tell that the earth is slowly shifting from a period of rest to getting ready to be productive and active. The ground thaws as the ice melts, last fall's leaves have started to become this year's new soil, and the early risers of the plant world are preparing to burst forth. With the right combination of sun, rain, and fertilizer, the earth becomes ready to bloom.

By the way, self-care isn't all about taking baths, getting a massage, and other lovely lux things. It can definitely include scheduling your annual physical, taking a class of some kind to stimulate your body or mind, going on a weekend retreat to reconnect with nature or perhaps some old friends, binge-watching a favorite movie or TV series, or doing something small to beautify your space that makes you feel good. Health and well-being are a mind, body, and spirit experience, so take this time to look at the whole you.

The Year I Ruined Imbolc for Everyone

Focusing inward can be a difficult experience. We are often our worst critics—honed and developed from years of absorbing everyone else's opinions and demands on us. So I would like to remind you that humor is a wonderful balm for the soul that can really help us gain perspective in new ways. It may seem like blasphemy, but getting a bit silly with our sabbat time can definitely give us a more realistic view of ourselves and the world. I believe that having some fun can make us better Witches all around. To aid in this lightening of mood, I'm going to share with you the story of what has come to be known as "The Year Tempest Ruined Imbolc."

Now, when I wake up in the morning, normally the first thing I do is rearrange my body around the one to four cats that have taken refuge on top of and/or around me in the night. Next, I look at my phone to see what time it is. (I stopped having a clock by the side of my bed years ago. The LED lights of the digital ones are too bright, and the ticking of traditional clocks can be maddening when insomnia hits.) Since it's a smart phone, I'm also likely going to get sucked into a message or email, look at the latest news, or just scroll my feed to see what's going on with friends before I start my day.

On the day I "ruined" Imbolc, I was scrolling through my feed, which was chock-full of people wishing others a blessed Imbolc, mostly with graphics mined from the internet. I saw one particular image easily over a dozen times in just a couple of minutes. It's one that's been around for quite a while—a photograph-like image of a nude woman who appears to be just waking up. She is somewhat sitting in a small underground cave or nook hidden underneath a tree's roots. With one hand, she is stretching up through the earth, breaking through the ground of a snow-covered forest, and there's a hint of a winter-cloaked figure in the background. All around her hand the mossy earth is turning green. To hide any revealing bits, a fire wraps around her body and snakes upward. As I said, the art has been around for a while, so I have seen it a lot. It's a perfectly lovely image. But that fateful morning, my pre-tea brain looked at the picture in a whole new way.

I don't know what sparked the reboot. Maybe it was the lack of caffeine, or perhaps it was seeing the image repeatedly in such a quick, repetitive sequence that caused the revelation. But I suddenly noticed something. Those flames that carefully wrap around her body? They appear to originate from behind her buttocks. To my eyes, her posture had also changed from "waking from sleep and stretching" to "I desperately need fresh air!" Connecting the flaming rear with her body language, my brain went down the road into teenager territory, and so an image of Mother Nature waking up became "The Goddess has gas!"

Naturally, I had to share this revelation with the internet, because that's what one does before they have the wisdom of tea in their body. I guess I thought it would get a few likes and silly comments, and that would be the end of my merriment.

But no, quite the opposite happened. Things escalated very quickly. Soon there were multiple posts, hundreds of comments, and many (luckily) good-natured folks informing me that I had forever ruined that image for them. Also, somehow burritos and tacos entered the conversation—likely used to explain what meal had caused her to have the gas issue. From there, a new tradition began: making or having tacos for Imbolc. It wasn't even a Tuesday.

A day or two later, I felt deeply inspired to create a new painting of Brigid—a task that had been sitting on my to-do list for a couple of years. Once I finished her, I posted a photo of the art as a way of saying, "Here, sorry I ruined your favorite art for Imbolc. Maybe this will make it up to you?" The painting was extremely well received. You may have even seen it on the cover of a major Pagan magazine. It appears that despite my heretical ways, Brigid was indeed pleased. In the end, new traditions were born, and art was made!

Here's the lesson within: It's okay to break loose and ride the silly wave for a bit. You never know what fun and inspiration can be stirred up. There are multiple ways to illuminate your path and to kindle your spirit. Sometimes "in the belly" means having some tacos and allowing yourself to laugh from the root of your soul.

Cosmic Sway

Ivo Dominguez Jr.

THIS YEAR THE SUN is at the 15th degree of Aquarius on the morning of February 3, which means that the customary calendar date for Imbolc pretty much overlaps with the astrological date for the holiday. The waning Moon will start the days of Imbolc in Virgo on February 1, move through Libra, and enter Scorpio on February 3. Mercury is retrograde in Aquarius and will remain so until February 20. Throughout the whole period there is a stellium, a cluster, in Aquarius composed of the Sun, Mercury, Venus, Jupiter, and Saturn. Mars and Uranus are forming squares to the stellium in Aquarius throughout Imbolc. The Moon also makes an opposition to Uranus in Taurus, and squares Saturn on February 3.

Imbolc is one of the four cross-quarter holidays. More often than not, whatever was going on at the previous solstice or equinox comes into fuller manifestation at the cross-quarter holidays. There was quite a bit going on at Yule that was bound to change the world on a broad scale, and at Imbolc these changes will be looming large. Moreover, the astrological conditions during Imbolc are powerful and likely to add to the strained atmosphere. At first glance it would appear that the astrological influences are at odds with the themes associated with Imbolc. They are at odds with each, but that just suggests that the inherent nature of Imbolc can be used as a counterbalance to the harshness of the times.

Mars in Taurus will be squaring the Sun and Jupiter in Aquarius. These aspects are adrenaline mixed with caffeine and can encourage rash action, accidents, and overreaction. Instead of giving in to reckless urges or irritation, redirect that energy toward the first stirrings of life and the lengthening days. Find evidence of plant life beginning to awaken in your area, whether it be crocuses, snowdrops, plump buds, patches where the snow has cleared, or whatever is local and represents Imbolc for you. If you work with candles, or have access to a fireplace or fire pit, feed that energy to the flames with the intention that you have chosen to enliven.

You may wish to celebrate Imbolc three days in a row as the Moon will be moving from Virgo to Libra to Scorpio February 1–3. The Moon will be waning during this time so you can use it to release things that burden your heart, dissolve or diminish obstacles, and wrap up and complete unfinished business. Depending upon where you live, you'll have to get up early on February 1 to catch the Moon while still in Virgo. If that doesn't work for you there is still special value in working with the Libra and Scorpio Moon. The waning Virgo Moon is especially good for determining and releasing what is unhealthy for you. The waning Libra Moon can be used to see all sides of the situation so that you can find justice and a more complete truth. The waning Scorpio Moon offers the gift of the phoenix so that you may re-create yourself and rise refreshed like the world, which is awakening at Imbolc.

The Scorpio Moon on February 3 makes an opposition to Uranus in Taurus and squares Saturn. These aspects will call forth powerful tension between the desire to follow what is serious and well known versus the desire to break free and to innovate. There is also a strong sense of being pushed and pulled by forces that are larger than you. If you are up to the task, put your hand on the rudder of this ship in a storm, and find the way to what is true and best for you. Or you can stay home and ride out the storm and tend to your home fires. Regardless of which choice you make, make kindness the guiding principle for yourself and others. The aspects can make you forget that people are a priority.

Throughout this holiday, we have a cluster of five planets in Aquarius: Sun, Mercury, Venus, Jupiter, and Saturn, with Mercury being retrograde. It is the Sun at the 15th degree of Aquarius that makes Imbolc a cross-quarter day, one that falls at the midpoint between a solstice and an equinox. This year having Mercury, Venus, Jupiter, and Saturn line up with the Sun in Aquarius gives the holiday more intensity and more complexity. Imbolc is the quickening of things, the first proof that growth is occurring. Saturn brings the gift of pattern and structure and organization to whatever you're putting into motion. Jupiter gives the knowledge of how things fit into the bigger picture of your life. Venus will tell you the meaning that new things coming into your life will bring. Retrograde Mercury will ask you to think clearly and contemplate what it is that you want to begin in this new cycle of growth.

To make the best use of the celestial energies available during this holiday, make sure you include some form of divination in your rituals and celebrations. Divination during Imbolc is traditional, and you may already have customs of how you approach this work. This year consider specifically asking how best to use each of the planetary forces in the stellium for the best possible outcomes. You may also wish to take the opportunity offered by this lineup of influences to bless and charge candles, oils, or ritual implements that you plan on using over the course of the year.

If you have any plans for Valentine's Day, or Lupercalia, make sure that your plans are mellow and low stress. The Moon will have moved into Aries, and Saturn in Aquarius is making a square to Uranus in Taurus. This may stir up conflicts around independence and how decisions are made. When we add in the waxing Moon, it becomes more volatile as there will be a tendency to leap headlong into things without thinking. More than ever it is important to consider the value of partnership and mutual appreciation.

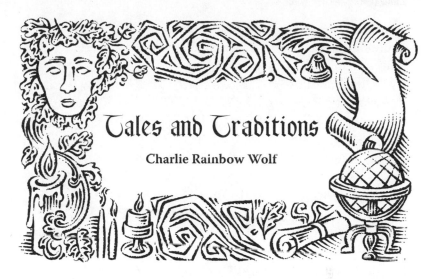

Tales and Traditions

Charlie Rainbow Wolf

ISN'T IT PECULIAR HOW some traditional festivals like Samhain and Yule grew in popularity over time, while others such as Imbolc seem to have faded into the background? Today, Imbolc is often acknowledged as the Christian ceremony of Candlemas, but there are still many of the old ways associated with this time of year, some of which you might not have even considered. They come from a wide variety of cultures and backgrounds, seeping into our customs seemingly unnoticed.

Divination and the Dark Lady

The Feast of the Purification of the Blessed Virgin celebrates the ritual cleansing of the Virgin Mary forty days after the birth of Jesus. In Jewish traditions, women couldn't go to the temple until so many days after they had given birth (forty for a baby boy, sixty for a baby girl), and they had to go through the purification rite before they were allowed back inside. Even though Candlemas has now been adopted into Christianity, some even older beliefs remain. For instance, there are many divination customs associated with Imbolc. Even during Candlemas it is said the candles were lit to drive away malevolent spirits, and that should a candle drip down one side during the festivities, it was an indication that there would be a death in the family during the coming year.

Divination

Divination seems to be a popular theme at this time of year. In the US, February 2 is the date when Punxsutawney Phil—a real groundhog with a somewhat mythical pop culture following—is watched carefully to see whether he casts a shadow. If the skies are clear and he casts a shadow, it is said to indicate there will be six more weeks of winter; but if the skies are cloudy and he does not cast a shadow, then spring will arrive early.

This custom isn't new to America, though. The practice was brought to the US by German immigrants who used a badger to predict their seasons. The outcome was the same; a shadow meant winter, and no shadow meant warmer weather was on its way.

Much of the forecasting depended on seeing animals as signs and portents of things to come. For example, seeing a hedgehog or hearing a lark sing was meant to indicate good luck for the coming season. Firegazers often looked to the flames of the hearth to see what shapes and animal spirits might present themselves. Sometimes different amulets or talismans were burned in the fire, and the ashes were read the following day in order to forecast future events and trends.

Weather magic always seemed to be interwoven with the augury practiced at this time of year. I previously mentioned the groundhog seeing its shadow. Rain on this day supposedly indicated a fair and pleasant summer. If it was particularly blustery, this was meant to predict harsh weather for the month of March.

There are some differences of opinion as to the best time for Imbolc divination practices. Some people say that they should be done after the ritual bathing but before the feasting, so that the person doing the divination is clean inside and out. Others say that after the feasting is the most appropriate time, when both body and soul are full and nourished.

There is no hard and fast rule; if you are including divination into your Imbolc festivities, plan for it at the time that feels right to you.

Holda, The Dark Lady

Holda is represented as the maiden, the mother, and the crone, and is the goddess of winter. She appears dressed in white. She has rulership of the household, and her craft is spinning flax on the spinning wheel. She is the weaver of destiny, the giver and taker of life. She is the leader of the home, and all domestic arts from baking bread to raising children come under her domain—and woe betide you if you are lazy or try to shirk your responsibilities!

Holda's darkness comes because she is the gatherer of children's souls. In some cultures, children were named only after they were nine days old, and should a child die before that time, they would cross into the underworld unnamed. The underworld in this instance is not a negative or fearful place, but it would mean that—without a name—this little soul would not be connected to its ancestors. Holda gathered these wee souls so that they had a family; her family.

Holda's gifts are integrity and endurance, particularly to those overworked mothers who seem to always have tasks left undone at the end of the day. Holda will readily teach you how to be more efficient at all the domestic arts—including the mystical art of knot magic—but she comes at a cost. The price? Pay it forward. Do something kind for another woman who is struggling. Offer an hour of kindness to a sister in need, and Holda will ensure you are richly rewarded.

Honoring the Ways

For something different this Imbolc, you might want to try a fiber festival to honor Holda and the gifts she brings to the hearth. There are many ways this could unfold. Holda was the "domestic goddess" in every sense of the word! In the past we have invited everyone to bring a ball of yarn, and those who knit and crochet taught those who wanted to learn.

This is a good time to explore different methods of divination too. Going back to Holda again, her presence in the underworld means that she can be used to travel through the realms for divination purposes. Her element is water, and if you have never tried hydromancy—water scrying—this is an excellent time to do so. In fact it is believed that her entrance to the underworld comes by traveling through water, as opposed to walking the path of the dead.

I have two methods I use to water scry. The first is to put the water into a dark bowl and simply meditate on it, waiting for the images to appear. This is more of a solitary practice than the second way, which is to take a bowl of water and drop pebbles or beads into it and interpret the way that the ripples form. This would make a good group activity, discussing what was seen and what it could potentially represent.

Also associated with this festival are many items that were made to keep away misfortune and the malevolent spirits that might cause it. Perhaps you have made the Brighid's cross ornaments from straw or long grass, or maybe woven one from colored yarn. These were made to protect the household from fire and lightning strikes as well as for ornamental purposes.

If you choose to honor Holda, don't forget that she will ask a price for her aid; pay it forward in some way before you seek her assistance. You can make a game out of this by having everyone write down a simple wish, such as "bring me a cookie" or "brush my hair for me" on a piece of paper and put them all into a bowl or bag. Have everyone draw out a wish and perform the task that is on the paper.

For your feast, you might choose to make snowflake-shaped sugar cookies or gingerbreads and decorate them with lacy icing, representing the snow that Holda brings. In Scotland, bannocks— sometimes called skillet breads—are a staple food, quick to make and delicious to eat. The Imbolc bannocks were often called Bride's bannocks and were handed out to little girls who carried a likeness of St. Brighid.

Reference

Andrews, Ted. *Animal Speak: The Spiritual & Magical Powers of Creatures Great & Small.* Woodbury, MN: Llewellyn Publications, 2006.

Feasts and Treats

Sue Pesznecker

WITH IMBOLC, WINTER'S COLD begins to ebb, and we feel the first stirrings of fire as the life cycle swings up. Imbolc is traditionally known for lambing, but it's the time of year when all farm animals give birth and the mother's milk begins to flow. Foods associated with Imbolc are the grains, pickled and preserved foods, and root vegetables that sustained us through the long winter, as well as all things milk- and dairy-related.

Cheese Board

A cheese board is always a wonderful way to start a meal, or can be a meal in and of itself. The best version will have two or three different cheeses, one or two types of bread or cracker, and an assortment of goodies to be eaten with the cheeses. Be aware of varieties in texture, crunchiness, shape, acidity, sweetness, saltiness, and so on as you plan your board. The more contrasts you can incorporate, the better!

Prep time: 30 minutes
Servings: varies

Select from some or all of these categories (suggestions given):
Soft cheeses: Brie, Camembert, goat cheese, burrata, Humboldt Fog
Semi-soft cheeses: Stilton, fontina, Havarti
Semi-hard cheeses: Swiss, cheddar, Gouda, Gruyère
Hard cheeses: Parmesan, Asiago, extra-sharp cheddar
Bread or crackers: something soft but sturdy and something crisp
   or brittle, such as baguette slices, seeded or multigrain crackers,
   breadsticks
Fresh fruit: grapes, cherries, currants, sliced pears, fresh raspberries
Dried fruits: apricots, figs
Meats: thin-sliced deli meats, salami, prosciutto
Sweets: fig or apricot jam, cherry preserves, honey
Tarts/acids: pickles, chutneys
Salty/spicy: olives, tinned cocktail oysters, olive tapenade, spicy or
   hot mustard, hot pepper jellies (delicious alone or spooned over
   a small block of cream cheese)
Nuts: walnut halves, Marcona almonds, candied pecans, pistachios
Garnishes: spears of rosemary, parsley sprigs, edible flowers

Select an attractive board or platter for your cheese plate. Remove the cheeses from the refrigerator about an hour before serving; bringing them to room temperature makes them softer and heightens their flavor.

Choose and assemble your ingredients in a pleasing arrangement. Don't hesitate to surf the web for layout ideas. Provide utensils or cocktail picks to help your guests serve themselves.

Baked Potato Bar

What's more satisfying than a hot, fluffy baked potato stuffed with one's choice of fillings? This meal also gets people involved as they sit around the table together, building their dinners. Tasty and fun!

Prep time: 1 hour
Cooking time: 1 hour
Servings: 4

Potatoes

5 good-sized russet potatoes

Preheat oven to 450° F. Wash the potatoes, pat dry, and poke each one deeply two or three times with a sharp knife. Place the potatoes directly on a middle oven rack and roast for 50–60 minutes, until the potatoes are soft when probed with a knife.

To serve, cut a longitudinal slice into each potato and push the ends toward each other to create a potato bowl. Offer an array of toppings and let everyone fill their own potatoes.

Béchamel Sauce

1 quart whole milk
½ cup unsalted butter
½ cup flour
1½ teaspoons kosher salt
½ teaspoon pepper
½ teaspoon nutmeg
1 garlic clove, minced
2 tablespoons parsley, chopped
½ tablespoon fresh thyme, chopped (or ¼ teaspoon dried thyme)

Bring milk to a simmer in a saucepan and remove from heat. Melt butter in a 2–3 quart saucepan over medium heat. Add flour and cook, stirring, until the flour just slightly begins to change color, about 2–4 minutes.

Whisk the hot milk into the flour mixture all at once and continue whisking until smooth. Add the salt, pepper, and nutmeg. The sauce should be thick enough to coat a spoon; if it isn't, cook another 2–3 minutes until it thickens. Remove from heat and stir in garlic, parsley, and thyme. Use this sauce to create the variations.

Stroganoff Variation

1 pound ground beef (not the lean variety)*
6 ounces fresh mushrooms, finely chopped

½ cup full-fat sour cream
Salt and pepper
*Vegetarian option: Leave the meat out and double the mushrooms. Adding a teaspoon of soy sauce, miso, or tamari will amp up the umami factor.

Brown the meat and mushrooms together, draining off all excess fat. Stir in half of the béchamel sauce, then begin adding sour cream—one spoonful at a time—until you reach a desired stroganoff flavor. Season with salt and pepper.

Broccoli-Cheese Variation

Salt
1 head broccoli, cut into florets
1 cup sharp cheddar cheese, grated
Salt and pepper

Fill a saucepan with an inch of water and add 1 teaspoon of salt. Bring to a boil then add the broccoli, cover and steam until it's tender. Drain. Add half the hot béchamel sauce and all of the cheese. Stir to melt, then season with salt and pepper.

Purist Variation

Butter
Sour cream
Sharp cheddar cheese, grated
Bacon bits

For the purist variation: No béchamel needed! Just offer a more traditional array of butter, sour cream, grated cheddar, and bacon bits.

Gluten-Free Fudgy Chocolate Cookies

In these easy-to-make cookies, we have a simple but decadent treat that everyone can enjoy—a fitting end to any celebratory meal. If you've ever been skeptical about gluten-free baked goods, these will change your mind.

Prep time: 15 minutes
Cooking time: 15 minutes
Inactive: 30 minutes or 2–3 hours
Servings: several!

3 cups confectioner's sugar
¾ cup unsweetened cocoa powder
¼ teaspoon salt
3 egg whites
1 teaspoon vanilla
1½ cups semisweet or dark chocolate chips
Optional:
1 cup walnuts, chopped
Flaked sea salt

Preheat oven to 350° F.

In a large bowl, blend the confectioner's sugar, cocoa powder, and salt.

Add the egg whites and vanilla, stir until thoroughly combined. Fold in chocolate chips and walnuts.

Chill for at least 30 minutes; 2 or 3 hours is better.

To bake, drop large spoonfuls onto a parchment- or silicone-lined baking sheet (prevents sticking).

Bake for 11–15 minutes, just until the edges begin to crack. The cookies will still be very soft. Sprinkle with sea salt, if desired.

Cool for 30 minutes on baking sheets, then remove (carefully) to wire racks.

DIY Milkshakes

We'll follow up the baked potato bar with a DIY milkshake bar. Provide tall or deep glass cups for each diner (pint canning jars work well), an assortment of stir-ins, and cans of whipped cream, and you'll have an instant party. Don't forget the long spoons!

Prep time: 5 minutes
Servings: varies

Ice cream, one flavor or multiple
¼ cup ice-cold whole milk per shake
An assortment of stir-ins: chocolate syrup, caramel sauce, crushed
  cookies, chopped candy bars, crushed fruits, honey, maple
  syrup, nuts, etc.
Canned whipped cream
Sprinkles!

For each shake, spoon ice cream into the glass, almost to the top. Add cold milk and begin to stir until the mixture reaches shake consistency. Add any stir-ins, top with whipped cream, and add sprinkles. Bam.

Crafty Crafts

Tess Whitehurst

IMBOLC IS A PROFOUND and mystical time. In many parts of the world it's still wintery, and yet you can feel the days lengthening and the light returning as we begin to awaken from our winter hibernation and move steadily toward the spring.

For many, the beloved, fiery-haired Celtic goddess Brighid is synonymous with the holiday of Imbolc. Since ancient times, Brighid has been known to bestow blessings related to poetry, creativity, divination, healing, feminine mysteries, and magic of all varieties. As illustrated by her dominion over both hearth fires and sacred wells, Brighid is equally associated with two elements: water and fire.

At Imbolc, both water and fire are invoked for their cleansing and healing properties, as well as their support with both divination and blessing rituals. Water cleanses and heals by washing away negativity and toxins from mind, body, and spirit. Fire cleanses and heals by warming, transforming, and disinfecting. As for divination, water gazing is an ancient oracular art, and candles and fire are often lit to bring illumination to predictive activities such as tarot reading, dowsing, and reading the runes. And, of course, both water and fire are used to bless and consecrate people, objects, spaces, and ceremonies.

Fire and Water Candles

This craft merges pure water and fire to invoke Brighid's unique presence and power. While it doesn't get much easier than these candles, you'll find they will bring a mystical mood and whimsically witchy appeal to any Imbolc décor.

You can actually use any color food coloring, but I chose pink because it is a color traditionally associated with Imbolc. In *Imbolc: Rituals, Recipes & Lore for Brigid's Day* (from the Llewellyn's Sabbat Essentials series), author Carl F. Neal includes pink in the list of Imbolc colors and lists its properties as "harmony, affection, tenderness, love, spiritual healing, virtue, spring, honor, contentment" (Neal 2015).

Materials

One quart-size mason jar for every candle you'd like to make

Blue decorative glass gems (The ones that look like flattened marbles)

Water

Pink or fuchsia gel food coloring

Butter knife or chopstick (to stir)

Iridescent glitter (optional)

Floating candles

Long matches or a long-reach candle lighter

> *Cost:* $15–$20
>
> *Time spent:* 5–10 minutes

To assemble one candle, simply fill the bottom fifth or quarter of the jar with the glass gems. Add water until the jar is about ⅔ full. Add one drop of the food coloring and gently stir it into the water with a butter knife or chopstick. If you'd like, you can lightly sprinkle the top of the water with iridescent glitter. Then add a single floating candle to the jar, wick side up. When you're ready for a magical glow, light the candle with the long lighter or a long match.

Take a moment to invoke Brighid's blessing. Invite her into your home and feel her fiery, watery, healing, and empowering presence arrive.

Imbolc Healing Pendulum

As mentioned above, divination is one of the magical activities traditionally associated with Imbolc. A pendulum is a wonderful divination tool for connecting with your body's intuitive wisdom for healing and personal empowerment.

Here's how to make a pendulum specifically aligned with the energies of Imbolc.

Materials

Hemp twine

A large garnet bead or pendant

1 smaller, round aquamarine bead
1 smaller white agate bead (make sure all the beads have holes large
   enough to fit on the hemp twine)
Optional: essential oil of basil
Scissors
   Cost: $5–$10
   Time spent: 5–10 minutes

Cleanse all the beads by running them under cold water and placing them in bright sunlight or by a fire for about 5 minutes. Cut a length of about 7 or 8 inches of hemp twine. Tie a knot in the hemp twine and thread the garnet through the other end. Pull it through until it's resting on the knot. Trim the excess twine near the knot if desired. Then string the aquamarine bead so it's just above the garnet. Thread the other end of the twine through the agate bead and tie it tightly with a knot so the agate is secured at the opposite end. Optionally, anoint the hemp twine with a drop of essential oil of basil.

Garnet is a fiery stone that warms the heart and heals the blood. It boosts immunity, illuminates mysteries, and awakens the fire within.

Aquamarine is a watery stone that brings clarity to the mind and helps to heal the body by balancing, harmonizing, energizing, soothing, and detoxifying.

The white agate will help center your energies and align you with the wisdom of the earth. Its white color will promote purity and spiritual nourishment.

Basil is an Imbolc-aligned herb that helps strengthen our connection to our divine guidance and blesses all forms of divination.

Before using the pendulum, bathe it in bright sunlight and call on Brighid to bless it with accuracy and a clear connection to Spirit.

To use the pendulum, hold it in your dominant hand. Relax your entire arm while simultaneously keeping it stable. Take some deep breaths and clear your mind. Say, "Show me 'yes.'" Feel and sense the bright light of divine wisdom moving through your elbow, wrist, and hand. To allow this free flow of energy, you will want to be sure your arm is steady but not rigid.

Now, energy will move through your arm, which will cause the pendulum to move. For some, it will move forward and backward for yes. For others, it will move in a clockwise circle. Be open to whatever movement arises.

Once you are clear on what your yes answer looks like, say, "Show me 'no.'" Again, relax your arm while also holding it steady. Popular no movements include a side-to-side movement or a counterclockwise circle. Again, allow your no answer to look however it looks.

Now that you know how you can use your pendulum as a divination tool, you are free to work with it however you choose. Many

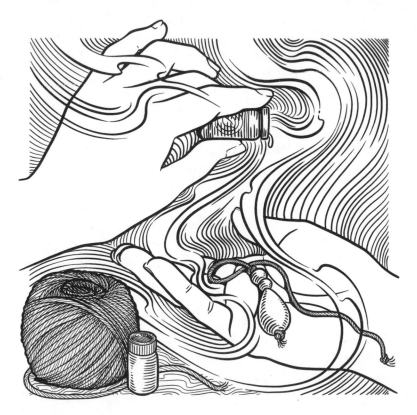

magical practitioners like to use a pendulum to check in with their bodies about what herbs, supplements, and foods will most nourish them and which ones their body doesn't need or prefer. A pendulum can also be an excellent tool for validating intuitive hits or gaining more clarity on a tarot or oracle card reading. You may also like to use it when you'd like a little extra guidance making a decision. It works with your body as a channel for divine wisdom of energy, so it is uniquely suited to help you gain insight into what is best for you personally in a number of situations.

Creating your pendulum at Imbolc will infuse it with the uniquely purifying and healing magic of this time of year. But of course, you can use it year-round!

Reference

Neal, Carl F. *Imbolc: Rituals, Recipes & Lore for Brigid's Day.*
Woodbury, MN: Llewellyn Publications, 2015.

Spells

Michael Furie

THOUGH SPRINGTIME MAY FEEL as though it shall never appear, the magic of the Imbolc sabbat assures us that it will. The power of this time reminds us that even though things appear to be at their darkest point, there is a spark of light growing in strength that will emerge to bring about spring and a reawakening of the earth. This is such a powerful time of renewal and potential when the energy naturally available to us offers a fresh start, new blessings, and power to create and strengthen our bonds to Spirit.

Locking In Your Personal Correspondences

Over the generations, a wealth of lore concerning which herbs, trees, stones, et cetera align with each other, and with which magical intentions, has been built. While these traditional correspondences are very useful, they may not always speak to us personally. For example, if the smell of an herb leaves you feeling nauseated or reminds you of an unpleasant memory then it is best omitted from a spell even if it traditionally corresponds to your goal. Applying this idea to Imbolc, though lamb and dairy products are very traditional fare for this sabbat they're not always something desirable for a holiday feast. What if you're vegetarian or have an allergy? In these cases it's a good idea to modify the menu, substituting food better suited to the tastes and needs of the participants. My solution to this is to formally draw and declare my own correspondence between what I choose to eat and the energy of the holiday. This simple spell can be used for any ingredient, food, herb, stone, or anything else used in magic.

Materials

Journal and pen
A symbol of the magical intention desired
Item to be redirected (or a photo or symbol of it)
1 white candle

To begin, make a journal entry for Imbolc, listing the traditional correspondences at the top such as candle colors, herbs, foods, and symbols, being sure to include the ones that you do not intend to use. Below this, make a list of the items that you wish to align with Imbolc for you such as vegetarian burgers (vs. lamb) or the color gray (vs. or in addition to red and white since Imbolc is gray and rainy where you live). Do whatever best suits you. Once the list is complete, draw a single line through any of the traditional correspondences you don't wish to use, symbolically striking them out, then place the journal on your working table. Charge the candle with your intention, holding it in your strong hand and squeezing it firmly while focusing on your desire to draw the alignments for your correspondences, that the items you have selected shall now be equated to Imbolc.

Set the candle down behind the journal. As you light it, say:

In greater web of cosmic sway, the threads I seek to create a bond; from point to point, connections placed, my own correspondences are hereby drawn.

Allow the candle to burn for as long as desired, then extinguish.

Magical Lampshades

A key hallmark of Imbolc for many is lighting every lamp in the house in order to welcome back the light and warmth of the sun. Aside from the celebratory and symbolic aspects of this action, a magical element can be added to harness the extra energy during this sabbat. A simple way to add a touch of spellwork into the holiday is to magically charge lampshades so that when they are lit, the spell is released. An excellent activity for the day before Imbolc is to create and empower the shades so that when the time comes to light them, the magic can be released all at once. Ideally, you could use lampshades in a color symbolic of your goal and embellish them with a corresponding rune or sigil, but if you do not wish to permanently alter a shade, items symbolizing your intent, such as money for wealth, a heart for love, a pentagram drawn on paper for protection, et cetera, could be taped or clipped to the shade for the spell and removed later.

First, settle on a magical goal (one per lampshade), then decide which items or symbols would best represent that goal and how they would be best displayed on the lampshade. Next, remove the shade from the lamp and dust or clean it as necessary, then apply the symbols for your spell. Finally, hold the shade with both hands and visualize your goal so that the shade is energetically charged with your intent. Move to the next shade if you are making more than one until all are ready. Once all have been made, put them back on their respective lamps, leaving them unlit until you are ready.

If lamp lighting is a usual part of your Imbolc ritual, then simply wait until that time, but either way, when the time comes to light all the lamps, light the spell lamps last with the words:

Shining lights, hope's bright beacon, hurry forth across the span; manifest the goals I'm seeking, as the sun returns to warm the land; Imbolc magic, work my will, with harm to none, my wishes fulfilled.

Leave the spell lamps on for at least an hour so that the magic is fully released. The next day, the symbols and items can be removed from the shades but should be kept somewhere safe until the goal has manifested.

Imbolc Self-Blessing

Imbolc doesn't have much ancient public lore attached to it, but one of the things we do know to be traditional is a ritualized washing of the head, hands, and feet. The practice is an excellent self-blessing rite, which can be strengthened by the addition of the powerful herb juniper. Juniper is not only protective against danger, accidents, and theft, but also cleanses and blocks evil entities and forces. Juniper berries can usually be found in stores that carry natural foods. If the berries or other plant material cannot be obtained, a suitable alternative is gin.

Gin's primary flavoring ingredient is juniper. Though some brands contain other herbs as well, they all must contain juniper and, since alcohol is also cleansing, it remains ritually appropriate. To perform this self-blessing, there are three options: juniper incense smoke, juniper oil, or gin. After the option is chosen, prepare the juniper. For incense, obtain some dried berries and grind them together and prepare a censer and incense charcoal. For the oil, take two tablespoons of the juniper and add it to a quarter cup of vegetable oil, then simmer it on the stove over low heat just until you can smell the herb in the air. Remove from heat, allowing it to cool before straining and bottling for use. If using gin, simply pour about a quarter cup into your ritual chalice.

Before performing the blessing, shower while paying special attention to washing your head and hair, your hands, then your feet. After the shower, dry off and, using your chosen method, conduct the blessing. If using the incense, hold the smoke up to eye level and turn around in a clockwise motion so the smoke encircles you, repeating this at waist level and again at ground level. If you are using either the gin or oil, anoint your forehead, the back of each hand, and the sole of each foot. Finally, close your eyes and envision white light surrounding you, neutralizing any disharmonious energy in your body while saying:

Cleansed and refreshed, vitality renewed, of energy blocks I am free; charged and empowered, with magic imbued, returned to the world; blessed be.

Imbolc Ritual

Laura Tempest Zakroff

YOU'VE PROBABLY HEARD THE expression "going into the belly of the beast." If you're not familiar, it typically means finding yourself in a potentially dangerous or precarious situation, possibly venturing into unknown or enemy territory.

Healing the Beast in the Belly

So what then is the beast in the belly? Within several traditions of Witchcraft, there is the concept that our souls have three parts—a divine or god-self, a conscious self, and a subconscious instinctual self—which align as the spirit, mind, and body respectively. This last self can be called the fetch or the animal spirit, but for this ritual, we're referring to it as our beast. The beast is primal, focused on our most basic needs for living and thriving. Carnal pleasures and needs make up the majority of its focus: eating, drinking, breathing, sleeping, procreating. Our gut feelings of intuition, instinctual reactions, and reflexes all largely originate from the beast.

But you may wonder: Why is it in your belly? Well, I often use "The Cauldron of Poesy" as a means to teach mind/body/spirit awareness through ritual movement (Zakroff 2017). "The Cauldron of Poesy" is an ancient Irish poem that aligns very well with the threefold soul concept. We have the Cauldron of Wisdom, which resides in our heads and connects us to the divine. We have the Cauldron of Motion, which is stationed in the center of our chests and is what moves us through life mentally and emotionally. Then, last but not least, is the Cauldron of Warming, which is situated in our bellies. Its job is to take care of our physical health and well-being. This lines up well with the beast, and so it resides in our bellies.

So why does it need healing? Well, for centuries, human society has had a tendency to place greater importance on our godly and mental selves, eschewing the physical and dismissing it as sinful, ungodly, or shameful. But our bodies are beautiful and amazing—in all the shapes, colors, abilities, and ages they come in. Our beast in the belly is our root connection to the world around us and each other. The more healthy connection we have with our beast, the more powerful our practice can be.

As I mentioned earlier, through the blessings of Brigid, Imbolc is associated with animals, the hearth, healing, fire, and sacred waters. So for this ritual, we are going to tap into all of those aspects to make a wonderfully satisfying experience for your beast.

Preparation

Time of Day: I recommend evening, as you can incorporate dinner into the ritual. Plan the ritual at least a day in advance so that you have any ingredients you may need and have time to do any necessary tidying.

Meal: You will start the evening by preparing and enjoying a favorite meal that will leave you feeling satisfied, but not too full. (May I suggest tacos, as they are simple to make for a variety of diets? Or if you're more skilled, pull in the traditional Imbolc corn dolly for inspiration and make tamales!) Be sure to also plan to have an appropriately refreshing beverage.

Location: Indoors—your kitchen and bathroom (unless you have an outdoor hot tub). Both spaces should be free of distraction and physically clean. Have a fresh towel handy for later.

Attire: Whatever makes you feel good and is safe to cook in.

Music: Instead of looking at your phone or the TV, put on some music for the background of your meal and for your bathing time. Create a playlist that makes you feel relaxed, yet happy and energized.

Altar: Your kitchen is your hearth altar, and you can set up a small altar in your bathroom if space allows. Technically your bathtub or shower will be your cauldron.

Supplies

A tall white candle in a holder to carry from the kitchen to the bathroom

Sea salt (waiting in the bathroom)

The Ritual

Get into your (cook-safe) attire and set up your altar according to your path. If you have a specific way to craft your sacred space—by casting a circle or another method—do that now so that it encompasses both your kitchen and bathroom.

Before you pull out the ingredients and begin cooking, take a moment to close your eyes. Put your hands on your belly and take three slow breaths in and out. Visualize what sort of beast resides in your belly. What does it look like in your mind's eye? Is it familiar or strange? What kind of mood is it in?

Open your eyes, set the space for where you will eat, and light the candle, visualizing it illuminating your beast within. Start your music.

Next gather your ingredients, taking time to consider each one and where it came from. Every item is something of the earth that is an offering to your beast. See how it is transformed as you combine them, add heat, and make your meal. Tip: Try to clean up your cooking instruments as you go so that you don't have a big mess to deal with afterward.

Once the meal is ready, sit down before the candle, and be mindful of the aroma, flavor, and texture of every bite. Savor it, and think about how it nourishes the beast, which in turn makes your body do what it needs to do every day. Give thanks to it.

After you have completed your meal and tidied up, it's time to take a bath (or shower if that's available to you). Move with the candle and your music into the bathroom. Disrobe. As you start the water, sprinkle in the sea salt, focusing on purification and cleansing. When the temperature is right, get in. As the water covers your body, again close your eyes, place your hands on your belly, and take three slow breaths. Concentrate on how the beast feels now after your meal. Does it feel soothed by the food and the rushing water? Does it feel content and sleepy? Feel closer to it, the beast is a major part of you. Your body is an amazing vessel, full of power. Honor, love, and be kind to the beast.

When you feel ready, end your bath (or shower), and dry off. In front of the candle, with hands on your belly, repeat the following three times:

> *Beast of my belly, creature soul*
> *Healed within this sacred bowl*
> *Nourished now and all around*
> *With my words an oath is sound*
> *Carnal being of body mine*
> *Three to one and spirits divine!*
> *(Extinguish the candle)*
> *So mote it be.*

Prepare for bed and sate any other physical needs you may have. Do pay attention to your dreams. In the morning, write down any animals or messages that may have come to you while you slept. They may have words of wisdom concerning future care of your beast.

Reference

Zakroff, Laura Tempest. *The Witch's Cauldron.* Woodbury, MN: Llewellyn, 2017.

Notes

Notes

Ostara

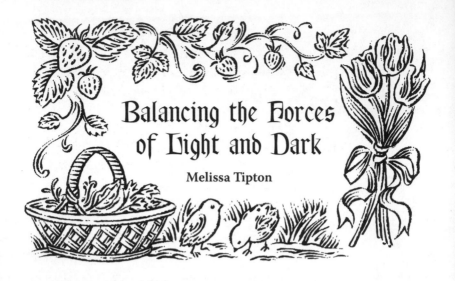

Balancing the Forces of Light and Dark

Melissa Tipton

OSTARA, CELEBRATED ON THE Spring Equinox when day and night are poised in momentary balance, heralds new beginnings. As such, it's a powerful time to reflect on the seeds you are planting during this especially fertile phase, because they will take root and shape the year to follow. Are these plantings in alignment with your highest truth? To go deeper with this question, we'll explore four qualities that capture the essence of Ostara, and by working more intentionally with these energies, you will be able to weave powerful magic during this sabbat.

Light

Ostara is named after the Germanic Ēostre, goddess of the dawn, without which there would be no life, and therefore no conscious awareness. Thus, light is often a symbol of consciousness, and it is also the spark of fresh beginnings, so here we will be using the light of our own consciousness to plant new seeds with wise intention.

Fertility

Ostara is associated with creation and fecundity, the Ēostre hare being one potent symbol of these qualities. We might think of this fertility as the rich, loamy soil that gives birth to life, called forth by the power of (sun)light. Without both—light and dark—there would be no creation.

Growth

During Ostara, life is energetically primed to flourish. I'm reminded of this during my woodland hikes: Once spring arrives, the entire forest is positively bursting with new energy, from the hypnotic trilling of tree frogs to the sprawling abundance of greenery everywhere I look. It's important to plant with intention now more than ever, because the seeds we sow are falling on fertile soil.

Balance

Being the Spring Equinox, this is a time of balance, particularly between the forces of light and dark, the necessary ingredients for creation. Here we will be personalizing and relating to these forces, primarily in the form of the conscious (light) and unconscious (dark) selves.

We create the very stuff of our lives using a mixture of these two energies—the activating light of consciousness and the fertile darkness of the unconscious. When there is an imbalance, our creations take on a characteristic feel. If the creative process is overly directed by the conscious mind, without the enlivening unpredictability of the unconscious, our creations lack vitality and do not nourish us on a deeper level. This might take the form of a lackluster job, a sense of trudging through our days without the fire of meaning, or a tendency to micromanage ourselves (and possibly others).

On the other hand, if the creative process is largely directed by the unconscious mind, our creations might feel "other"—like they're happening *to* us instead of *through* us. To paraphrase Carl Jung, when the contents of our unconscious self remain hidden from our awareness, we project this material out onto the world and call it "fate." If you find yourself engaged in familiar patterns that crop up regardless of how much the people or the scenery change, you are

likely creating more from the unconscious self. A common senti-
ment when the unconscious is dominant is, "Why is this happening
to me?"

During Ostara, the energies are in your favor to find balance
between these creative forces and to use them when planting new
seeds in alignment with your whole self. To begin, it's helpful to
take stock of what you've already generated in your life, to give you
a sense of how your creative energies are currently being expressed,
and I like to do this a week or so before the sabbat. This isn't a call
for shame and blame, but rather an invitation for greater clarity and
self-compassion. How nourished do you feel in the following areas?

- Relationships (you might divide this between primary rela-
  tionship(s), friends, and family, or whichever categories feel
  useful)
- Work and finances
- Health (physical, mental, emotional)
- Spirituality and meaning
- Play and rest

List what sustains you in each category and what depletes you.
Do you notice any patterns across categories? For example, perhaps
you feel taken for granted both at home and at work, and this feels
connected to your physical health in the form of chronic exhaustion
and susceptibility to colds and flus. Again, this isn't about assigning
blame; this is about getting clearer on your current reality so you
can plant the seeds of empowering choices.

Now, keeping in mind that this list is composed of material of
which you're currently conscious, now it's time to invite the unconscious self to the table, and there are numerous ways to do this;
here, we're going to focus on dreamwork and journaling. You can
use this practice as often as you like, but in preparation for Ostara,
I would recommend at least a full week of dream journaling. From
the work you did with the categories listed above, choose to focus
on one pattern or question that arose from this self-inquiry. Before

bed, take a few moments to calm and center yourself, eyes closed, and set the following intention: "I open to receive my highest guidance through my dreams tonight in relation to [pattern or question]. Thank you."

The next morning, as soon as you wake up, and before you brush your teeth or otherwise start your day, journal anything you can recall from your dreams, no matter how insignificant. Know that the simple act of writing this material down, even if you don't fully understand what it means, is forging a bridge between your conscious and unconscious selves, paving the way for more productive dialogue over time. If you have any initial thoughts as to the meaning of the dream, write that down as well. Then set the journal aside and state the following intention for your day: "I open to receive the insights that will help me grow in relation to [pattern or question]. Thank you." Throughout the day, pay attention to any thoughts, memories, or feelings that arise, treating them as potential messengers from the unconscious, and if something resonates, even if you're not entirely sure why, add it to your journal.

At the end of the day, give yourself fifteen to thirty minutes of undisturbed contemplation time, and optionally mark the occasion with the lighting of two candles: one white, one black, representing the conscious and unconscious selves you are seeking to unite. With your journal at hand, gaze at the two candles with a soft focus (or simply close your eyes and imagine candles, if they're not physically present), and sense the heat and energy of the flames merging, blurring the lines of where one begins and the other ends. Feel the boundaries within yourself, between what you know about yourself and what you don't, start to soften and fuzz, allowing more interplay between these inner aspects. Bring your focus pattern or question to mind, and spend some time holding this idea gently in your awareness while in this liminal space between conscious and unconscious. Don't force the agenda of figuring things out; simply let the question exist while the various energies within you interact with it.

When you feel ready, open your eyes and begin to free write in your journal anything that comes to mind. When this feels complete, go back and read your morning journaling about your dream—do any new knowings arise? Imagine that a response to the focus pattern/question exists in these words, and begin playing with possibilities. For example, if you were wearing a raincoat in your dream and your question was, "Why do I feel taken for granted at home and work?" imagine that the answer is that you need to wear a raincoat. What might this mean to you? Do you perhaps need a barrier between yourself and the intensity of other people's emotions (emotions often being symbolized by water)? Would imagining donning this energetic raincoat in conversations allow you to be more present to your *own* emotional experience, because you're not feeling bombarded by another's energy? Or perhaps in the dream you had the urge to fling the raincoat aside and dance in the rain. What does this evoke within you? Perhaps a desire to be more in contact with your emotional experience, to really savor the way emotions unfold in your physical body, bringing you deeply into the present moment and giving you valuable information about what you want and need right now.

One of the biggest barriers to working with dreams is believing that there is one right way to interpret them. The magic lies in being aware of what your dream images trigger for *you* personally— thoughts, memories, emotions, sensations—and following these clues, like a trail of breadcrumbs. I like to think of dreams as letters from my unconscious, and as I try on different meanings by asking myself questions like, "How can I put on a raincoat in my daily interactions?" "What does dancing in the rain feel like?" and "Are there times in waking life when I would like to feel that way?" I engage in dialogue with this unconscious self, and new insights bubble up from the inner depths. So toss out any ideas that you're doing this wrong, and play with the details, like a sacred word jumble.

As you feel yourself nearing the end of your dream exploration for the evening, see if you can identify one insight that resonates with you, such as, "I want to learn how to create more space in conversations to help me sense where my emotions end and another's begin," or "I want to practice focusing on what *I'm* feeling in conversation, rather than being hyperfocused on someone else." And then prepare for your bedtime intention setting once more. You might repeat the original intention: "I open to receive my highest guidance through my dreams tonight in relation to [pattern or question]. Thank you." Or you might modify the phrasing of the pattern or question to include a new insight that arose during your dreamwork this evening. For example, you might ask to receive insights that will help you remain more focused on your own emotional experience when in conversation with others. Remember, this entire process is a way for you to go deeper into the original pattern or question, bringing both your conscious and unconscious selves to the discussion, so feel free to adapt as needed to honor any new questions that arise throughout this work. As the week progresses, you will see an intention taking shape: this is the seed that you will be planting on Ostara. Using the above example, this might be as simple (yet oh-so-powerful) as "I remain present to my own emotions in conversation with others."

If you carry out this practice for, say, the week prior to Ostara, when the sabbat arrives, your inner light and dark will be more in balance and ready to sow the seeds of your newly-forged intention. On the day of Ostara, weave this intention into the ritual practices of your choice. You could keep it short and sweet by selecting a literal seed, holding it in your palm while focusing on the intention, sending the intention's energy into the seed, and then planting it in your garden. Like with any new life, tending to its growth regularly will help it flourish, so check in with yourself in the days and weeks to come, perhaps setting the reminder to revisit self-contemplation work every new moon. How is this intention unfolding in your day-to-day life? Are there any additional actions or shifts that could be made to support its growth?

This practice is a powerful means of tapping into the energies of Ostara in order to bring more balance to your creative energies, paving the way for a year of empowered choices and supercharged growth. Blessed Ostara!

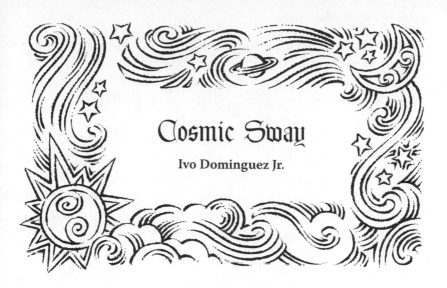

Cosmic Sway

Ivo Dominguez Jr.

THE SPRING EQUINOX, OSTARA, will be on March 20. The waxing Moon and Mars are both in Gemini with Mars forming a trine to Saturn in Aquarius. Mars is also sextile to Chiron in Aries. The day before Ostara, the Moon and Mars are conjunct. The day after the Spring Equinox, Venus enters into Aries as well. Venus cannot be seen in the sky as it is approaching a superior solar conjunction on March 26. A superior conjunction is when a planet moves behind the Sun and thus cannot be seen from Earth. Chiron is 3 degrees from the Sun and Venus during the superior conjunction.

The Full Moon is on March 28 in Libra, opposing a triple conjunction of the Sun, Chiron, and Venus in Aries. The Moon is also in a loose grand trine with Mars in Gemini and Saturn in Aquarius. Mercury is also moving toward a conjunction with Neptune in Pisces.

The Spring Equinox is when we get our bearings, find our balance, and jump into action. The Sun is accompanied by Venus and Chiron during the balance point between night and day. This suggests that quite a bit can be accomplished in matters of healing of the heart, patterns of thinking, and relationships with people in your life. Venus above all else is the indicator for the most important things in life. Chiron is the great healer and teacher that shows what needs to be adjusted to bring balance. The Moon is waxing as the Sun reaches the tipping point for the days to become longer and the nights shorter. This means that both the solar and the lunar tides are working together and can be used to increase abundance, vitality, and so on.

This Ostara is also a good time for doing self-dedications, self-initiations, and other acts of professing connection to, and relationships with, powers of the universe and deities. Rituals or ceremonies to renew vows of love, spiritual commitment, or the beginning of a new role or career would also be served well by these aspects. If you have felt unbalanced, uncentered, or adrift in what direction your life might take, then this Ostara can be used to seek your way forward. Whatever work you begin at Ostara you may wish to continue on March 26 when Venus slides behind the disk of the Sun. Think of it as the moment when the phoenix is aflame and will shortly reemerge refreshed and ready to greet the world. Another way of thinking of it is that like all the green life of the earth that is awakening and arising with the spring, you are filled with the pulsing, fiery force of life.

The Full Moon after Ostara can also be used for magic to bring health and wholeness. You will find that the Sun setting in the west sees the Full Moon rising in the east. It is only at the equinoxes that the Sun and Moon actually rise and set along the east-west axis. Try to be outside to feel the energy exchange between them. Let yourself become the center around which they move while thinking on whatever healing or change you want to call forth. Furthermore, the Moon is alone on one side of the chart with all the other planets on the other side. This directs more power into this Full Moon with some emphasis on matters of the home, the heart, nurturing self and others, and how we collectively offer care in society.

The threefold gathering of Sun, Venus, and Chiron in Aries is echoed by the Moon, Mars, and Saturn all being in air signs, forming a loose grand trine. Communication, written or verbal, is reinforced and clarified, so if you have a writing project or an important conversation that you have postponed, the time to do it is now. Plan your social and spiritual events around the idea of a coming together of hearts, minds, and hands. The hands part is important because these aspects also favor doing work together, physical tasks. Perhaps something along the line of a symbolic tree planting would be in order. Making a plan of action for the remainder of the year is also favored by these celestial influences.

The conjunction between Venus and Chiron may also shake loose some long-buried or denied feelings. Since this is in Aries, you may be urged to act on these immediately. Try to slow down and convince yourself that exploration and examination of your feelings is also a form of action to appease that Aries energy. This may also mark a shift in your life priorities and goals. Another way this can play out is as a test of the depth and nature of the love that you have for yourself and others.

Although it is always a good idea to set out water to charge under the light of the Moon, it may be especially useful to do so under this Full Moon. You can use that water by itself or as an ingredient to continue whatever work you started at Ostara or the Full Moon. A drop rubbed between the palms of your hands can help you to remember what you have chosen to do and to feel the impetus to do so.

It is very likely that there will be plenty of turmoil still rolling through the small and large details of your world from the last several months. In the days before and after Ostara and the Full Moon, take a moment to breathe in the balance and the power. After doing so, review what has occurred, how you are responding, and what you need next. Take some seeds and tell them what message or petition you need them to carry to the powers that be. Plant them and, if you collected Moon water, pour a libation on them. Alternatively, you could do the same with a slip of paper that you bury. If you use paper, write on it with the energy of your words, not with pen or pencil.

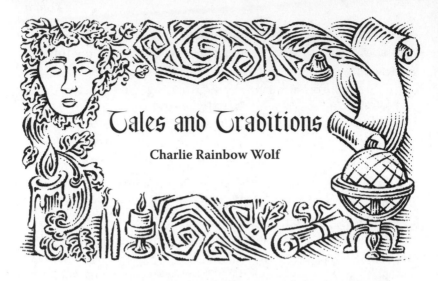

Tales and Traditions

Charlie Rainbow Wolf

OSTARA IS WHEN THE Western calendar marks the "official" start of spring, but to me it is the middle of the season. The early flowers are already blooming, and the early planting has already started. It is a time of growth and preparation, a time of expectancy and anticipation.

Venerating the Sun and Moon

We think of Ostara as being a celebration of the goddess Ostara (also spelled Eostre or Eastre). It's not a long stretch to see where the name for the Christian holiday came from! The name Eostre is related to the Greek goddess of the dawn. In the Wheel of the Year, springtime occupies the same space as morning in the wheel of the day.

Eggs are a big part of this season's decorations. The shops are filled with chocolate eggs, plastic eggs, and all manner of kits and materials to decorate hen's eggs in a variety of colors. Eggs are a symbol of renewal and new life, both themes of this time of year.

In Bosnia, there are street festivals featuring large vats of scrambled eggs, shared freely to those who come to welcome the spring.

Over the last few hundred years this activity has grown in popularity, and people now travel from all over the country to the town of Zenica to participate in the event.

The Green Man and Other Effigies

You will also see an upsurge in the Green Man at this time of year. Garden centers proudly display wall art and other items with the friendly face looking out of the decorative leaves. Some are quite whimsical, with vines coming out of the nose or tendrils snaking around his eyes. However he is depicted, the Green Man is a symbol of growth, fertility, and abundance.

Not all seasonal effigies have to do with the coming of the warmer weather. In Switzerland, people gather to watch the ceremonial burning of a snowman's representation. This custom dates back some five-hundred years and is often accompanied by fireworks. In Poland, straw dolls called Marzannas are thrown into the river to depict the end of winter's wrath. Over the years this has become quite a procession, with giant dolls being paraded through the streets before meeting their eventual demise. In both of these instances, it is the passing of winter that is the focus of the activity.

Honoring the Ancestors and Welcoming the Sun

In Japan, Ostara is celebrated in a week-long festival. Much of the time is spent eating and visiting under their beloved cherry trees. It's a time for family reunions and for celebrating their lives and the lives of their ancestors. On the date of the equinox, it is customary to visit the graves of their deceased loved ones, cleaning and tidying them and leaving fresh flowers and other decorations as a sign of respect and appreciation.

In Mexico, there really isn't any winter to banish, but the equinox is celebrated all the same. This is a time when citizens and visitors alike pay homage to the ways of the ancient civilizations at the shrines and temples left behind. Many of these structures act as timekeepers, with specific architectural features that mark the passing of the seasons.

At the Kukulkan temple in Chichén Itzá, the afternoon sun casts a shadow that looks like a serpent winding down the building. People come from far and wide to observe this rare event, which happens for a few days on either side of the equinox and lasts for an hour or so.

Teotihuacan is another popular spot to visit at this time of year. People come from all over, dressed in white clothing, to climb up the steps and extend their arms to the sky to absorb the strong energetic vibrations of the day.

Cheesy!

In Gloucestershire, England, they roll a cheese down a hill every spring. Go ahead, laugh—I did when I lived over there and first saw it on the television! Called the Cooper's Hill Cheese Rolling and Wake, it's held at Cooper's Hill near Brockworth. It used to be just for the locals, but over the years it's gained worldwide notoriety, with many international winners.

It's uncertain how the cheese roll started. The first recorded evidence comes from the early nineteenth century, but even then it is noted as a much older custom. It may have arisen from the rolling of different breads and sweets down a hill to appease the gods and ensure a good harvest. There is also speculation that it once could have had something to do with grazing rights on the land.

Today the cheese that is rolled down the hill is a Double Gloucester cheese, a hard, round wheel weighing about nine pounds. It's put into a protective wooden case, which is then decorated. As fun and entertaining as this all sounds, it is not for the faint of heart. There have been many recorded injuries as well as notable victories.

Homage to the Moon

My Cherokee friends hold one of their sacred festivals around this time too—the First New Moon of Spring Festival. This is a gathering that marks the start of planting. It's a time when those who haven't seen each other for most of the winter join together for fellowship and feasting, and to discuss their ideas for the coming season. It is a time of renewal and healing, of planning and purification.

The fire is a central part of this ceremony. The Fire Keeper lights a new fire and places a clinker in it from the last council fire. All fire pits and fireplaces are thoroughly cleaned at this time, and everyone in attendance of this festival will take home a cold cinder from the festival fire to put in the first fire they light at their own hearth, thus bringing the energy of the gathering home with them. This echoes the theme of newness and purification that permeates this festival, which traditionally lasted (including preparation time) for around a week but now tends to happen over a weekend.

Honoring the Ways

As you can see, there are many ways you can deviate from the traditional eggs and bunnies yet still honor Ostara. If you wanted to reenact one of the above activities you could do so by hosting an egg-based potluck supper, making dolls to symbolically drown, or even reproduce your own version of the cheese rolling! This is also a good time to visit the graves of your loved ones as the Japanese do, and freshen them up to welcome in the spring.

This is a very busy time of year, with garden preparations and nature bursting forth in readiness for growth and renewal. It's easy to get too busy, to become too overanimated with plans and projects. Another good activity for Ostara is to take time out, enter into the inner sanctuary of your soul, and remember what peace can be found by doing so. If you're working with a group, you might want to consider a guided meditation, giving your spirit a chance to slow down to the speed of life. If your work is solitary, this is an excellent way to end your Ostara observances.

Ostara is a wonderful time to practice your divination skills too. We once held a "flower sentience," where our friend Joan brought a huge bouquet of mixed flowers. We each chose a flower upon entering, and one by one she told us the meaning of the flower we had chosen, what its magical influences were, and why we were drawn to that particular bloom—what it had come to teach us. If you are unfamiliar with the divinatory meanings of flowers, *Cunningham's Encyclopedia of Magical Herbs* is a very good place to start.

References

Basford, Kathleen. *The Green Man.* Rochester, NY: D.S. Brewer, 2004.

Cunningham, Scott. *Cunningham's Encyclopedia of Magical Herbs.* Woodbury, MN: Llewellyn Publications, 1985.

Seabright, Colin and Jean Jeffries. *Cheese-Rolling in Gloucestershire.* Cheltenham, UK: History Press Ltd, 2002.

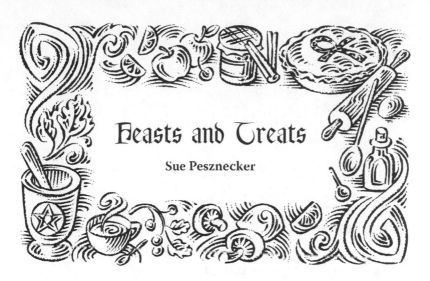

Feasts and Treats

Sue Pesznecker

OSTARA BRINGS THE SPRING Equinox, and for most of us it means that spring has really and truly arrived. The world suddenly seems full of baby animals, soft-sky mornings, and everything green. Foods that we associate with Ostara include eggs and all of those wonderful spring herbs, greens, and vegetables. What better way to honor this sabbat than with an eggs-and-greens-centered brunch?

Custom Quiches

This quiche, full of milk, eggs, cheese, and green goodies, is emblematic of the season—and both the eggs and the quiche's round shape remind us of the life-giving sun.

Prep time: 30 minutes
Cooking time: 23 minutes for crust; 30 minutes for quiche
Cooling time: 30 minutes
Servings: 6–8

1 unbaked pie crust, rolled and fitted into a 9-inch pie plate, chilled
     (make your own or buy your favorite premade)
Parchment paper
Pie weights, or about 2 cups of dried beans or split peas
½ cup whole milk

¾ cup heavy cream

4 eggs

1 egg yolk

½ teaspoon salt

¼ teaspoon black (or white) pepper

¼ teaspoon ground nutmeg

Mix-ins: cooked bacon or ham; grated cheese (up to 1 cup); chopped, cooked, or sautéed vegetables (leeks, onions, mushrooms, and shallots are amazing); fresh herbs (parsley, basil, oregano); slivers or fresh greens (spinach, kale, chard)

Toppings: sliced green onions, additional grated cheese

Start by partially "blind baking" your pie crust—baking the crust without anything in it helps it keep its texture once the quiche custard is poured into the shell. Preheat the oven to 400° F. To blind bake, line the well-chilled pie shell with parchment paper and fill with pie weights (dried beans work well for this).

Bake for about 15 minutes, or just until the edges start to brown. Remove from oven. Remove the parchment and pie weights, prick the entire bottom with a fork, and return to the oven for another 8 minutes. Set on a wire rack.

Reduce oven temperature to 350° F. Prepare the custard filling: Use a whisk or immersion blender to combine the milk, heavy cream, eggs, egg yolk, salt, pepper, and nutmeg until well blended.

Scatter the mix-ins evenly over the cooked pie crust. Pour the custard mixture over the crust, and top with toppings.

Bake at 350° for about 30 minutes. The quiche should be lightly browned, and a knife inserted between middle and edge should come out clean.

Cool for 30 minutes before cutting.

Sausage Patties

Making your own sausage patties is lots of fun—kitchen experimentation at its finest! Children will enjoy this too.

Prep time: 10 minutes
Cooking time: 15 minutes
Servings: 4

1 pound ground pork
1 tablespoon fresh sage, minced
1 tablespoon fresh thyme, finely chopped
1 tablespoon fresh parsley, finely chopped
1 teaspoon fresh rosemary, minced
1 garlic clove, minced very finely
1 teaspoon salt
½ teaspoon black pepper
1 tablespoon maple syrup
Optional:
¼ teaspoon red pepper flakes
⅛ teaspoon cayenne pepper

Using your hands, mix all ingredients in a bowl until combined. Separate into 8 pieces and pat each one loosely into a small patty. Don't overdo it; the sausage will stay juicier if handled minimally.

Fry in a skillet over medium heat, 4–5 minutes per side. Serve with a drizzle of additional maple syrup if desired.

Peach Caprese

This is my very favorite spring and summer salad, and I wait for it all year. It's sweet, creamy, tart, and fresh—everything a salad should be. It's a spin-off of the traditional tomato caprese, and I think it's better!

Prep time: 5 minutes
Servings: 4

4 peaches, ripe (use canned peach slices if ripe peaches aren't
    available)
1 8-ounce container of ciliegine mozzarella (small mozzarella balls)
A handful of fresh basil leaves

Good quality olive oil
Balsamic vinegar
Optional: lettuce leaves or greens

For each salad, peel and slice one peach into a bowl. Top with 5–6 ciliegine pieces, each cut in half. Chop a few leaves of basil and scatter over the peaches and mozzarella. Drizzle the mixture with olive oil and stir to mix well. Serve with balsamic vinegar, allowing diners to apply their own.

Note: This can also be made as one large salad. Layer lettuce or greens on a platter; top with sliced peaches, halved ciliegine, and basil, and drizzle with olive oil.

Mimosa bar

Top off your spring brunch with a mimosa bar—just the thing for welcoming spring.

Prep time: 15 minutes

Servings: varies

1 bottle champagne, sparkling wine, or prosecco, makes 6–8 mimosas
Fruit juices: orange, grapefruit, cranberry, pineapple
Fruit nectars or purees
Toppers: fresh berries, thin citrus slices, fresh mint leaves, pomegranate seeds, rosemary sprigs
Optional: sparkling water or lemon-lime soda for a "virgin" mimosa

Each person makes their own mimosa by filling a glass half full of fruit juice or puree, filling it the rest of the way with champagne, and adding toppers.

Notes: Choose champagne flutes or any small, attractive glass for your mimosas. Be sure to keep the champagne and other sparkling beverages on ice throughout brunch. Use glass decanters for fruit juices and decorative bowls for the other components.

Crafty Crafts

Tess Whitehurst

OSTARA IS THE SECOND of three festivals that celebrate the spring; the first is Imbolc and the third is Beltane. While Imbolc observes the earliest stirrings of spring and Beltane commemorates the full expression of spring, Ostara is springtime in its adolescence. In this way, it is the springiest of springtime sabbats. Eggs, baby animals, the initial springtime blooms such as daffodils and lilacs, unopened flower buds, and verdant newborn grass are among the symbols of freshly burgeoning life that traditionally appear at this magical time.

Like other sabbats, Ostara is a portal: a liminal time when we move from one quality of energy to another. Unlike other sabbats, Ostara—also known as the Spring Equinox or vernal equinox—is midway between Imbolc and Beltane. During this time, the days and nights are of roughly equal length, but the days are growing longer. We can tap into the balance of this time to bring harmony on all levels, and we can also make use of the transitional quality of this time to open up our psychic awareness and receive messages from the divine and invisible realms.

These bath salts interweave a number of magical factors to bring balance, harmony, purification, blessings, and psychic awareness. These factors include the powerful symbolism of rabbits, the transformational dynamic of aromatherapy, the purifying magic of herbs, and the cleansing aspects of water and Epsom salt.

The goddess Ostara, for whom many believe this holiday was named (the actual history is not crystal clear), often appears with a rabbit, whom you might say is her familiar or her fetch. At least in modern Paganism, Ostara is generally seen as a springtime and fertility goddess who spreads her magic across the land, awakening beauty, vitality, and new life. Rabbits, of course, are famous for their fertility and are also aligned with magic, mystery, and the moon. They are highly sensitive and can help us awaken and enhance our awareness of the subtle realms. In *Animal Speak*, Ted Andrews writes, "The rabbit...is active both day and night, but is most visible at dawn and dusk. These are times long associated with the Faerie Realm of life, and...the rabbit is often seen as an animal that can lead one unknowingly into the Faerie Realm" (Andrews 1993).

Essential oil of lemongrass is highly purifying to the mind, body, spirit, and aura. It is vitalizing and stimulating, and it awakens intuition and psychic awareness.

Jasmine absolute possesses a sweet floral scent that aligns us with the sensual beauty of the spring. In *Magical Aromatherapy*, Scott Cunningham writes, "Jasmine's powerful scent directly affects our emotional centers, making it an excellent choice for use in love rituals...Jasmine's calming, soothing fragrance is also of tremendous help in relaxing our physical bodies" (Cunnginham 1989). He also writes that inhaling the scent before going to sleep may promote psychic dreams.

Peppermint—even though this craft only calls for a single drop—is energizing, enlivening, and purifying. It brings clarity, enthusiasm, and inspiration. In *Aromatherapy for Healing the Spirit*, Gabriel Mojay writes, "Traditionally classified as a Visionary Herb, mint was thought not only to uplift the Spirit, but to bring dreams of prophecy...peppermint oil enhances our receptive capacities on both mental and spiritual levels, and...benefits those in need of insight" (Mojay 1997).

Together, this blend of lemongrass, jasmine, and peppermint evokes the cheerful scent of fresh green grass and the bright floral breezes of spring.

Epsom salt is magnesium sulfate, which purifies and relaxes the body.

Sparkle Bunny Bath Salt

There are two parts to this craft: the jar and the bath salt.

Materials for the jar

A pint-sized (16 ounce) mason jar
A plastic lid from something else that fits the mason jar (I used a mayonnaise lid)
Acrylic craft paint in a pastel color (I used lavender)
A paintbrush
Fine glitter that matches the craft paint (I used light purple)
A tiny rabbit figurine
Glue (I used Elmer's)
Craft glue matte finishing spray (I used Mod Podge brand)

Materials for the bath salts

1½ cups Epsom salt
1½ teaspoons iridescent Spectra glitter
4 drops green or teal gel food coloring
6 drops essential oil of lemongrass
¼ teaspoon essential oil of jasmine absolute diluted with jojoba (now available as a separate essential oil)
1 drop essential oil of peppermint
A medium to large bowl for mixing
A spoon or chopstick to mix with
> *Cost:* $12–$15
> *Time spent:* 20 minutes, plus 4+ hours for glue to dry

To make the jar, begin by gluing the bunny to the center of the top of the plastic lid. Allow the glue to dry, perhaps overnight. Paint

the entire lid (including the rabbit) with the craft paint. Allow it to dry for 10 minutes or so, then paint it with a layer of glue and sprinkle it with the glitter. Lightly shake off any excess glitter and allow it to dry.

Carefully follow the instructions on the finishing spray can to seal the glitter on the lid. Make sure you are outdoors when you spray, and allow it to dry completely before taking it back inside.

To make the bath salt, add the Epsom salt, glitter, food coloring, and essential oils to the bowl. Mix well in a clockwise direction until all the food coloring is evenly distributed. As you mix, say:

Cleanse and bless and birth anew
Awaken love and magic too
Purify with springtime light
And summon all that's sweet and bright.

Carefully transfer the salts to the jar and close the lid.

This bath salt will purify your energy, awaken your intuitive abilities, lift your spirits, and align you with the verdant and vibrant energy of the spring. It will also make your bath water a light and refreshing shade of green or teal. You can use it before your magical work or as a bath ritual all on its own. It will help you draw beautiful new conditions and opportunities, open you up to romance, and call in blessings of all varieties.

If you'd like to do magical dream work, or to summon a psychic message in your dreams, bathe with this salt before bed.

Of course, don't use this bath salt if you have extremely sensitive or easily irritated skin or if you know you have a sensitivity to one of the ingredients.

To use, light a white or pastel candle in your bathroom. Draw a warm bath and add ⅓ cup of the bath salt. Swirl the water in a clockwise direction until the salts are dissolved. Then soak for at least 20 minutes.

References

Andrews, Ted. *Animal Speak: The Spiritual & Magical Powers of Creatures Great & Small*. St. Paul, MN: Lllewellyn Publications, 1993.

Cunningham, Scott. *Magical Aromatherapy: The Power of Scent*. St. Paul, MN: Llewellyn Publications, 1989.

Mojay, Gabriel. *Aromatherapy for Healing the Spirit: Restoring Emotional and Mental Balance with Essential Oils*. Rochester, VT: Healing Arts Press, 1997.

Spells

Michael Furie

THE VERNAL EQUINOX, THE time when the Earth has shifted in her orbit enough for the sun to shine directly over the equator, heralds a point of balance not only between night and day but also between both halves of the Earth. On the solstices there is an area of zenith and nadir, with one hemisphere having the longest day and the other having the shortest, but with an equinox the entire globe experiences a moment of balance. When our hemisphere experiences the Spring Equinox we are gifted with the opportunity to work toward growth and abundance. What we shape now has the potential to grow into blessed vitality.

Balance Toward Growth Prosperity Spell

The energy of the vernal equinox is that of balance since the hours of day and night are nearly equal with the sun positioned over the Earth's equator. Though this same position is seen during the autumnal equinox, the difference lies in what comes next, and with the Spring Equinox, growth shall follow. This is a good time for prosperity magic, and this spell requires only a few ingredients.

Materials
A green or gold candle
A stick of sage incense
Two clean jars
An equal amount of coins

To begin, separate the change into equal amounts of the same types of coins; two stacks of each kind, ideally quarters, dimes, nickels and pennies. On your working table, set one jar and half of the coins on the left side and the other jar and the rest of the coins on the right. When ready, light the incense and candle, placing them behind the jars and coins. Hold your hands over the coins and close your eyes; visualize having the money you need whenever you need it. Feel prosperous and free of stress.

When you feel ready, open your eyes and begin to put the coins in each jar, being careful to add the same types in the same amounts simultaneously. Once all the coins have been added, say:

Power of spring bring to me, abundance and prosperity; what is now in balance shall begin to grow, money comes freely and good fortune flows.

Leave the jars open and in a place where you can see them often. Whenever you have spare change, add it to the jars. Be careful to only add equal amounts so that the magic continues to grow.

Plastic Egg Divination Spell

A common feature of Ostara is an abundance of eggs: plain eggs, dyed eggs, candy eggs, and plastic ones, all in bright colors to celebrate them as symbols of life. Though plastic is not exactly known for magical ability, the plastic eggs made to hide candy and treats can be used for a seasonal divination similar to drawing lots or rune stones.

Materials

13 plastic eggs of the same size
A permanent marker
A piece of cardstock
A piece of cardboard or construction paper
A basket to hold the eggs

Cut the cardstock into 13 squares small enough to fit in the eggs. Draw a large circle on the cardboard or construction paper as well as two lines dividing it into four sections. The solar cross paper will be used as the divining board and should be placed on a table with the cross forming an "X." On each of the paper squares, draw an individual symbol: a dollar sign for prosperity, a heart for love, a crown for power, a pentagram for protection, an airplane for travel, an infinity sign (an "8") for spiritual guidance, a crescent moon for magic, a circle for wholeness, a "yes" answer; a circle with a line through it for blockages, a "no" answer, a cauldron to indicate that spellwork is needed, an eight-spoked sun disc for healing and strength, a god symbol (circle with two horns) for the masculine divine, and a goddess symbol (the triple moon) for the divine feminine.

Place one of the thirteen squares in each egg, close them, and then put all the eggs in the basket. Set the basket on the paper with the solar cross drawn on it and hold your hands over it. Mentally charge the eggs, basket, and paper with energy as you say:

Charged by my associations, bring new insights to my mind; symbols of life and divination, reveal to me what I must find.

To use the eggs in divination, you can ask a yes or no question and then slowly pour the eggs out of the basket onto the divination board. Whatever eggs roll away aren't significant; only the ones on the paper matter. Paying close attention to where they fall, open each egg and place its token back on the board. The upper triangle represents the spiritual, the lower represents the physical, the left shows what you are drawing to you, and the right shows what you are releasing. The center represents the present time. Interpret the symbols as they relate to your question. If you see the direct yes or no token, the remaining tokens reveal the circumstances and forces surrounding the question. If they both appear, look to the sections in which they land to find where you are supported and where you are being blocked. Multiple readings can be done for greater insight. This system can be used again and again or just at Ostara if preferred.

Making Your Own Good Luck Charm

At this time of growth and greenery, and just after Saint Patrick's Day, our thoughts may dwell on lucky clovers and leprechauns, flowers and happiness. Since this is a time of growth and increased energy, creating a charm to bring good luck into our lives is an excellent way to take advantage of the extra power available at this time. Luck is really all about choices, timing, and trusting our instincts. When a good luck charm is working, it helps keep us tuned into our intuition so that we stand a much greater chance of making the correct choice. Much the same as with a money charm, I've always felt that workings for good luck should not be expensive or risk defeating their own purpose.

An effective charm can be created from nothing more than a coin that was minted in your birth year. Once you have found the correct coin (it can be of any denomination), cleanse it by soaking it in saltwater overnight. The next day, rinse the coin in cold water and dry it thoroughly. The coin can now be charged with its purpose. Hold it with one hand clasped over the other and visualize green light streaming from your hands into the coin while feeling lucky, prosperous, and hopeful. To seal the intention, say:

Lucky coin of my birth year, increase my chance of success; with this charm a path shall clear, leading me forward, happy and blessed.

Once the coin is charged, carry it in your wallet or purse in a spot where you will not accidentally spend it. Whenever you feel in need of a little extra luck, take out the coin and hold it in your hand.

Ostara Ritual

Melissa Tipton

ONE OF THE MOST important ingredients of successful magick is a unified will, meaning that, as much as is humanly possible, all parts of you are fully on board with experiencing the desired outcome of your magick. I find it helpful to visualize the unified will as an arrow. Through breathwork, meditation, ritual, and other practices, I gather my energies into this arrow, and then I aim it using a clear intention. When our energies are scattered, the "oomph" of our arrow is lessened, making it more difficult to effect powerful changes with our magick. One of the primary reasons for scattered energy is a disconnect between our conscious and unconscious selves.

Ostara, celebrated at the Spring Equinox, is a time when day and night, potent symbols of the conscious and the unconscious, exist in equal measure, making it easier to find this balance within to create a powerful, unified will. Ostara is also a time for beginnings and fresh starts, so once we have forged this unified will, we can direct it with intention into new creations.

Unifying the Will

For the following ritual, you will need two black candles, three white candles, and a small fireproof vessel. Optionally, one of the white candles and the fireproof vessel can be replaced by a campfire if you are performing the ritual outdoors. You will also need an intention of your choosing, written on a slip of paper. Ideally, phrase your intention in the present tense and be specific. For example, instead of "I want to be happier at work," try "My work fulfills me on all levels: emotionally, mentally, spiritually, and financially."

Four of the candles will be used to mark the directional quarters, and you are welcome to call in any deities or guides of your choosing for each. We are using white and black candles to emphasize the contrast between night and day, and you will be performing your ritual in the balance between these polarities. For this reason, I like to situate the elements so that fire and water are opposite each other; ditto with earth and air.

I love to perform this ritual at daybreak on Ostara, in honor of Ēostre, goddess of the dawn, but feel free to choose a time and location (indoors or out) that works best for you. You might choose a time when you don't often do ritual (another reason I like working at dawn) to help you slip more easily into a liminal, out-of-the-ordinary mindset.

Arrange the four candles so one is marking each of the four directions (north, south, east, and west) with a white candle opposite a black one, making sure that the candles are situated safely so they won't topple over. If outdoors, you can ready the makings of a campfire in the center, but otherwise use this spot for the third white candle and a fireproof vessel for burning your intention.

Cleanse the space with the method of your choice, such as sage smoke, a ringing bell, or clear intention, and, standing inside the candles, prepare to cast a sacred circle. I like to take a few moments first to connect to earth energy rising up through the soles of my feet, out via the crown of my head, and sky energy cascading down into my crown and out through the soles of my feet, imagining these streams feeding an ever-expanding swirl of energy at my heart center. Then I send this energy out through my hand, index finger pointed, to cast the circle, tracing the boundaries in a clockwise direction, making three full passes around the space. Optionally, you can speak the following as you cast, one sentence per pass:

I cast this circle to protect me from harm on all levels.

This circle exists beyond the bounds of space and time, centered between the worlds.

I charge this circle to be a temple of balance, within and without, above and below.

So mote it be!

Light each of the candles in turn, using the quarter calls of your choice or the following framework:

I call upon the powers of the [north/east/south/west]! Please lend your magic to this ritual. Hail and welcome!

Feel free to call upon the deities or spirits of your choice within the sacred circle, or use the following evocation:

I call upon Ēostre, goddess of the dawn. Please guide and aid me in this magic. Hail and welcome!

I call upon Máni, god of the moon. Please guide and aid me in this magic. Hail and welcome!

I call upon the Great Spirit, heartbeat of the universe. Please guide and aid me in this magic. Hail and welcome!

Light the central white candle or build a campfire, readying your intention slip for later use. Within this ritual space, take some time in meditation to sense the polar energies holding the boundaries of your circle: north and south, east and west. Slow your breathing and tune into your heartbeat. Begin to sense the larger heartbeat of all that is, and feel your individual rhythm begin to meld and blend into this greater pulse. In this space, experience the interplay between "opposites"; you might even start to sway back and forth, feeling into the still point balanced in the middle. Allow this process to slowly gather your energies into the central balance point, which you might experience at your heart or perhaps your lower belly. Feel the unification of your entire being focused at this middle point, your own inner equinox.

When ready, open your eyes and hold your intention slip. Feel your unified energies like an internal arrow, poised and ready to be loosed. Read your intention aloud three times, visualize and feel your energetic arrow shooting into the cosmos, carrying out your will, and then surrender the intention slip to the flames. As the paper burns, your attachment to outcome dissolves, freeing any last remnants of energy to move freely through time and space to bring about the fulfillment of your magick.

Feel free to do anything else you wish inside the circle, such as blessing cakes and ale, and then close the circle by reversing the opening steps. Start by thanking and releasing any deities or spirits:

Thank you, Ēostre, for your guidance and aid. May there always be harmony between us. Hail and farewell!

Thank you, Máni, for your guidance and aid. May there always be harmony between us. Hail and farewell!

Thank you, Great Spirit, for your guidance and aid. May there always be harmony between us. Hail and farewell!

Snuff out the central white candle or put out the campfire. (You can also allow the campfire to burn if you plan to celebrate longer, being sure to put it out fully before you leave.) Then release the quarters in the reverse order, snuffing out each candle in turn:

I thank and release the powers of the [north/west/south/east]. May there always be harmony between us. Hail and farewell!

Walk around the circle once in a counterclockwise direction, using your finger to energetically pull back the "curtain," opening the space. You might intone the following as you do so:

I cast this circle out into the cosmos as a sign of my magick. This circle is undone, but never broken! Blessed be.

Ostara blessings!

Notes

Beltane

Beltane: Rekindle Your Spiritual Fire

Kerri Connor

AH, BELTANE! THE TIME of year when spring is giving birth to summer. Our plans and goals have turned from the inward to the outward and burst forth into the light. Life, love, and lust fill the air. We are renewed and rejuvenated as we rekindle our fires within. We complete our spring cleaning, we pull back the curtains, throw open the windows, and let the fresh air in to cleanse away the old, both inward and outward. We feel alive and share in the joy of life erupting all around us.

Or at least we should.

We often take these little miracles for granted. The daily miracles of life, joy, beauty, and peace. Being Pagan, however, we should be incorporating these aspects of our spirituality into our daily lives. We get busy, we get distracted, and we end up cutting ourselves off from our own spiritual self without realizing it. Our connection to the natural world is paramount. Even if you live in a densely populated city, you can still feel and celebrate this connection. When concrete is under your feet, turn your face to the warmth of the sun. Feel the breeze on your skin. Nature is all around us. Even when we hide from it or ignore it, it is always there.

One thing I realized about my spirituality over the years was that I was often keeping it a separate part of myself. Definitely not hidden—but also certainly not integrated on a daily basis. Yes, there were normal, everyday moments when I would feel a sudden strong connection to my spiritual self, but they were seldom occurrences outside of ritual.

I loved those moments, I cherished those moments, I missed those moments that were so few and far between. I finally realized I could have those moments as often as I wanted. I simply had to *choose* to have them. Why hadn't anyone ever shared this nugget of knowledge with me before?

I was brought up in a Christian church. For years as a child my understanding of a higher power was only the Christian God—an authoritative father figure that you needed an intermediary (such as a reverend) to speak with on Sundays. As a child, and in my limited experience, I can remember thinking pastors, reverends, and priests were all lawyers in front of God, God being the ultimate judge. Being in church felt like being in a court room. There was no such thing as a personal, close, relationship with God. It was all very formal. We had to put on our Sunday best for services. We had to sit still. We couldn't fidget. We had to stay awake.

It should have been no surprise to my family that the little girl in pigtails who loved to walk barefoot through the acres of dandelions would end up finding herself and her spirituality out there in the wild, and not on a hard wooden pew where she wasn't allowed to feel the grass under her feet or the wind in her hair or the sun on her skin. My parents gave birth to a child of the earth and had no clue.

It was years before I fully understood what an intimate relationship with deity could be like. It was several more years before I realized I could have that relationship as a daily open part of my life and not centered around rituals only. My spirituality did not have to be a "Sunday" thing.

I could choose to integrate my spirituality—my connection to both deity and nature—with the rest of my life as much as I wanted to, so I did. The peace and joy it brought with, well, it was truly divine. My eyes opened to many things I hadn't even realized they were closed to.

Integrating your spirituality into your daily life—a true, full integration—involves letting go of that which you cannot control and shifting your view to find the positive in those situations that leave you feeling down, betrayed, or harmed. This isn't to say forgive and forget; it is to say control what your response is. Choose what road you take. Choose the obstacles you can avoid. Life is not a race. It is an experience.

Beltane is the perfect time to renew a commitment to your spiritual self, to rekindle your spiritual fire, and to recognize and honor your spiritual self in your daily activities. It is a time of cleansing, both physically and spiritually. It's a time for growth. It is a time of celebrating new life—whether the "new life" is your own or the new leaves on the trees that uphold their promise of abundance. As the plants and trees convert energy created from a combination of air, water, fire (sun), and earth into growth, so must we. We too must grow by harnessing our own energy and then sending it where we need it to go.

One of the customs often associated with Beltane is that of the Maypole. While the Maypole is often thought of as a phallic symbol of fertility, it is also a symbol of abundance and energy. The Maypole originated as a dance performed around fruit trees to instill them with magical energy and blessings, boosting their production and giving a more abundant yield. Look at the energy put into performing a Maypole dance! It is easy to see and feel the energy build as dancers get set in a rhythm and find their colors weaving into patterns. Pushing harder and rushing faster as they go until they reach the climactic end and release their own energy into the universe, often rolling in the grass afterwards, both out of a need to ground and pure exhaustion.

This building and release of energy can obviously be done when working with a group, but the pole is only a symbol; the dance is what brings the true energy.

The energy from dance can be built, used, and released anywhere you want. It can be done inside or outside. Day or night. In private, in the open. Anywhere you feel comfortable (that doesn't involve illegal trespassing or some type of insane danger), you can dance.

Dance is not only physical and energy-raising, it can be an extremely spiritual experience if you allow it to be. The key is to literally dance like no one is watching. Let down your guard and your inhibitions and just dance.

Dancing is known to release endorphins, which often allows the dancer to experience a cathartic release of stress and other negative emotions. At the same time, the dancer builds energy to send toward a positive intention. Dancing releases serotonin and norepinephrine. Not only does this make you feel good, it allows you to open yourself more fully to spiritual experiences. These are just some of the reasons dancing has been a historical aspect of many spiritual practices. Once I decided to start using freeform dance as a part of my daily exercise, I was quickly reminded of the spiritual connection I had felt years earlier when I was learning to belly dance. I used to love to dance, but had put it aside as something I was too busy for. Now it is something I make time for daily due to a massive priorities shift. That new shift puts my health and spirituality above things like TV time.

Dancing outdoors, in particular, allows you to form a universal connection to the natural environment around you. (If you partake in cannabis use, you can feel this connection even stronger.) In the warmer months of northern Illinois, my dancing takes place either on my deck or in a spiral labyrinth I built on my property (we have just over two acres and are building a mini spiritual retreat). But when it's cold (and temperatures in the single digits and below zero temps are common), my dancing takes place inside. Dancing indoors just doesn't have the same connection as outdoors does. Nothing compares to nature, but you can still dance up an emotional release and build energy to send into the universe.

Another important aspect to discuss is what you will dance to. Obviously, unless you have your own drum troupe to follow you around, you will most likely need some sort of an electronic device to play music for you. Whether it's MP3s, CDs, or some streaming app, you will need not only the device, but the actual music. I have several playlists stored that I use. I use services like Pandora and Amazon Music to discover new and fitting songs and then add them to the appropriate playlist. Build your playlists up, making them as generic or as specific as you want. Also keep in mind the order of songs in your playlist. Some of my playlists have songs in a very specific order. (I also use these playlists on shuffle for my daily dance time, so they serve a dual purpose.) I start with slower songs, then move into faster and faster ones to allow my movements to increase with the music. In order to create a building of energy, you need the music to match. You may want to include one or two last cool down songs for after your release, but that's completely your own personal preference.

What if you don't know how to dance? You do. It's that simple. Your body knows how to dance, you simply have to allow it. You don't need to take lessons or know fancy steps. All you need is to learn to let go and allow your body to go where it wants, to move how it wants. Feel the music, don't just listen to it. Remember the old saying from earlier? Dance like no one is watching. Because no one is. Your dance is what you need to do. Do what feels good and avoid what doesn't. Try different steps. Use your hands and arms— they are great for building energy! You have hips—shake them, twist them, let them gyrate. Your dancing is for you, your deity, your connection with nature. It is an expression of yourself. No fear necessary. If you aren't used to dancing, it might take some getting used to, both physically and mentally. You may be moving muscles you haven't for quite some time. Work up to it. Don't wear yourself out. Don't hurt yourself. When I first started dancing again, I could barely make it through a few songs, and I would be covered in sweat and out of breath. Now I sometimes go for a couple of hours at a time. Know what your limits are and use that to set up how many songs you will need on your playlist. I highly recommend working yourself up to a minimum of twenty minutes, including a song or two for cooling/winding down. Once you build more stamina, you can create your playlist to reflect several waves of building, climax, cool down, and then continuing the cycle back toward release.

You can incorporate dance into your spiritual life as much, or as little, as you want, but I do highly encourage you to make it a permanent part. It is truly an exercise of the mind and spirit along with the body.

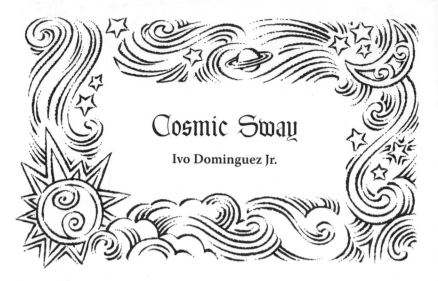

Cosmic Sway

Ivo Dominguez Jr.

ON MAY 1, the Sun, Mercury, Venus, and Uranus are all in Taurus. The waning Moon is in Capricorn, as is Pluto, which makes for a significant concentration of planets in the element of earth. Overall, the planets are all on one side of the chart as well. The Sun is tightly conjunct to Uranus. Mercury is trine to retrograde Pluto in Capricorn.

May 5 is astrological Beltane when the Sun is at the 15th degree of Taurus. Mercury will have entered Gemini on May 4. Saturn in Aquarius is square to the Sun and Uranus in Taurus. Retrograde Pluto in Capricorn is trine to Venus in Taurus. Venus is also square to Jupiter in Aquarius. The New Moon is in Taurus on May 11 with an applying trine to retrograde Pluto.

Like all the sabbats, Beltane is complex and contains many meanings and possibilities. As always, Beltane is all things Taurean. It is joy in the beauty of the living world. It is the passion and sensuality that arises from the gift of being embodied. It is the promise of the flames and the flowers of May. The astrology of this particular Beltane brings some specific themes to the forefront. You are probably aware of customs involving the crowning of a May Queen and King. For the purposes here, let's expand that to say May Monarchs, as that phrase contains more possibilities. One of the tasks at hand is the claiming of your personal sovereignty. It is your divine birthright to be the ruler of your life. If you use it well, this Beltane season is your personal coronation. It can also be thought of as an initiation into the mysteries of your life.

The Sun's conjunction to Uranus also increases your need and ability to express your individuality. It is a good time to reinvent yourself in any and all ways. This can run the full gamut from your appearance to your living situation. Change is in the atmosphere, so it is better to choose your changes rather than simply going with the flow. The restless energy that this aspect brings is best used by remaining active. It is in the doing that you will find answers and insights, not in contemplation during Beltane.

The clustering of all the planets on one side of the chart, and the preponderance of the element of earth, will also bring out a longing for completion and your counterpart. This may surface as a longing for someone or something that fills the empty side of the chart. This is a challenge and not the answer. Be wary of obsessions and preoccupations. The rest of the influences are calling for you to step up and be a monarch. Summon the courage to discover the parts of your psyche that you have hidden from yourself. Claiming your whole self is the key to taking the next step in your life.

Mercury's trine to Pluto magnifies all powers of persuasion, whether this is directed inward or outward. Your capacity to see deeper, unveil hidden things, and unravel complicated situations is sharpened. Telepathy is stronger during this aspect as well. During Beltane this arrangement also facilitates spirit travel so that the Maypole symbolically becomes like the World Tree, the omphalos, a bridge between the worlds. Communications with non-physical beings will be easier during Beltane.

As we approach astrological Beltane on May 5, the influence of Saturn square to the Sun-Uranus conjunction takes hold. The Uranus part of this Saturn square will shake up the boundaries between duty, desire, and aspirations. It will become very clear what things are out of order and need mending or discarding in your life. Don't overreact or give in to irritation; instead ask to be shown the middle way between the extremes of action or opinion. The Sun part of this Saturn square encourages a sense of heaviness and the frustration of being blocked. Make use of the lively and vigorous energy of Beltane to counteract this melancholy influence. Keep moving; movement is life, and procrastination now will lead to a great cost.

The Venus aspects at this time turn off the color and sound on emotions, passions, love, attractions, and old unrequited needs that yearn to be acknowledged. Your self-control is weakened so it may be wise to reinforce promises, pledges, and good habits. In particular be careful not to lower your standards. These aspects can make you fun and overly optimistic, so be wary of how you spend your time and money. Many of these influences are at odds with each other. If you work with ideas and imagery of your crown of sovereignty and the bridge between heaven and earth of the Maypole, the turbulence will resolve into abundance and comfort.

Should anything need further course correction or adjustment, you have one more chance to set things right at the New Moon on May 11. We began the Beltane season with a waning Moon in Capricorn, and whatever rituals or workings you've already done can be refined or continued at the New Moon in Taurus. The New Moon holds the power of transformation and is in the sign of the season. Even if things are going the way that you like, you may still want to plan a working to speed things along. Remember that a New Moon is a conjunction with the Sun. This joining of Sun and Moon is very evocative of the themes of Beltane as well as the rest of the starry influences of this season.

The New Moon is also making a trine to Pluto, which opens up psychic abilities and makes magic flow more easily. This aspect can also be used for ancestral work or delving into secrets of the past, especially those from your family tree. Family bonds with the living can also be enhanced during this time. Self-nurturance is easier to accomplish, and healing work directed toward you will have a greater affect. There is also a possibility that whatever was set into motion at Samhain in 2020 will come to its culmination now.

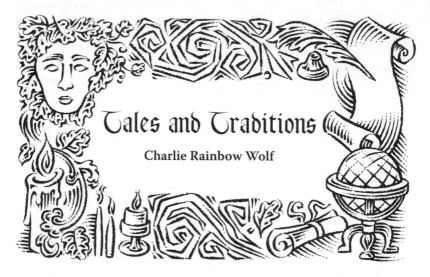

Tales and Traditions

Charlie Rainbow Wolf

BELTANE IS THE FIRE festival that takes place around the first of May. Many cultures around the world celebrate May Day, but did you know that not all of them see this as a fire festival? In some areas of the world, such as England, this is very much a water festival too. Even though the calendar says that it happens in spring, it is noted as the first of the summer gatherings.

Samhain and Saint Walburga

The festivities of Beltane are rooted in glorification of fertility and union. This was even turned into a verb. To go "Maying" meant that partners would disappear into nature and spend the night together, then decide whether they wanted to develop this connection into a relationship.

Today Beltane is sometimes portrayed as a festival of orgies and debauchery, but that is a far cry from the way it honored the sacredness of life and the opportunity to enjoy living to the fullest.

Dig a little deeper and it makes sense that this is a sabbat that honors both the gods and goddesses, for both masculine and feminine are needed to create new life—the theme of this festival. In some observances, a May Queen is crowned, and she is then to be given to the May King, in a representation of the divine union. She is the personification of spring and summer, the entity that holds her own against the coming of the winter, providing harvest and bounty to sustain life during the cold and bleak months ahead.

Halloween in May?

Beltane isn't the only festival honored at this time of year. In Europe, Walpurgis Night is a very old and time-honored tradition. While it is said to honor Saint Walburga, the revelry does seem to be more like Samhain than anything from the Christian customs! Once again, we have a blending of beliefs: the Christian saint after whom the ceremony is named and the Viking bonfire rituals to ensure good weather, fertility for their farms, and the absence of malevolent spirits.

Beltane is opposite Samhain on the calendar. In some places this is thought to be the last night that unruly spirits can gather to create mayhem before the spirit of springtime awakens the land once again. Many activities are similar to those of Halloween—bonfires to ward off evil entities, masks worn to disguise a person's identity and confuse malevolent energies, and homes decorated to protect people from negativity.

Bonfires are a big part of Walpurgis Night. There's a practical side to this history; in the spring the farmers would turn their livestock out to graze. The young would be easy prey to wild animals, so fires were set to deter predators from coming close. The fires were often accompanied by the farmers and shepherds who would make a lot of noise and move around to create further discouragement.

These activities evolved over time into a more ritualistic practice. Today, people will often bring offerings to the fire in the shape of things that represent what they need to purge from their lives.

Sometimes this is even the object itself, such as worn-out clothing and other household items. By offering them to the fire, they rid themselves of any negative energy that may have been attached to them.

Walpurgis Night is also a time when children dress up and make mischief. In Bavaria, pranks are pulled similar to our Western custom of throwing toilet paper into trees or covering glass windows with soap. In Germany, little girls dress up as their favorite witch. In Finland, you may see people running wildly around the streets, sharing drinks and animated chatter. On the farm where I lived in Lincolnshire, England, we hung cowslips over the doorways and placed them on the window sills so that the spirits would pass by our home. It may have helped that we lived next to the churchyard too!

Dances and Digestible Delectations

May Day is celebrated in many different ways in England, and one of the more popular activities is the Maypole. The pole symbolizes the divine masculine, and the girls dancing around it are the divine feminine. The pole is lavishly decorated with ribbons hanging from the top, and the girls duck and dive in a dance, weaving the ribbons around the pole in a pattern to ensure fertility and abundance for the coming season.

Morris dancing is one more English custom. It is a form of folk dancing that was often performed only by men, although that has begun to change in the last century. The dances are ancient and have been handed down from generation to generation, one dancer to another, and many are over five-hundred years old. They are accompanied by music that is indigenous to the dance team's region, and the dancers have uniform clothing in a specific style that identifies their location and their dances.

Like all festivals, food and drink was a focal point of May Day. In England, we celebrated it with the first strawberries of the season because nothing quite says "summer" like British strawberries and cream or a traditional cream tea! Also, the seeds on the strawberries represented a time of fertility and plenty.

Honoring the Ways

There are numerous ways you can add a different theme to your Beltane festivities. You've heard of Christmas in July; perhaps you could have Halloween in May and celebrate Walpurgis Night! Morris dancing is another challenge you might wish to try to master. While you may not have access to your own band of morris dancers to teach you, there are many YouTube videos of the dances and the clothing worn while performing them.

The fairies and nature spirits are thought to be particularly lively around Beltane. Activities to honor them are both fun and beneficial—no one wants the wrath of an angry fairy! Over the years we've made it a practice to add something new to the yarden (yard + garden = yarden), whether it's planting a perennial or placing a statue. This year we began clearing space for what will be the actual fairy garden: a rockery decorated with miniature pottery items and sown with stonecrop and other miniature perennials. It doesn't matter if you don't have an outside area in which to do this. Many lovely fairy gardens are built in giant flower pots or other receptacles, and those have the added advantage that they can be transported to different locations or brought inside if you live where the winter is harsh.

It could also be a bit of fun to bring in some Samhain traditions for May Day. In many cultures, the mirror image of something, or doing something backward, is considered to be sacred. What better way to recognize that hallowedness than to bring out your All Hallows' Eve traditions for Beltane? My friends usually jump at this idea, for most of them see no reason not to celebrate Halloween year-round! Then again, we do call the Halloween aisles in the shops our "home decorating supplies"!

References

Cutting, John. *History and the Morris Dance: A Look at Morris Dancing from Its Earliest Days Until 1850*. Hampshire, UK: Dance Books, 2005.

Raedisch, Linda. *Night of the Witches: Folklore, Traditions & Recipes for Celebrating Walpurgis Night*. Woodbury, MN: Llewellyn Publications, 2011.

Rawe, Donald R. *Padstow's Obby Oss and May Day Festivities: A Study in Folklore & Tradition*. London: Francis Boutle Publishers, 2007.

Feasts and Treats

Sue Pesznecker

BELTANE IS SPRING IN full flower. Everywhere one looks, something is growing or blooming. Most farmers markets have opened for the season and are rich with fresh greens, flowers, vegetables, and berries. It's the time of year when the earth is fecund and life is full of promise, and the recipes in this section honor that bounty in all its richness.

Fresh Pesto with Pasta

For me, pesto is summer in a bowl, all ripening herbs and salty cheese and gorgeous aroma. It's easy to make and elegantly impressive all at once—a real crowd pleaser.

Prep time: 10 minutes
Cooking time: varies by kind of noodle
Servings: about 4

Salt
Pasta of your choice—I prefer a standard spaghetti with this
2 tablespoons toasted pine nuts
1 garlic clove, peeled and cut into 4 pieces
1¼ cups of loosely packed basil leaves
2 ounces (about ½ cup) grated Parmesan cheese*

2 ounces grated Pecorino or Grana Padano cheese*
½ cup extra-virgin olive oil*
Additional salt and pepper to taste
Additional basil leaves
Additional grated Parmesan cheese
*For best results, use the highest quality cheese and olive oil you can
    find. If possible, grate the cheese yourself.

Gather all the ingredients you need for the pesto.

Start a 4–6-quart kettle of water boiling. Season with 2–3 table-spoons of salt; the water should taste very salty.

Add the pasta to the boiling water and set a timer.

When the pasta only has three minutes left to cook, place the pine nuts, garlic, basil, and cheeses into a food processor. Process in bursts, scraping down the sides often, until the mixture is evenly chopped.

Turn the food processor on to its continuous setting. Using the feeder tube, add the olive oil in a steady stream. Scrape sides as needed and process in additional bursts—you're aiming for a smooth, slightly flowing green pesto that will still have a somewhat rough texture. If it seems too thick or too solid, add a bit of additional oil. Taste and add salt and pepper as desired.

Drain the cooked pasta, pile into bowls, and spoon large dollops of pesto atop, allowing diners to mix their own. Garnish with a few fresh basil leaves if desired. Serve with additional cheese on the side.

Notes:

- Don't have a food processor? You can make pesto with a large mortar and pestle, although this is rather challenging.
- Have fun customizing your own pesto or swapping out ingredients because of allergy or food sensitivity. Use different nuts or seeds in place of pine nuts. Try different herbs or cheeses or different varieties of olive oil.
- Add leftover pesto to scrambled or deviled eggs, salad dressing, potato salad, or anything else you can imagine.

- Leftover pesto also freezes beautifully in small containers, ice cube trays, etc. Top with a thin film of additional olive oil to keep the basil from browning.

Amanda's Roasted Beet, Walnut, and Goat Cheese Salad

I never was a beet eater, but this recipe from my friend Amanda convinced me to change my mind. Sweet, tart, savory, crunchy, soft, salty...Whatever you want, it's here. Enjoy this!

Prep time: 30 minutes
Cooking time: 1 hour
Servings: 4

½ cup walnuts
2 teaspoons olive oil
¼ teaspoon salt
¼ teaspoon black pepper
6 medium beets
⅓ cup red onion, thinly sliced
6 tablespoons olive oil
2 tablespoons red wine vinegar
¼ teaspoon sugar
Kosher salt and pepper to taste
½ pound fresh spinach or baby greens (or mix thereof)
3 ounces fresh goat cheese

Preheat the oven to 300° F. Combine the walnuts, olive oil, salt, and black pepper, mixing well to coat the nuts. Toast them for about 5 minutes on a cookie sheet in the oven.

Preheat the oven to 400° F. Wrap the beets in a large square of foil that is closed tightly around them. Roast for 45–60 minutes until they are soft.

Peel the roasted, cooled beets and slice in ½-inch wedges. Place in a bowl with the toasted, seasoned nuts and sliced red onion.

Combine the olive oil, red wine vinegar, and sugar in a lidded jar. Shake until well blended. Taste and add salt and pepper as desired.

Pour the dressing over the beet mixture and toss well. Let sit at room temperature for at least 1 hour.

To serve, place spinach or greens on individual plates or a large platter. Arrange beet mixture on top. Crumble the goat cheese over to finish. Pass additional dressing to be used as desired.

Roasted Baby Turnips

I first heard the good news about baby turnips three years ago, and I've been hooked ever since. Seriously. I stalk them at our early spring farmers markets because you'll only find them during that time. Baby turnips are a whole different deal than their full-grown relatives. When roasted, they're sweet and tender with their own unique, earthy flavor. A perfect icon of spring feasting!

Prep time: 15 minutes
Cooking time: 20–25 minutes
Servings: 4–6

½ cup extra-virgin olive oil
1 tablespoon white wine or apple cider vinegar
1½ teaspoons whole grain mustard
1 scallion, minced
1½ tablespoons flat-leaf parsley, chopped
Salt and freshly ground pepper
24 baby turnips (about 2 pounds), washed, stems trimmed to 2 inches

Combine ¼ cup of the olive oil with the vinegar, mustard, scallion, and parsley in a lidded jar. Shake to combine.

Preheat oven to 425° F.

Cut the turnips in half (cut larger ones into fourths). Toss with the other ¼ cup of olive oil and place on a foil-lined baking sheet. Roast for 20–25 minutes, until the turnips are soft.

Cool for 5–10 minutes, place in a serving bowl, and drizzle with the vinaigrette.

Savor...

Wicked Quick-Pickled Good Green Beans

Every good meal needs a balance of textures and flavors, and adding a bit of crunchy-sweet-tartness is guaranteed to accent whatever you're serving. These pickled green beans are easy to whip up and can be served as a condiment or even as the perfect martini or Bloody Mary add-on. For variety, swap out the beans for slices of sweet onion, sweet pepper, or summer squash.

Prep time: 30 minutes

Cooking time: no cooking unless you decide to water-bath can your jars

Inactive: 2 days to 2–3 weeks

Servings: varies

Beans

1 pound fresh green beans, ends and strings removed
Optional additions (per jar):
1 dill head, or 2 teaspoons whole dill seed
2 cloves garlic, peeled
½ teaspoon black peppercorns
½ teaspoon mustard seed
½ teaspoon crushed red pepper flakes
¼ teaspoon coriander or fennel seeds

Vinegar mixture

1¼ cups apple cider vinegar
1¼ cups water
⅛ cup kosher salt
1 tablespoon sugar

Select 3–4 pint-sized jars; wash well and sterilize with boiling water—lids too. Trim the green beans so they will stand upright in the jars with ½-inch clearance.

Load each jar with any of the optional additions, then stand the trimmed beans vertically on top of them. Set aside.

Bring the vinegar, water, salt, and sugar to a boil in a saucepan, stirring until everything is dissolved. Pour over the green beans in the jars to within ¼-inch of the tops of the jars. Screw on lids, cool to room temperature, and place in the refrigerator.

Store these in the fridge. The beans will be ready to eat in two days, but if you can wait 2–3 weeks, they'll be even better.

For longer storing, use pint canning jars with two-piece canning lids. After pouring the vinegar mixture, wipe the rims with a clean, damp cloth and screw on the lid fingertip tight. Process for 10 minutes in a boiling water bath. (If you aren't a canner, please look up detailed instructions.) Store in a cool, dark place for up to a year; once opened, store in the fridge.

Crafty Crafts

Tess Whitehurst

AT BELTANE, THE VEIL between the worlds of humans and fairies lifts. At this time of year, those of us who can sense fairies become even more awake to their presence.

Even if you don't think you can sense fairies, you probably can. For example, have you ever been in nature and suddenly noticed your senses were heightened? If so, can you also remember how your experience of beauty became more intense and you also lost track of time? This was the realm of the Fae—the magical consciousness of nature—beckoning you back to your wild, free, and undomesticated state.

Many ancient cultures have stories about the spirits that live in nature. And in truth, we are all part Fae. We all have wildness encoded in our DNA. When you laugh genuinely, dance unselfconsciously, express unfettered creativity, enjoy music on a deep level, or run barefoot on the earth, your inner fairy is awakened and your joyful aliveness blooms.

Fairy Footwear

Another way to awaken your inner fairy? Put on your fairy shoes. Here's how to make some.

Materials

An old pair of faux-leather shoes. I used boots I found at a thrift store, but any old pair that speak to your inner fairy will do: ballet flats, buckled clogs, etc.

Gold or silver metallic acrylic craft paint

A paintbrush

Faux flowers and leaves (be sure to choose colors and shapes that speak to your inner fairy)

Scissors or wire cutters

A hot glue gun and hot glue sticks

Newspaper to cover your workspace

Optional: adhesive rhinestones or craft gems, vetiver essential oil

Cost: $10–$20

Time spent: 30–40 minutes, plus time for glue to dry

Here's a tip: Play fairy music while you make these! Traditional Celtic music, Native American flute, or Japanese folk music would all be appropriate choices.

If necessary, first clean your shoes with a damp cloth and allow them to dry thoroughly. After covering your workspace with newspaper, paint the entire external surface of the shoes (except the soles) with the metallic craft paint to create a burnished look. While the paint is drying, use the scissors or wire cutters as necessary to separate the faux blossoms and leaves you'd like to use to adorn your shoes.

And now for the fun part: Use the glue gun to affix the flowers and leaves to the outside of your shoe in any way you like. If your shoes have buckles or straps, you can nestle the ersatz botanicals in and around them, or simply glue them to the surface in any way your creativity dictates. You may like to cover the entire surface of the shoe with flowers and leaves, or simply employ them as accents.

If you're using gems, glue or adhere those to the surface of the shoes as well. There's no right or wrong here—follow your intuition about where to put the jewels. Do keep in mind, however, that fairies love things that sparkle, so don't hold back!

If you'd like, you can anoint each sole with a small amount of vetiver essential oil. This will awaken the magic of your fairy shoes and help you summon the luck and prosperity of the earth each time you put them on.

Ideas for what to do in your fairy shoes: dance, make music, go to a party, work magic, attend a Pagan gathering, garden, or sprinkle fairy summoning dust around your yard. Speaking of which, here's how to make some.

Fairy Summoning Dust

Beltane is a wonderful time to summon the fairies. When fairies live in your yard, you'll know because birds and butterflies will hang around more often. Your flowers will be blessed with more blossoms, your fruit will be sweeter, and your vegetables will grow to immense proportions. Depending on where you live, you may even see more wild critters than usual. For example, after I dusted my yard with this powder, it wasn't long before I saw a grown moose and her adorable calf right outside my window. They camped out for an hour or so. It's rare that you get to see moose up close like that without being in danger of being trampled. It was almost like I was spying on unicorns.

The lilac blossoms in this craft help open the lines of communication between fairies and humans—they sensitize humans to fairies and fairies to humans. Reishi is a sacred mushroom that awakens the power and magic of the earth and blurs the boundaries between the human and fairy realms. Chamomile soothes stress and promotes the joyful simplicity that invites and welcomes our fairy friends. And, of course, fairies love treasure—the crystal offerings will first draw them in and then entice them to stay.

Materials
A glass bowl or mason jar
1 cup dried lilac blossoms (you can substitute lavender)
A mortar and pestle

1 tablespoon dried, powdered reishi mushrooms or reishi mushroom tea

½ cup dried chamomile

A wooden chopstick or wand

9 tiny crystals (I used quartz, rose quartz, carnelian, and garnet, but any tiny gemstones or gemstone beads will do)

Cost: $8–$12

Time spent: 5–10 minutes

Crush the lilac blossoms with the mortar and pestle. Then place in the bowl or jar and combine with the mushrooms and chamomile by stirring in a clockwise direction with the chopstick or wand. As you stir, envision the powder being filled with sparkly golden light. Say:

Nature spirits, realm of Fae
Creatures of both night and day,
I invite you now to dance and play,
And hope that you will choose to stay.

Go outside and sprinkle the fairy dust around the perimeter of your yard. As you do, mentally or aloud let the fairies know this is an offering and an invitation, and that you'd love for them to live in your yard and bless it with their magic. Also place each gemstone in your yard as an additional offering and incentive.

Once the fairies have accepted your invitation (which shouldn't be long), be sure to keep them happy by offering gifts regularly. For example, keeping a hummingbird feeder stocked with fresh nectar is an excellent offering to the spirits of nature. So is a traditional birdfeeder continually stocked with birdseed. Fairies also appreciate libations of beer, champagne, cider, or ale. You can serve it to them in walnut shells or simply pour it straight onto the earth. Mirrored gazing balls delight fairies, as do fairy statues and fairy houses. Or, you can keep it simple: Each time you water your yard, you can say blessings over the water and offer up its positive vibrations as a gift to the fairies.

Spells

Michael Furie

THIS DAY, AS THE sabbat that officially welcomes the light half of the year, is all about life, vigor, strength, growth, health, energy, and desire. We can celebrate what we've achieved, protect what we have, revel in the power of longer days, and harness the magic of Beltane to make our wishes into reality.

Faery Protection Spell Bottle

Though the more positive and friendly aspects of faeries are the most often highlighted in this modern era, an older view of the Fey is one of foreboding and precaution. It is certainly possible to develop a good working relationship with members of their realm, but it is also wise during this time (Beltane is a very active time for the faery) to set up protections against any malevolent members of the faery kingdom. Old tales speak of people being taken by faeries—switched with changeling doubles left in their place. Other tales warn of humans and animals being stricken by "elf shot," an attack that results in shooting pain.

Whether or not we need to worry about such things, it is better to be safe than sorry at this time of high activity. One protective herb that has been in use for generations against faery magic is fennel. All parts of the fennel are protective against malevolent faeries, but the seeds are the easiest to work with for this magic. Foxglove has been associated with the faeries for centuries and is also protective. The seeds can usually be found for sale in small packets since foxglove is grown as a decorative flower.

Materials
1 bottle with lid or stopper
¼ cup fennel seeds
1 packet of foxglove seeds (*Digitalis purpurea*)
Water
Funnel
1 small pot

The amount of water needed will vary depending on the size of the bottle chosen. The easiest way is to simply fill up the bottle with water and then pour it into the pot. Add the fennel seeds and simmer for about ten minutes. Remove from heat and allow it to cool completely. Once cooled, using the funnel, open the foxglove seed packet and pour the seeds into the bottle. Then pour the fennel brew (without straining) into the bottle as well. Hold the bottle in your hands and visualize the bottle acting as a battery of sorts, radiating a protective field large enough to secure your home from any malevolent forces. After this, seal the bottle tightly and place it in a hidden spot in your home where it will not be disturbed.

A Crystal Wish Spell

Beltane is the sabbat that brings in the light half of the year, so it is one of the two most powerful times (the other being Samhain) and has an energy that encourages all forms of growth and increase. This spell can be used for any purpose as long as it involves growth, expansion, and increase. Tapping into this earth energy can be as simple as making an offering back of a portion of that which has been taken. Since the rise of the New Age culture, the extraction of quartz crystals from the land has increased to meet the commercial demand. This spell is a way of giving a small piece back to the earth in the spirit of gratitude. For the spell you will need a clear quartz crystal that you can release; don't use one you intend to keep.

Materials
1 small clear quartz crystal
1 small trowel or shovel
1 small bottle of water

Before casting this spell, find a spot in nature beside a tree that you feel drawn toward. Once you have decided upon a magical goal, hold the crystal in your strong hand and focus on your desire, seeing and feeling it as strongly as possible. When ready, take the crystal, water, and trowel to the tree and dig a small hole big enough to bury the stone. As you place the stone into the hole, again strongly visualize your goal and say:

Magical gift taken from the land, I ask my wish be granted; returned to the earth with joy and thanks, I leave this stone enchanted; may my goal be reached with comfort and ease, for highest good, so mote it be.

Bury the crystal in the hole, water it, and then leave the area without looking back.

Four Thieves' Vinaigrette Spell for Good Health

For this spell, the famous Four Thieves' Vinegar has to be made. This vinegar is said to have originated in Europe during the time of the bubonic plague. Four thieves allegedly used it to avoid catching the plague while they stole from the sick. Everyone wondered how they managed to remain healthy despite exposing themselves to the illness so often and were anxious to uncover this secret. Once the thieves were captured, it is said that they traded the oil's secret formula for a means to escape.

Though not the nicest origin story ever, the vinegar is indeed a powerful mixture that can be used for both healing and banishing.

We will be focusing on an edible healing version. It is best to make it yourself as purchased varieties are not usually created to be taken internally and may contain harsh-tasting or inedible ingredients such as wormwood. The formula requires four ingredients (one from each thief) to be added to apple cider vinegar.

1 cup apple cider vinegar
1 tablespoon sage
1 tablespoon rosemary
1 tablespoon thyme
2 cloves garlic, crushed
1 small pot

In the pot, warm the vinegar and the garlic over low heat for a few minutes, being careful not to let it boil. Remove from heat and allow it to cool, then add the herbs. Bottle it for use. To use it in the vinaigrette, pour one part of the vinegar into a shaker bottle, adding three parts olive oil, ½ part Dijon mustard, and salt and pepper to taste. Shake the bottle to mix and charge it with the intention that it will strengthen the body and preserve good health by saying:

Healing potion from ancient lore, banish all illness, good health ensure.

Repeat the spell at least three times as you shake and then pour some of the vinaigrette onto a fresh green salad to take in the power of the vinegar. This vinaigrette can be eaten as often as desired.

Beltane Ritual

Kerri Connor

I HAVE DISCUSSED SOME of the basics of spiritual dance in the earlier introduction to Beltane, so in this ritual we will work with a direct intention and focus, using dance as our energy-building catalyst to release our intentions into the universe. After learning how to prepare for this ritual, you will have a format you can use to set up other dance-based rituals to suit your needs.

Rekindle Your Spiritual Fire with Dance

This ritual will require prep work, so be sure to give yourself time to prepare. This may take days.

Your first step is to determine the length of your ritual. You will be dancing throughout most of it. How much can you safely dance? If you can, I highly recommend a minimum of twenty minutes, but you know what will work best for you and will leave you energized and not collapsing. Now that I can, I keep mine to about sixty minutes total.

The music you choose is up to you. Your taste may be far different from mine. I will offer suggestions, but these are not required. You might find something you like, or it may lead you to something else you like, and if so, perfect!

On that note, I suggest:

"Weaving the Summer" by Spiral Dance
"Beltane Fire Dance" by Loreena McKennitt
"Oak, Broom and Meadowsweet" by Damh the Bard
"Firebird's Child" by S.J. Tucker
"The Greenman" by Michelle Mays
"Come to the Dance" by Emerald Rose
"The Celts" by Enya

There are several songs by Jethro Tull, Kelliana, and Jenna Greene each that are fitting. Drum music is also a necessity; no matter what kind of drumming you like, have a few songs available for your playlist.

Set up your playlist in the correct order. You will need to begin with a song you can spend a few minutes meditating with, and then move to something with a slower beat for warm-up. Follow this with songs with a faster, stronger beat to create more energy to build and continue until your release. Finish with a softer, slower, relaxed song or two for cool down and grounding.

You will also need to find a location you can use for this amount of time. If you don't have your own private area outdoors where you would feel comfortable dancing, don't give up. Look at other options, like parks, forest preserves, gardens, or friends' homes. Some metaphysical shops now offer courtyard garden areas that can be used for these types of purposes. If you are only doing this for a one-time ritual, that makes it extra special, and therefore worth putting forth more effort. Perhaps you will discover a perfect location right under your nose that you never knew about. Ask around.

If your options are limited, we can work with that! The simple act of cracking open a window allows for a partial disintegration of the wall between us and the outside world. While not a full immersion, a wafting is preferable to total enclosure. Prepare your area by bringing in natural items—plants, cut flowers for an offering, a bowl of dirt or salt, a bowl or pitcher of water (in addition to cut flowers in water), or even a small water fountain, stones, shells, feathers, antlers, fruits, vegetables, leaves, seeds, broken branches, bark, and so on—any of these items can be used to attune your inside world more with the outside world.

If you are working outside, you can use items like these too. Use them to decorate the ground in a circle around where you will be performing your dance. Be sure to make your circle large enough to give yourself room to move, if the space is available.

If you are indoors, space may be minimal. If you can safely make a circle on the floor with your natural items, do so. If not, place them in locations throughout the room to help distribute the energy evenly.

Open your ritual as you normally would.

Begin your playlist.

The intention you will set for this ritual is to rekindle your spiritual fire through dance. Take some time to sit in quiet meditation on the ground in the center of your circle during the first song of your playlist to think about what that means to you. What do you need to cleanse from your spirit to be able to rekindle your spiritual fire? Is there something holding you back? What dampened it in the first place? Are you just discovering it? What does your spark need you to feed it to become a full blown blaze? Make a commitment, a promise to yourself, your deities, the Earth, and all her life to rekindle the spiritual fire within yourself. Make this promise out loud so you know you mean it.

When your first song finishes, rise to your feet and begin your cleansing dance. Imagine as you move that the air that flows past you is cleansing your spirit. The floor or earth below your feet grounds your spirit.

Increase your enthusiasm in your dance as your songs change. Let yourself go, free from worry, free from any cares. It is just you in your place in the universe. Take the hand of your deity and dance with him or her. Envision yourself at one with nature, at one with the universe.

Find your spark inside of you.

Hold onto it with your mind's eye and blow life into it. Fan the flames so that your spark grows bigger, stronger, more furious, but never out of control. No matter how large it gets, you are in control.

Build with your dance until you meet your moment of release, timed to your music. Send the energy of your flame shooting into the universe. Allow it to burn down to a temperate flare, brighter, more vibrant than it was before you began.

Follow along with your music to wind down and ground.

Finish your ritual with a quiet meditation and reflection on your working. Open your ritual when you are ready.

Notes

Notes

Litha

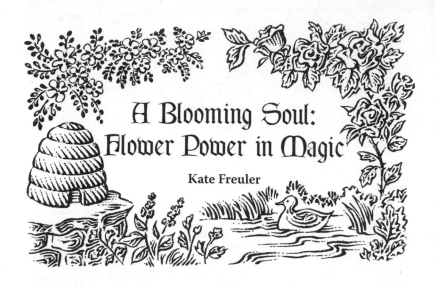

A Blooming Soul:
Flower Power in Magic

Kate Freuler

LITHA, ALSO CALLED THE Summer Solstice or Midsummer, occurs in late June in the Northern Hemisphere. The sun rises earlier and sets later than it will on any other day and is at the absolute height of its power. This celebration marks the time when the goddess is heavily pregnant and about to give birth, and the god is about to become a father. This is reflected in nature all around us, in the blooming of flowers, the abundance of ripening fruit and vegetables, and the birth of baby animals. The fullness of the sun represents the pregnancy of the earth and how it is ready to burst forth with new life. After this day, sun exposure starts to lesson bit by bit as the Wheel of the Year cycles into its waning months, even though the hottest days are still to come.

Traditionally fires were lit and tended on Midsummer's Eve, burning throughout the entire night and following day to celebrate the sun. Fairies are thought to be about on this day, and people often leave food out for them such as milk, honey, and butter and bread.

Another thing associated with Litha is, of course, flowers. Flowers are the very soul of summer. They're not only pretty and fragrant; they encompass the meaning of the solstice: life, abundance, brightness, growth, and hope. It makes me feel happy to be alive to look out at a field of wildflowers basking in the sunshine, bustling with insect life and ground-dwelling animals, and dripping with pollen for bees and nectar for butterflies. Flowers are at the peak of their lives when they bloom, their open faces celebrating the full power of the sun as they reach up towards it.

Flowers are rich with symbolism across cultures and throughout history. They've been important to people for various reasons for so long that their meanings have become contradictory in some cases. For example, the marigold's sunny face represents life but, due to its strange smell, is associated with death. When including flowers in your magic, intent is very important in determining what energies they will contribute to a spell.

In celebration of our flower friends that bloom during Midsummer, here are some easily found or obtained flowers to integrate into your working. This is a list of plants that naturally blossom in late June, making them perfect for Summer Solstice crafts and amulets. You may find some of them in your own garden or growing wild in fields and parks. Remember that some flowers are poisonous and shouldn't be used in creations you'll be putting on your skin or ingesting.

Flower Meanings

Black-Eyed Susan: These cute yellow and brown flowers represent encouragement, inspiration, and motivation.

Buttercup: Buttercups encompass cheerfulness and child-like happiness. They're excellent for adding to spells for joy, or you can place them around your house to encourage happy, carefree energy to enter.

Carnation: Carnations have a long history and therefore many different associations, including bravery, pride, hard work, and love. They've even been called an aphrodisiac. On the other end of the spectrum, they're associated with death; in the Christian faith it is said that they appeared after the death of Jesus Christ. As with many flowers, the color of a carnation is important:

- pink: encouragement and maternal influence
- red: love and romance
- white: purity and devotion
- yellow: disappointment and rejection

Chicory: Chicory represents unconditional love. It is said to aid with releasing emotions and attachments, and can be included in spells for removing obstacles. Chicory is a good ingredient in workings for letting go of a relationship in a loving, healthy way.

Columbine: The flower of the columbine contains a five-pointed star, linking it to the pentacle symbol. Many associate the pentacle with warding off negativity or providing protection. Columbine represents victory, determination, and courage.

Cornflower: The cornflower is an excellent sky-blue flower to grow near your home. It represents family love, a peaceful household, and good friends and neighbors. It is also associated with loyalty and consistency. The blue color of the cornflower associates it with the blue sky and divinity.

Daisy: Pluck the petals from a daisy one by one while saying, "They love me, they love me not," to divine whether or not someone is interested in you romantically. In this way, daisies can represent choice. They're believed to attract love, warmth, and non-materialism. Daisies encompass the simple joys of young love.

Echinacea: Echinacea represents strength, integrity, and the self. It is popular for its medicinal properties and is taken to strengthen the immune system during cold and flu season, making it a good addition to healing rituals. Include Echinacea in spells and crafts to bring inner strength and resolve. It can be added to any spell to enhance its power.

Geraniums: Geraniums can be planted around the home to attract love, fertility, and protection. This is another flower in which color is important to its meaning:

- pink: finding a mate, love, romance
- red: protection, especially of the home
- white: fertility

Gerbera Daisy: Gerbera daisies are associated with active, cheerful energy, love for life, and excitement.

- orange: dispelling negativity
- yellow: emotional stability
- red: deeply-passionate love
- white: childlike open-mindedness
- pink: open adoration

Iris: Irises are believed to purify the area all around them, cleansing unwanted energy. They're associated with faith, authority, and victory, but also the pain of unrequited love. The root of the Iris can be carved and worn as a protective amulet.

Lavender: Lavender was burned at Midsummer as incense to honor the deities as expecting parents. It's used in handfasting rituals and is associated with love. Lavender's most common use is in love spells and to induce a peaceful sleep.

Larkspur: According to folklore, larkspur scares away ghosts. It can be included in protection spells, especially of the spiritual variety, such as if there are negative energies or beings in your space.

Lilies: There are too many types and colors of lilies to list here, but in general due to its reproductive ability, the lily represents mother goddesses. Lilies represent long-term relationships, pride, and devotion. They can even be used to break love spells. Some different types and colors of lilies are:

- Easter lily: innocence, purity, divinity
- tiger lily: courage, determination, fierce fire energy
- pink stargazer lily: wealth, prosperity, opportunity

- white stargazer lily: simplicity
- lily of the valley: cheerfulness, choice between two opposites

Marigold: The folk name of this flower is Bride of the Sun or Summer's Bride, which tells us a lot about its meaning. Carry marigold to make yourself as charismatic as the sun. Keeping them near you when you sleep can bring prophetic dreams. The marigold represents life and solar energy, but also death, and is often planted in graveyards.

Pansy: Pansies invoke memory, loyalty in marriage, and loving thoughts. They're especially useful in love divination, so keep some near your tarot cards or oracle of choice while asking questions about your romantic life.

Peony: Peonies represent marriage, union, and a happy future. They guard against evil spirits. The root is especially protective; dig it up only at night and carve beads from it to make an amulet.

Poppy: Poppies are said to encompass opposites. Life and death, good and evil, abundance and lack. Beautiful on the outside with potentially poisonous seeds on the inside, the poppy has appeared in mythology all over the world. They represent memory, sacrifice, blood, death, rest, and sleep.

Rose: The rose is the queen of all flowers. Over time it has represented beauty, love, and excess, as well as purity and virtue. Today, the colors of the rose give the flower its most well-known meanings:

- red: romantic love
- yellow: get well, cheer up
- pink: friendship
- white: truth, honesty

Sunflower: Big, bright, and bold, the sunflower represents strength, confidence, happiness, and virility. It signifies devotion and is said to aid in granting wishes.

Vervain: It is said that vervain in the home will bring peaceful emotions and a happy disposition to babies and children. In magic it's used for protection and warding off negativity, and to enhance the efficacy of spells.

Yarrow: Yarrow dispels fear and enhances psychic abilities. It represents long-term relationships and is believed to attract those you want to see most, making it useful in communication spells.

Flower Power Oil

A flower in full bloom is a powerful but fleeting thing. Only for a short time are we gifted with the scent and beauty of each blossom before it withers, which seems to make it that much more special. One way to harness the ephemeral energy of fully-opened flowers is to make a magical oil out of them. Creating an actual essential oil like what you'd buy at a store requires a lot of expensive equipment and larger quantities of flowers than are available to the average person. However, the simple oil recipe below can be just as effective in magic, if not more so because you have made and empowered it yourself. This oil will not have the strong scent of concentrated, commercially-sourced oils, but it definitely holds a far more powerful energy.

Materials
A carrier oil such as jojoba, almond, or olive oil
A selection of blooming, fresh flowers, chosen according to your
    intent. Make sure to avoid poisonous flowers.
A jar with a tight-fitting lid

It's best to create this oil immediately after picking the flowers to capture them at the peak of their power.

On the day of the solstice, fill your jar with oil and gather some blooming flowers. The more the merrier, but be sure not to disturb their natural setting or take so many they cannot reseed themselves. Once you've gathered all your flowers, find a quiet spot outdoors if possible. Sit in the full power of the sun and imagine its fiery energy infusing the oil in the jar. If you hold the jar up to the sun and look through it, you can see the sun's light blazing inside of the oil.

Hold the flowers in your hands. Feel how they're ripe with life and bursting with energy. Place them in the oil and tightly cap the lid.

Let the oil sit in the sun for 3 days around the solstice, infusing it with the energy of the flowers and sun. Then strain it through cheese cloth and store in jars. Now you have the power of the fertile, blooming solstice in oil form to use in the following ways:

- Use it to anoint yellow or orange candles dedicated to joy and warmth during times of darkness.
- If you used non-poisonous flowers, add a drop or two to your bottle of hand and body lotion to imbue it with joyous, fertile energies. When you rub it into your skin you are attracting these energies to yourself.
- Anoint your chakras when they're feeling blocked. For example, to help your heart center bloom, dab a small amount on your chest. To open your throat chakra for communication and connection, rub a small amount onto your throat.
- Incorporate into spells for growth, progress, and abundance by wearing a bit on your pulse points during ritual.
- Place some on coins and carry them with you to attract prosperity.

References

Cunningham, Scott. *Cunningham's Encyclopedia of Magical Herbs.* St. Paul, MN: Llewellyn Publications, 1985.

Darcey, Cheralyn. *Flowerpaedia: 1000 Flowers and Their Meanings.* Double Bay, NSW, Australia: Rockpool Publishing, 2018.

Heilmeyer, Marina. *The Language of Flowers: Symbols and Myths.* Munich, Germany: Prestel Verlag, 2001.

Impelluso, Lucia. *Nature and Its Symbols.* Translated by Stephen Sartarelli. Los Angeles, CA: J. P. Getty Museum, 2004.

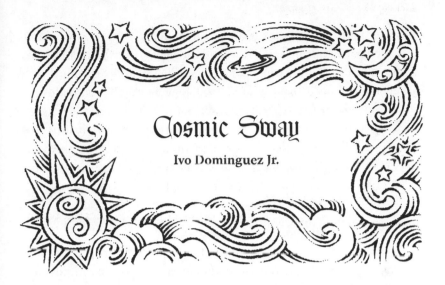

Cosmic Sway

Ivo Dominguez Jr.

THE SUMMER SOLSTICE IS on June 20 with the Moon in Scorpio a few days shy of the Full Moon in Capricorn on June 24. Four planets are retrograde: Mercury in Gemini, Jupiter in Pisces, Saturn in Aquarius, and Pluto in Capricorn. Venus in Cancer is trine to Neptune in Pisces. Venus is moving into opposition with Pluto. The Sun is trine to Jupiter in Pisces, which is its old domicile and grants it more power. There is a strong emphasis on the element of water, and the Moon is the recipient of much of the energy so there is more Scorpio influence than normal. Mercury will go direct on June 22 and Venus will enter into Leo on June 26.

Litha is the peak of the solar cycle in the turning of the year. It is useful to think of it as comparable to the Full Moon. This year these two cycles are close enough to being in sync that there is even more of a full sun effect. This energy can be used to empower whatever it is that you are trying to create or strengthen. It can be done with some finesse, but it does not offer assistance in the removal of obstacles. The Summer Solstice can be a peak experience, like standing at the top of a high hill and surveying your surroundings. It is a good time to take stock and assess what you are doing. The focus can be spiritual, mundane, or both.

Litha is also known as a time of gathering together to celebrate, as is Yule, and this includes beings without physical bodies. It may be the shortest night of the year, but it is filled with the comings and goings of the Fae, spirits, and divine beings. During this sabbat it is important that you mind your manners and remember the value of hospitality and reciprocity. Even if you are not in the middle of a ritual or a meditation, keep in mind that there may be unseen beings that are listening. In particular at this Summer Solstice, recognize the power of your words and deeds and that you will be held accountable for both the blessings and the challenges that these may call.

The Venus trine to Neptune favors creativity, singing, guided visualizations, and the appreciation of all forms of beauty. Your celebrations for the sabbat may want to take advantage of this flourishing of talent and aesthetic appetite. The downside that Venus brings to this holiday is its opposition to Pluto, which encourages a sensitivity that could lead to drama, suspicion, and mutual misunderstandings. The Scorpio Moon combines with this to intensify the depth of feelings, promote a fondness for brooding, and a tendency to see things as stark contrasts. The key to move past this test and to the best outcomes is to seek out the roots and reasons for things, thereby expending the emotional energy in a productive manner. Also remind yourself that Mercury is retrograde during Litha, and it is harder for people to communicate clearly, so ask for clarification as needed. The other retrograde planets also indicate a need for a careful examination of the meaning of experiences you have during Litha.

The Sun at its peak is trine to Jupiter, and that combination can provide some of the best options for getting the most from this sabbat. The more you connect consciously with your spiritual side, your higher self, the more you'll be able to connect with the kind of confidence and warmth that will make the intense energy feel comfortable rather than stressful. Also focus on the difference between happiness and joy. The distinction to be made here is that happiness is a reaction to what is occurring in the moment, such as enjoying a delicious treat. Whereas joy is a perspective that allows you to examine positive experiences and place them in context with the rest of your life so that even as the experience fades, it is replaced with a sense of gratitude rather than longing.

The Summer Solstice is the peak of the Sun, but also thereafter all the days grow shorter. It is the beginning of the decline of the light. You may wish to think on, to contemplate, to ritualize an exploration of this Sun–Jupiter interaction because it leads to the core of the mysteries of Litha. It is the resolute knowledge of continuity, renewal, and the power of generosity of spirit. From the pinnacle of the Sun, look around in all directions and know your place in the world, where you have been, and your next destination. You may wish to set out bowls or jars of water on Litha to absorb the sunlight for future spells or rituals. Another option is to use a magnifying glass to light a candle, but don't forget to protect your eyes. Let it burn for a few minutes and snuff it out while pulling the energy of the fire into the candle. Whenever you relight it you have access to the Sun at its peak. You may wish to use it to light your fires at Yule.

When Mercury stations to go direct on June 22 you are nearly at the Full Moon. This is the best time to push forward with whatever guidance or direction you received during Litha. If you didn't get a message, or it wasn't clear or complete, then do divinatory work or seek a diviner. If you have important written or verbal communications, you may want to wait until then. It is also an excellent day to leave offers or make libations. When Venus enters Leo on June 26, it will greet Mars waiting in Leo. If there are any disruptions in friendships or relationships this is the time for reaching out and pampering the connection. Self-care, rest, and recuperation are also a great idea. If you made plans earlier in the month related to finances or job hunting, this is also the time to follow up or renew your efforts. If nothing else say an affirmation that day to call sweetness into your home.

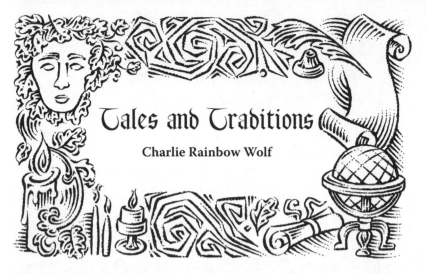

Tales and Traditions

Charlie Rainbow Wolf

I HAVE NEVER UNDERSTOOD why people talk about Litha being the first day of summer when the old name for this festival is "Midsummer"! It makes more sense for it to be in the middle of the season, for this is when the day is the longest. After this, it's all downhill until winter!

Celebrating Fire and Water

Litha isn't always celebrated as Midsummer in other parts of the world, though. In the Southern Hemisphere, their seasons are the opposite of ours, and this is when our friends in New Zealand start to prepare for the longer days and shorter nights! It all gets a bit confusing at times, doesn't it?

I was very fortunate when I lived on the coast in England, for it was one of the very few places on Earth where a person could watch the sun rise and set from the same vantage point. We were on a small peninsula that stretched out into the Irish sea to the west, Morecambe Bay to the north, and the River Wyre to the east. On Midsummer's Eve we would go down to the beach and light a fire. When the skies were clear the sun would nearly set in the west, just leaving a salmon and turquoise hue on the horizon. As we fellow-shipped with each other, we would watch that light travel along the top of the water from the west, to the north, and then to the east, where it gradually became lighter and day broke. These hours are among some of the most magical moments of my life.

Old Midsummer

Even though the solstice is celebrated at Midsummer, Midsummer hasn't always been celebrated at the solstice! There's an old Christian tradition held on June 11 that was considered to be the Midsummer celebration, the Feast of Saint Barnabas. Farmers saw this day as the time to start cutting hay, and because Saint Barnabas is said to protect from hail and storms, it is easy to see why he would be asked to intercede for good weather while the hay was drying and baled.

After the hard work out in the fields, it was time for feasting and festivities. It's interesting that the history of this date actually has links with Glastonbury, famous for Arthurian legends. English folklore relates a tale about a walnut tree in Glastonbury Abbey that only bloomed on Saint Barnabas's day.

So, why the confusion? Why does the old Midsummer fall well before the solstice? You can blame the timekeepers for that. Today it's frustrating when we change the clocks for an hour in the spring and the autumn; imagine having to shunt them forward for nearly two weeks! Yet that's exactly what happened during King George II's reign. Back when Queen Elizabeth I was on the throne, Britain used the Julian calendar, but the rest of Europe was using the Gregorian calendar, making Britain quaintly out of sync with everyone else. Parliament argued this fact until 1751, and over the next two years the days were manipulated until the Gregorian calendar was adopted. However, many still celebrated the Old Midsummer on June 11. Why pass up a chance to make merry?!

Fasting and Fires

Up until recently, it was customary for men in England to fast overnight in the church, burning candles and praying for renewal and cleansing. Bonfires and beacons were lit and kept burning throughout the night. This practice still occurs in some rural areas, particularly down in Cornwall where a week-long festival is held.

The bonfires and vigils were both spiritual and practical, warding off evil spirits and potential predators alike. Many people believed that this was a time when the veil between the worlds was thinner, making it easy for spirits to pass from their realm into ours. It stood to reason that the brighter the fires and the louder the party, the less likely the malevolent entities would want to try to cause trouble.

After the reformation of the church in the sixteenth century, the ruling clergy declared these festivals far too hedonistic for their puritan ways and banned many of the practices. In an attempt to force their Christian beliefs into activities they knew people were going to participate in anyway, they even renamed this "The Feast of Saint John the Baptist!" For this reason, we can only imagine what activities and other heritage associated with Midsummer may have been lost over time.

A Festival of Water

Not far from where we lived in England the practice of well dressing was very much alive. This is another ancient practice that faded away over time thanks to the intervention of the church, but it is now seeing a resurgence in popularity. Well dressing starts in May, climaxes around Litha, and continues until Mabon, giving every community a chance to celebrate the water and to promote their own decorations. We had a huge stone well on the farm, and I dressed it with flowers for many Midsummers in an attempt to appease the water spirits, for the well had long been filled in with the arrival of city water.

Many villages in the nearby Peak District decorated their wells by designing a pictorial story or image on a board and then filling it in with colored flowers. The materials are those which are in season, and it can take up to a week to fill in the picture and display it on the well. Nowadays different towns decorate their wells at different times to capitalize on the tourist trade as people travel to view their dressed wells.

A lot of churches in England held their flower festivals on or around Midsummer, and these were frequently accompanied by the ringing of the church bells. We would sometimes ring a quarter peal at a church; or, if we were making a day of it, we would travel to many different bell towers and ring a touch—a short series of changes—in each one. We would follow the bellringing in the time-honored way with a large meal and good ale in the nearby public house!

Honoring the Ways

In England, one of the main news stories for Litha always centers around the megalith circle at Stonehenge. There's a huge organized vigil there, where thousands come to watch the Midsummer sunrise. No one really knows why the stones are there or what they were actually used for, but every year there are countless people who go to visit them, in awe of their enigmatic majesty.

Stonehenge isn't the only stone circle; it's just perhaps the most famous. Our local stone circle was Castlerigg, nestled in the rolling hills of Cumbria. You don't have to visit a stone circle to tap into that ancient energy, though. You can build your own stone circle of any size, and this is a wonderful way to mark Midsummer.

If you gather in a ritual meadow or other regular area, one activity might be to have everyone bring a large stone or small boulder to build your own stone circle. If you meet inside someone's home, or you don't have a regular gathering place, then small stones or crystals can be used to lay out a stone circle on a floor in which to do your ritual. In the past, we've even set the stone circle on a tabletop to harness the energies.

As always when magic is concerned, it's not what you do, it's the intent in which you do it that makes things happen. Build your stone circle, announce your intent, call your deities, and perform your Litha ritual. Afterwards, discuss how the energies of the stones added to your observance. You may be surprised at what you find!

References

Chambers, Robert. ed. *The Book of Days: A Miscellany of Popular Antiquities in Connection with the Calendar Including Anecdote, Biography & History, Curiosities of Literature, and Oddities of Human Life and Character.* Chambers Harrap, 2004.

Naylor, Peter, and Lindsay Porter. *Well Dressing.* Ashbourne, UK: Landmark Publishing Ltd, 2004.

Roy, Robert L. *Stone Circles: A Modern Builder's Guide to the Megalithic Revival.* White River Junction, VT: Chelsea Green Pub., 1999.

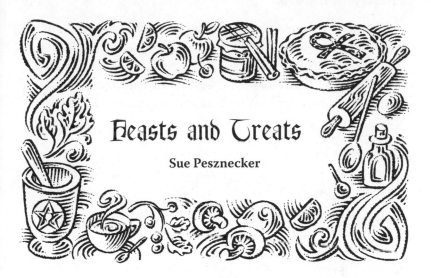

Feasts and Treats

Sue Pesznecker

WITH JUNE COMES THE Summer Solstice and the beginning of summer proper, at least according to the astronomical calendars. Earth's fecundity is in full flower, and we head to the farmers markets to avail ourselves of the season's best. In the coming group of recipes, we celebrate the breakfasts of summer. Does that sound like a Beach Boys song? Make it so!

Strawberry Freezer Jam

I don't think there's any better way to capture summer than in fruit preserves. Opening a jar of homemade strawberry jam in snowy, cold January feels like the best kind of decadence.

Prep time: about an hour, including the 30-minute resting time
Servings: several jars

About 5 pints fresh seasonal strawberries
¼ cup fresh lemon juice
1 2-ounce box powdered pectin (I have always used MCP pectin)
4½ cups sugar

You'll need a large stoneware or glass bowl and 6–7 jam-size lidded glass jars or plastic containers.

Before beginning, rinse the berries, scatter them on a cotton towel to dry, and pick over them, throwing out (or composting) any that are overly ripe. Do not throw out berries that seem under-ripe! Underripe fruit contains more pectin than ripe fruit; including some orangey berries will help the jam gel and set.

Using a food processor or potato masher, crush enough berries to equal 3¼ cups. Be careful not to liquify the berries; just crush. You still want some nice big chunks in your jam.

Empty the berries into a large stoneware or glass bowl and add the lemon juice.

Slowly stir the box of pectin into the crushed berries—this should take 2–3 minutes. Once done, pop the bowl into the microwave and process at full power for 30 seconds. This will just barely warm the mixture and will help it process.

Let the berry mixture sit on the countertop for 30 minutes, stirring every 5 minutes or so. This helps the pectin dissolve into the berry liquid and sets it up for the gelling process.

After 30 minutes has passed, slowly stir half of the sugar into the jam. Pop the bowl back into the microwave for another 30 seconds, and then continue adding sugar, stirring constantly.

As soon as all the sugar is added, continue stirring until it's fully dissolved and the jam doesn't feel gritty. It should be starting to gel by this time.

Spoon the jam into your prepared jars—leaving ½-inch of head space—and screw on the lids. The jam now needs to sit on the kitchen counter (out of direct sunlight) for 24 hours. After that, refrigerate and use within a month, or freeze for up to a year.

Note: If freezing, loosen the lids, then come back when the jam is fully frozen and tighten them up.

Fresh Cream Scones

You've made the jam; here's something to put it on. Scones are easy to make, and they're best eaten fresh (and warm!). If you can't finish all your scones, pop them into the freezer; thawed and briefly re-warmed, they'll be good as new.

Prep time: 10 minutes
Cooking time: 15 minutes
Inactive: 15–20 minutes
Servings: 6–12

3 cups flour
1 tablespoon baking powder
1 teaspoon salt
⅓ cup sugar
1 teaspoon vanilla
1½ cups heavy cream
Additional heavy cream, for brushing on scones
Additional regular, sparkling, or raw sugar for sprinkling
Toppings: butter, jam, honey, heavy cream, clotted cream, lemon curd

Preheat oven to 425° F and set the upper oven rack to the middle position.

Place the flour, baking powder, salt, and sugar in a large bowl. Add the vanilla to the heavy cream; pour this mixture over the dry ingredients. Combine with a spoon or your fingers, mixing just until the dough comes together. The less this dough is handled, the better.

Sprinkle a bit of flour on a clean work surface. Divide the dough into two equal pieces. Pat each one out on the floured surface, aiming for a 5–6-inch circle of dough that's about ¾-inch thick on the sides and thicker (about 1 inch) in the middle.

Cut each circle into 6–8 wedges, pizza style. Place the wedges on a parchment-lined or silicone baking sheet, allowing about an inch between each one. Use a pastry brush to brush each scone lightly with additional heavy cream and sprinkle with sugar.

Place the baking sheet in the fridge or freezer for 15–20 minutes before baking.

After the brief chilling, slide the baking sheet into the oven and bake for 11–15 minutes. The scones will be nicely risen and browned when done.

Allow to cool briefly, but eat these as soon as you can, split and filled with your favorite toppings.

Breakfast Sweetie Biscuit Sandwiches

Enjoy this quick, easy recipe while sitting outdoors in the morning sun with a fresh cuppa coffee or tea and a favorite book on the side. And a couple of napkins! This is also a great dish to make with children.

Prep time: 25 minutes, including preparing eggs and sausage
Servings: varies

Breakfast bread: toast, English muffins, biscuits, or the cream scones you just made above
Fruit jam: strawberry, sour cherry, or strawberry-rhubarb are excellent options
One fried egg, per person
One grilled sausage patty, per person (see Ostara recipes)
Goat cheese
Arugula

Toast, grill, or warm the bread items.

Split the breads. For each sandwich, place a sausage patty on the bottom bread item. Add the egg, top with a spoonful of jam, and crumble a layer of goat cheese over the jam. Top with arugula and the second bread item as a lid.

Quick Blueberry Mug Cake

A perfect snack for a spring evening or a fun way to serve breakfast.

Prep time: 2 minutes
Cooking time: 1 minute
Servings: 1

3 tablespoons flour
¼ teaspoon baking soda
2 teaspoons honey or maple syrup
1 tablespoon milk
1 tablespoon vegetable oil (not olive!)
1 egg
1 tablespoon fresh or frozen blueberries
Optional: Add more maple syrup and blueberries

Whisk together all ingredients in a microwave-safe mug, mixing until there are no lumps.

Microwave for 50–60 seconds (based on a 1200W microwave). A toothpick inserted in the center should come out clean.

If desired, top with a little maple syrup and more blueberries.

Fruit Shrub

The fruit shrub— also called a vinegar shrub—is a vintage drink that predates conventional sodas. And it's delicious! Since the shrub mixture works via natural yeasts and fermentation, it comes with the proposed health benefits of modern fermented foods, like kombucha. Topping off the list of why shrubs are amazing is the way they allow you to use up bits of ripe fruit —no doubt a trick the grandmothers used when every bit of food was precious.

Prep time: an hour of fiddling and several days of fermenting
Cooking time: 30 minutes
Servings: varies

Fresh or slightly overripe fruit (berries work well, but any fruit can be shrubbed)
Apple cider vinegar
Sugar

Wash fruit—stone fruits need not be peeled. Chop or crush the fruit and measure it by volume or weight. Place the fruit in a glass or stoneware (nonreactive) bowl.

For each 6 parts fruit, add 1 part vinegar. Mix well, cover, and set aside undisturbed for 4–5 days. (Be sure the cover is snug enough to keep out fruit flies!)

After 4–5 days, remove the cover, skim off the foam, and strain through a fine sieve or cheesecloth. If you have time, straining two or three times will make the shrub extra clear.

Measure the strained juice and add 1 part sugar to 2 parts juice. Boil the mixture until it reduces to a syrupy consistency. Pour this into clean, lidded jars.

Store in the refrigerator for up to a year or tuck into the freezer. If you're a home canner, process in a water bath canner for longer storage.

To serve, add two or three tablespoonfuls of shrub to a glass of chopped ice and water. There's nothing more refreshing on a hot summer day!

Crafty Crafts

Tess Whitehurst

THE SUN IS OUR world's ultimate superstar. It's not only at the center of our solar system; it is also what defines us. Our eyes evolved to perceive the light of the sun. This is the same light that drenches our world, not only making everything grow, but also orchestrating each organism's very existence so that it can thrive on a planet that revolves around this radiant, white-hot star.

With solar energies at their pinnacle at Midsummer, the world is saturated with magical power. While each sabbat possesses its own unique magic, this is the time when magic in general is at its peak. That's why magical work related to divination, dreams, manifestation, cleansing, and blessing are all extra powerful at this time of year. In short, it's magical high noon.

Can you feel it? If you're in a particularly hot climate, you'll be most likely to sense this magical intensity at the sunrise and sunset, or even at midnight. If you're in a more temperate climate, you'll be able to sense it all throughout the day, and especially when the sun is high in the sky. It's almost as if you can hear the sun shining, taste the stars twinkling, and feel, deep in your heart, the expansion of every green and growing thing.

In *Midsummer: Rituals, Recipes & Lore for Litha* (from the Llewellyn's Sabbat Essentials series), author Deborah Blake writes,

"The most common representation of Midsummer is the sun itself. Whether it was the actual sun overhead, flowers that resembled the sun, or any of the symbols such as fire, wheels, or disks that were used to stand for the sun, almost all Midsummer celebrations focused on the sun's position high in the sky, as well as its power and energy" (Blake 2015).

Mosaic Mandala Light Catcher

This craft depicts the sun in symbolic form, while also creating a beautiful focal point for sunlight to shine through. It's very easy, but it does require a bit of patience while you wait for the glue to dry. You may want to start it a good 4 or 5 days before the solstice if you want to have it ready to hang by Midsummer's Eve.

The sun itself is a circle, and all of the planets move around it in sacred geometrical patterns. In fact, the entire solar system is essentially a mandala (a circular mathematical design). In *Mandalas in Nature*, author Sonia Waleyla writes, "The sacred mandalas of the world are well known—from Tibetan sand mandalas to the Celtic cross, from Navajo sand mandalas to the Hindu *yantra* drawings. These ancient symbols are tools for healing, spiritual realization, and the creation of harmony. But, as in all human endeavors, what humans create is inspired by what came before us—nature" (Waleyla 2010).

This craft also takes the form of a mandala, albeit a very simple one.

Materials

The lid from a standard-sized plastic container of something like hummus (I used the lid from almond milk cream cheese)

Clear glue (don't substitute regular—clear is the way to go)

Decorative glass gems—the ones from the craft store that look like flat marbles—in blue and at least one solar-aligned color such as orange, red, or yellow. (I purchased one container of various blue shades and one of various red shades)

Hemp twine

Something that will pierce a hole in the dried glue, such as an ice
pick or toothpick

Optional: a solar-aligned essential oil such as cinnamon, orange, or
tangerine

Optional: a suction cup with a hook (this is handy if you want to
hang it directly onto a window)

Cost: $5–$10

Time spent: 20–30 minutes, plus 4–5 days for glue to dry

Place the lid topside down so that it's like a small saucer or dish.
Fill the lid with glue just until the entire flat inside of it is completely
coated and there are no empty spots. (Stop there. If you add more
after that, it will take too long to dry.)

Now, create a sunshine shape in the lid with the red, orange, and/or yellow gems. Do this by dropping gems, flat side down, into the glue. If you need to slide them around a little after you drop them, it's fine. The number of gems you use will depend on the size of gem you're working with, but I placed one in the middle of the lid and surrounded it with six more to form a circle. Then I created the rays by adding two additional gems in a line extending outward from each of the six central gems. If possible, allow for a tiny bit of space between the edge of the gems and the rim of the lid.

Next, fill in the remaining glue area with the blue gems, to depict the sky. The size of gems I was working with allowed for a little triangle of three blue gems sandwiched in every gap between the rays.

Now, allow your craft to dry. This craft uses a lot of glue, so (as mentioned above) the drying process will take quite a while. Allow for 4–5 full days. After about three days, I noticed the glue beginning to curl up around the edges when it was mostly dry, but the middle bottom was still a bit sticky. If you'd like to speed up the drying process at this point, you can gently peel the mosaic away from the lid and turn it topside down on a magazine or newspaper to allow the back to dry. Otherwise, you can just leave it alone until it's totally dry.

Once the glue is indeed dry, peel it away from the lid (and recycle the lid). Gently pierce the dried glue somewhere between the gems, about one gem length in from the rim. Thread a short length of hemp twine through the hole, and tie it in a knot. If you'd like, you can anoint the hemp twine with the solar-aligned essential oil to bless your craft and to endow it with a delicious solstice scent. (Just be careful not to get it directly onto your skin.) Now, you can suspend it from a curtain rod so it's hanging in front of a sunny window. Or, you can affix a suction cup with a hook directly to the window and hang your light catcher on the hook.

You may like to say a prayer of gratitude to the sun when you hang it. Here's one that would be appropriate:

Central guiding star, the sun,
Light and warmth for everyone,
Primordial clock that shows the hour,
Powerhouse of magic power,
Shine your beauty, shine your light,
And arise each dawn after the night.
With gratitude and reverence true,
I celebrate and honor you.

References

Blake, Deborah. *Midsummer: Rituals, Recipes & Lore for Litha.* Woodbury, MN: Llewellyn Publications, 2015.

Waleyla, Sonia. *Mandalus in Nature.* New York: Sterling Innovation, 2010.

Spells

Michael Furie

THE SUMMER SOLSTICE MARKS the peak of solar power when we reach the longest day and shortest night. It is the strongest point in the light half of the year, when we can still look forward to a full three months of light, warmth, and vitality. This is a day to fully enjoy the richness of life and power of magic.

The Make-Life-Perfect Spell

Many years ago I was watching a "witch" television show and one of the witches sarcastically mentioned that there was no such thing as a "make-life-perfect spell," and from then on I was determined to create one. After a great deal of trial and error, I have finally crafted such a spell. Since the Summer Solstice marks the peak of active power from both the sun and the Earth, this sabbat is perfectly aligned with such large-scale magic. Now don't get me wrong, it is not likely that after casting this spell anyone will instantly turn into a billionaire (though with magic stranger things have happened), but it will begin to shape probability toward your personal vision of happiness.

Materials
1 clear tumbled quartz crystal
Paper
Pen
1 white candle
Matches
Heat-proof bowl or cauldron
Your favorite outfit, jewelry, and perfume or cologne

Place the candle, paper and pen, and matches on a working table. To begin, shower or bathe and dress up in your favorites. Then go to your working table. Hold the crystal in your dominant hand and meditate (ideally in the sunlight), and form as complete a mental picture of your ideal life as you can envision. Bask in this image and fill yourself with intense emotion: the feelings that you want to experience when your goals have manifested. Lightly squeeze the crystal and envision that the full intention (the image, desire, and emotion) of your goal is glowing, glittery energy that is being transferred into the crystal. Try to feel the energy move down your arm and into the stone. When your hand begins to pulse, declare to yourself that the power you have placed in the crystal shall renew itself for as long as the stone exists and remain unaffected by any other forces.

It is now time to come out of the meditation and take the crystal to your working area (if you meditated elsewhere). On the paper write the following:

I [your full name] *desire to manifest my ideal life plan which includes* [write as clearly yet concisely as you can what you wish to manifest]. *I ask that this be for the good of all with harm to none and that any goals both named and unnamed manifest and bring joy. In thanks and blessing, and so mote it be.*

Light the candle and read your paper aloud, then light the paper in the candle's flame and set it in the bowl to burn completely. The spell is now complete. Keep the crystal as a charm to keep the magic with you.

Midsummer Power Cord

Witch cords are a great way to harness and store power that may not always be present, such as the extra energy that is available during sabbats. Midsummer is such a peak of power that we can capture some of its essence and use it for virtually any purpose. In this way, if we need magic performed later in the year that would have been better suited to the summer season, we can use this cord to lend its stored power to the spell. To make a cord for Midsummer, gather three lengths of natural yarn or cord in the colors most associated with this holiday: red, yellow, and orange.

On Midsummer's Day, tie them in a knot at one end and then begin to braid them together, allowing your mind to relax in a meditative state as you visualize the summer sun at the peak of its power, warming the earth and revitalizing nature. Mentally send this energy into the cord as you braid it. When you reach the end, tie that end in a knot and coil the cord in your weak hand, holding your strong hand over it saying:

Witch's cord of Midsummer fire, charged and plaited to keep the power; held within until required, for future spellwork to empower; the work now fixed by my will, let this magic be fulfilled.

Keep the coiled cord in a safe place either at your altar or in a black magic bag until needed. To use the cord, simply incorporate it into the spell you wish to cast, such as using it to tie a spell pouch, encircling a candle with the cord (wide enough so that it will be safe) or tying charms and petition papers to it.

Triple Power Midsummer Herb Candle

This spell channels the power of Midsummer through candle magic to aid three important aspects of life simultaneously: love, health, and prosperity.

Materials
1 gold or yellow pillar candle
Candle holder
1 teaspoon sage
1 teaspoon peppermint
1 teaspoon basil
1 teaspoon rosemary
1 teaspoon thyme
1 teaspoon tarragon
1 tablespoon olive oil
1 piece of yellow paper and black ink pen

On the paper, draw a large circle and divide it into three equal sections. In one section write "love," in another write "health," and in the last write "prosperity." Write the goal you would like to achieve in regard to each section beneath its respective label and draw arrows from the center of the circle pointing to each word. Set the paper on a work table and prepare the herb mixture. On a tray or cookie sheet mix together the herbs and hold your hands over them. Envision your magical goals to charge the herbs with your intent. Next, anoint the candle lightly with olive oil from the tip to the base while again visualizing your magical goals; then roll it in the herbs so that they stick to the candle. Be careful to keep the wick area clean.

In the center of the paper, place the candle in a holder so that it is touching each section equally. Finally, light the candle with the words:

Midsummer magic bring to me, love, health and prosperity; I reach my goals and achieve my aims, with solstice power, magical flame; herbs of power, oil of peace, my spell is cast, the power released.

Allow the candle to burn for as long as safe, then extinguish. It can be relit each day until it burns out to extend the magic.

Litha Ritual

Kate Freuler

ON THIS DAY THE sun is at its most powerful zenith and the prime of its yearly life. It's a time to nurture that which is growing in the earth and to cultivate the dreams and wishes we have inside of us. The sunflower is an excellent symbol of midsummer because of the bright yellow petals that surround its face like rays of light and its large head that reaches toward the sky. If you look at a field of sunflowers over the course of a day, you can actually see the smallest buds turning their heads toward the sun as it crosses the sky. Fully grown sunflowers typically face east—toward daybreak. This is called heliotropism and mirrors the "sun worship" we perform on Litha.

The center of the sunflower is actually a series of tiny flowers, which are able to self-pollinate and produce seeds all on their own while also attracting bees and other pollinators. In this ritual you will place wishing seeds into the offering bowl alongside a blooming sunflower as a way of aligning their energy with that of the fruitful, fertile sunflower.

The Wishing Sunflower

This Litha ritual can be done alone or in a group and calls upon the energy of fire and the sunflower. It's best performed outdoors around noon, when the sun is high above your head. If this isn't possible, visualization will do.

Materials

The candles. Choose orange, yellow, or gold candles, one for each participant. If you're alone, you will only need one. They must be placed securely in a jar or holder that will protect them from wind and keep them upright. Novena candles, or 7 day candles, are excellent for this because they come in a glass sleeve. Prior to this ritual, the members of your circle can spend time decorating their candle to reflect their feelings about the solstice. Images can be painted onto the glass holder or carved into the wax. Some ideas for this are suns, flames, flowers, or positive words such as joy, abundance, fulfillment, or prosperity. After the ritual ends each participant will take their candle home and light it throughout the coming weeks to help manifest their wishes. You may also need a yellow taper candle for passing on the flame.

The sunflower. Find a sunflower and cut it from its stem near the head. Sunflowers are sold in nurseries and even grocery stores this time of year; however, if you're unable to get a real one, a false sunflower or a picture of one will do.

The sunflower seeds. You'll need four seeds for each participant. These seeds will represent wishes. They will be left outdoors for the wildlife to eat, so unseasoned and unsalted is best. They can be left in the husk or shelled.

Offering bowl. The bowl simply needs to be big enough to place the sunflower head in.

Lighter or matches

Place the offering bowl containing the flower on the ground and stand in a circle around it with each person holding their candle. The person standing in the east lights their candle first, holds it up toward the sun, and says:

Blazing, life-bringing sun
We ask for your brightest blessings.

Illuminate us, warm us, give us life and help us grow.
The sun gives us all energy, yet its own power never diminishes.
May we give love to others and to our planet in
The same selfless, never-ending way.
Today we ask the sun to smile down upon our hopes and dreams
To foster and nurture our goals into manifestation.

When they're done speaking, the person in the east turns to the participant on their left, lighting their candle from the flame of their own. (If you can't do this because of the holder, use a yellow taper candle to pass the flame.) As they pass the flame, they say:

The warmth of the sun fills your life and shines in your spirit. So mote it be.

The person who now holds the second lit candle turns to the participant on their left and passes on the flame, saying:

The warmth of the sun fills your life and shines in your spirit. So mote it be.

Each person repeats these actions and words, moving clockwise around the circle until all the candles are lit. Extinguish the candle that was used for passing the flame and set it aside.

Now everyone holds their lit candles up toward the sun, which is hopefully over your heads, directly above your circle. The person in the east now says:

Golden sun, we welcome you to our circle of fire. Shine your power through us and into others. Bring us courage, strength, health, joy, and love in the year to come.

Place the candles behind you out of the way, leaving them lit.

Give four sunflower seeds to each person. Each seed represents a wish: one wish for themselves, one for someone else, and one for the whole. The fourth seed is a secret wish they do not tell anyone.

Again, begin with the person in the east. This person will pick up their first seed and tell the group the wish they're making for themselves. Then they will place the seed in the offering bowl in the center of the circle. Next, they will hold onto their second seed and state their wish for a loved one. They place this seed into the bowl. For their third seed, they declare a wish they have for the whole and add it to the offering bowl. For their fourth seed, they are to silently say or visualize their secret wish and add it to the offering bowl. Below are some examples of wishes.

Wishes for the self:
- I wish for self-love.
- I wish for courage.
- I wish for prosperity.
- I wish for health of body and mind.

Wishes for a loved one:
- I wish [insert name] peace of mind.
- I wish for [insert name] to find the perfect job.
- I wish for [insert name] to be safe and secure.

Wishes for the whole:
- I wish for us to find ways to save the ecosystem.
- I wish for war to be resolved.
- I wish for equality for all people.
- I wish to protect endangered species.

Secret wishes:
- This can be anything! No one will ever know.

Move clockwise around the circle, having each person state their wishes and place their seeds in the offering bowl.

Now everyone picks up their candles. Starting in the east, blow out the candle. Next, the person on their right blows out theirs, and so on, counterclockwise, until the candles are all out. This releases the circle.

Place the flower and the sunflower seeds in a place where wildlife and birds like to look for food. Allow the flower to compost naturally.

Each participant can take their solstice candle home to light when they wish to bring solstice energy into their space.

Notes

Lammas

Lammas and Lughnasadh

Mickie Mueller

LAMMAS IS THE FIRST of three harvest festivals; it's the sabbat that falls between the Summer Solstice and the autumn equinox. Although most modern Pagan calendars mark the day as August 1, it is sometimes celebrated anywhere between July 31–August 6, depending upon tradition. Other names for this festival include Lammastide, Old Lammas, Bron-Trogain, and Lughnasadh, named after the heroic Celtic god Lugh on his feast day. At this point of the year the summer days have been hot and the earth, with any luck at all, has been fertile and is now yielding forth the beginnings of its abundance in the form of fresh fruits, berries, and various vegetables. Bounties of zucchini, the ripest tomatoes, and other summer favorites are either being toted in from backyard gardens or are available for purchase from local farmers markets. The harvest that we see most referenced in the folklore of Lammas, however, is grain.

The festival of Lughnasadh is a celebration associated with the Celtic deity Lugh, who's just one of those guys who seems to be good at everything and definitely someone who would be great to have in your corner. According to legend he is a skilled wheelwright, blacksmith, warrior, musician, poet, historian, craftsman, and sorcerer, among other things. Often the old festivals would last for days and would include feasting, drinking of beer and mead, music, and competitions to show off athletic feats such as tossing gigantic wooden poles (called cabers), boulders, and spears. In that spirit, lots of modern celebrants love to host outdoor activities for Lammas such as barbeques with music, drinks, and games like horseshoes, bean bag toss, or even water balloon fights. Some of the Lughnasadh traditions have survived through the ages as a time for communities to share skills, food, drink, and fellowship.

Lammas, or Lughnasadh, is often associated with the powerful connection between sex and death. Some people surmise that Lughnasadh was originally celebrated as Lugh's wedding feast, giving reverence to the Celtic god's symbolic marriage to the land. This is a very old concept of kingship where the bounty of the earth is tied in with the health and vitality of the king. This might be a good time of the year to consider the ways in which our own well-being, as sovereign rulers of our lives, connects to our personal abundance. The idea of it being a wedding feast is further reflected in the practice of Pagan marriage ceremonies—known as handfastings—performed at Lughnasadh. Another tradition was that of trial marriages that would last a year and a day, just to see if the couple was compatible. These trial marriages could be made permanent if it all worked out. Another suggestion is that Lughnasadh was born as a funeral feast and celebration for Lugh's stepmother, Tailtiu. According to legend this goddess of the earth died from exhaustion after toiling to clear the trees from the lands of Ireland so that the people could farm it. Because of this legend, it is also a season to keep gratitude in our hearts for the blessings that we have, as well as a remembrance of sacrifices.

Another concept associated with Lammas is that of the sacrifice of the spirit of the grain. One of the most well-known representations of this is John Barleycorn, the personification of the crops whose tale of death and resurrection is recounted in several versions of British folksongs. The tale of John Barleycorn uses the metaphor of a brutal sacrificial killing to describe the stages of barley cultivation, harvesting, and processing into malt liquor. Depending on the traditions of specific townships, the first grain gathered would be planted on a hill, and the first or last sheaf of grain harvested would be fashioned into a human figure of a man or woman. It would either be saved as a talisman for prosperity and abundance or burned as an effigy. In any case the spirit of the grain was very important because the harvest meant prosperity for all and assurance that the people would have enough food to survive through the winter.

There are many "first harvest festivals" celebrated in other cultures. In Nigeria they celebrate the harvest of yams around the beginning of August at the Iri-ji New Yam Festival, which has origins in the Igbo culture. Several Native American tribes celebrate August harvest festivals; the Hopi have several traditional dances that they perform to protect the harvest and ensure the fertility of the people and the land. When I lived in New Mexico the Santo Domingo Pueblo Feast Day and Green Corn Dance on August 4 was a blend of Catholic and Native American traditions with themes of gratitude and the beginning of the harvest season. The idea of the first food harvested being sacred is shared among many cultures worldwide. It's a symbol of the promise of abundance and is treated with reverence and importance. You don't have to take my word for it though, if you've ever planted seeds or seedlings and nurtured them until they produce food you can eat, you've felt that in your heart and soul. The years that Dan and I have put in a vegetable garden, that first tomato or little pepper to ripen is always treasured and sliced with bliss to be shared, even if it's just a mouthful. The fruits of your labor are sweet indeed and should be recognized as important.

The eight sabbats were originally aligned with the Celtic planting, growth, and harvest seasons, so where we live the weather, planting, and harvesting can sometimes be different than we might expect from the folklore surrounding each sabbat. Because the sabbats are tied in with the agricultural cycles of the land it can be challenging for those of us who live in cities or suburbs where we don't witness the cycles of planting, growth, or harvest that our ancestors relied on for their livelihoods. I used to live in an area of Missouri that was less developed; there were homes and businesses, but there were also still some farmer's fields in the area. There was even one that I could see from my backyard. I passed by a corn field and a wheat field every day when I drove to my office job. I watched those fields being plowed in the fall and spring, and I saw the plants that would eventually produce food sprout from the earth and slowly but surely reach towards the sky. They grew day by day as my car raced past on my way to the office to call print suppliers, track shipments, or manage spreadsheets. I watched the harvest as large machines rolled through, reaping the sheaves of various grains, and imagined how my ancestors used hand tools in the days of yesteryear.

Missouri grows mostly soft red winter wheat, which is planted in October and usually harvested between June and July. One year I do recall that it was Lammas and the weather had been unseasonably warm the previous Autumn, so the wheat planting and harvest was a bit behind, leaving the wheat still in the fields at the beginning of August. I was delighted to see a field of golden wheat dancing in the breeze Lammas morning on my way to work. The sun's rays streamed through the car windows as I breezed down the road, admiring the field, when a Led Zeppelin song came on the radio. I imagined the Celtic Lugh (rock star that he is) standing in the field with gilded waves of hair backlit by the sun like the stage lights on the hair of Zeppelin crooner Robert Plant, and I felt at one with the spirit of Lammas. I later created a piece of art that was inspired by that moment. Lughnasadh has that feeling of a summer rock festival to me. We often celebrate with beer, music, and boisterous fun, which is traditional as well.

One of the most common traditions that most Pagans, witches, Druids, and other magical traditionalists practice is the art and science of baking bread. After all, the name Lammas is derived from the Anglo-Saxon name "hlafmaesse," which means literally "loaf-mass." Yes, it's all about the bread. Even those who aren't skilled in the kitchen will often just throw a mix in the bread machine, make a loaf of an easy quick bread, or use frozen dough to bake fresh bread or rolls. Some create elaborate loaves shaped like the sun, or sheaves of wheat to be shared at their celebrations. I used to be one of the witches who always baked a Lammas loaf to recognize the beginning of the harvest season. This year I discovered that I, like many other modern humans, have unfortunately developed an intolerance to gluten—found in wheat and most other grains—and should avoid it for medical reasons. Like my vegan friends who don't eat eggs at Ostara, it's a bit of a quandary. I love gluten—seriously love it. Sure, I could just bake a beautiful loaf for everyone else and not partake myself, but that's just sad. I could just cheat and eat it on Lammas, but it seems counterintuitive to eat something that will wreck my health for weeks just because it's part of an old tradition. I've found that eating the things that are bad for me saps my magical energy too, so that doesn't seem like a very empowering idea. If you don't have a problem with gluten, have your Lammas bread and eat it too. Enjoy its crusty exterior and its stretchy soft middle, maybe warm with a little fresh butter and honey...but I digress.

Let's all remember that Lammas celebrates the spirit of harvest, and there are many foods that can represent that. Any seasonal foods can celebrate the first harvest, and if they're locally sourced, even better. I find that even if I don't have a garden, buying locally-sourced foods helps me connect with the spirits of the land and also helps my local community. If you really want to enjoy bread for Lammas, and like me aren't eating gluten, it's ok to use non-wheat, gluten-free baked goods. There are lots of gluten-free grains—like rice or oats— so you can still use a grain if you wish. My personal favorite is cassava flour, which is made from a root and bakes much more like real wheat flour. This year I plan to bless some fresh water under the Lammas sun and use it to bake a loaf of gluten-free bread topped with local honey to share with my loved ones.

The first harvest carries many themes. Among them: competition, love, gratitude, harvest, and sacrifice. One theme for Lammas that I keep coming back to in my heart and practice is community. All the themes of Lammas point to people coming together and sharing their food, talents, and fellowship, and that seems like something the world could use more of. As we come to the first harvest of the year it's a good time to contemplate our place in society. The spirit of the grain was felled in the field by the community, and that spirit lives in the wheat, bread, or ale and will rise again from the field in the spring. Historically the cycle of life in early agriculture was ushered in by everyone in the towns and villages because it was understood that the success of each individual farm meant the success of all. The dog days of summer feel celebratory as we savor the warmth, knowing that soon the air will feel crisp and cool. As we celebrate let's consider the importance of the Earth and the procession of the delicate seasons that sustain all life on our planet. As we celebrate life, death, and renewal at Lammastide let's all consider that when we care for our local communities and for the land that we love, we're also caring for ourselves.

Cosmic Sway

Ivo Dominguez Jr.

MANY CELEBRATE LAMMAS ON August 1, but astrological Lammas is early on August 7 when the Sun is at the 15th degree of Leo. Depending upon which time zone you live in, August 6 may be a better option. The 15th degree of Aquarius, Taurus, Leo, and Scorpio are at the midpoints between the Solstices and Equinoxes, so are more exactly the cross-quarters. The astrological influences are less intense and eventful during this sabbat. This is a relief because there is more than enough that is still in process from earlier events. You may wish to use the special qualities of Lammas to cope with ongoing matters.

On August 1, the Sun is conjunct Mercury and opposing Saturn in Aquarius. This is a superior solar conjunction, which means it will be behind the Sun, directly opposite the Earth. Venus in Virgo is trine to Uranus in Taurus. The Moon in Taurus is in its fourth quarter. Jupiter in Aquarius, Saturn in Aquarius, Chiron in Aries, Neptune in Pisces, and Pluto in Capricorn are retrograde. The planets are arranged in two clusters across from each other in the chart like a seesaw.

On August 7, the Sun in Leo squares Uranus in Taurus. Neptune in Pisces, its home, is sextile to Pluto in Capricorn. You may wish to do a two-part ritual or ceremony, with a start on August 1 and the completion on August 7. The planets are still arranged in a seesaw with five retrograde. The New Moon in Leo is on August 8. On August 22, the Full Moon will be in Aquarius and, since the last Full Moon on July 23 was also in Aquarius, it is astrologically a blue moon.

This year it may be productive to focus on Lammas as a holiday that celebrates skill, work, and altruism. The theme of the sacrifice of the first harvest is still present. It was a sacrifice to spend the hours necessary to learn the skills that you bring to your community. The hours you work for love or money are hours you do not get back. When you give of yourself to family, friends, community, or causes, it is self-sacrifice as well. Lammas is the cutting of the grain, the baking of the bread, and the filling of empty bellies. Lammas is also about the power of gratitude to make us whole and connected to the natural world and the world of human culture.

The Sun and Mercury opposing Saturn creates a restriction and offers a solution. You may feel a sense of isolation and have challenges in connecting with people and things that matter to you. If you are traveling, start early as the going may be slow. You may realize that you are judging yourself and others by too hard a measure. Choosing kindness can be the greatest offering you make this sabbat. Use that Sun conjunct Mercury to tell others how much they matter, and don't forget yourself. Whether as part of a ritual, celebratory feast, or a quick meal at the pizza parlor, savor the quality of the time spent together. Saturn rules time so make each moment count. If you are feeling low energy, reach out even if it is just a text message.

The two clusters of planets on either side of the chart, like a seesaw, add a dynamic to this Lammas that requires taking turns to keep things moving. You can only have drum beat when you have both sound and silence. A band plays best when all the musicians are playing their part and listening to the others. This arrangement also warns against trying to keep important parts of your life separate from each other. The most vitality comes when each part has time to shine, to be seen, and is acknowledged by the whole. Lammas is about community, and these celestial influences ask for harmony and fair play.

There are perfect Lammas-inspired uses for the five retrogrades that are in effect to better the common good. Jupiter retrograde in Aquarius asks us to reconsider our ideas and ideology in terms of who is served and who is harmed. Saturn retrograde in Aquarius asks us what structures and institutions need to be reformed. Chiron retrograde in Aries reminds you of your backlog of goals that need to be integrated into your life if they are ever to happen. Neptune retrograde in Pisces bids you to be quiet, for just a bit, so you can hear the soft but powerful voice of your divine spark. Pluto retrograde in Capricorn wants to show you things about yourself that you don't want to see. Trust the process and look at what is shown to you so you can move on and grow. These statements can also be prompts for ritual work, divination, or pathworkings.

On August 7 and 8, the Sun square Uranus, Neptune sextile Pluto, and the New Moon will shake things up on a personal and global level. It may feel like the Earth is moving under your feet. The unexpected outnumbers the predictable, and expectations are only loosely connected to reality. The best approach is to go with the flow and enjoy the show. Remain flexible and open to change, and when the dust settles there will be opportunities. Rely on your intuition as it is being helped by the Neptune-Pluto aspect. If you hold on stubbornly and rigidly to the status quo, you may get hurt as things flail about. Be a surfer riding the wave of change instead of hanging on to a rock in the crashing waves.

On August 22, in addition to a blue moon conjunct Jupiter, Uranus in Taurus will be trine to Mars in Virgo. If the question is when, the answer is now. Don't pass up the opportunity to take action and gain forward momentum in your life. These aspects embolden the heart and make the blood sing. Shake off doubts, dream big, and get to work on making those dreams real. The Uranus-Mars aspect being in the element of earth helps to make sure that you do not forget the practicalities. If you charged water or created a charged candle at the Summer Solstice, this is an excellent time to use it.

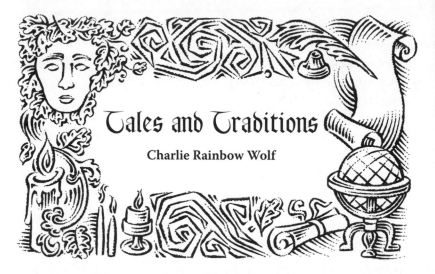

Tales and Traditions

Charlie Rainbow Wolf

WHEN I LIVED ON the farm in England, this was always considered to be the dawn of the fall season. We fervently watched the weather, hoping for fine days to ripen the grain and allow us to gather it at its best. This was when the fruit trees were heavy with their crop, when the elderberries down by the canal were at their ripest and sweetest, and where the skies started to lose the pastel blue of the summer in favour of the deeper and more vibrant turquoise as the days started to shorten. These were always my favorite days.

John Barleycorn and More

It was during my first Lammas as a young farmer's wife that I learned how to bake bread in the old cast iron wood-fired stove. I discovered later that this was a traditional practice, one that represented not just the harvest, but also an abundance of both the material and spiritual kind. A bounty of wheat and grain meant that the family would be fed when other food was perhaps scarce. It was a time to gather with others and share what had been reaped.

Corn, Wheat, and Barley

In the United States when someone talks about corn they're usually referring to maize—*Zea mays convar. saccharata var. rugosa*—the sweet corn that is eaten as a vegetable. However, in many areas of the world, the terms "corn" and "grain" are interchangeable. On the Lincolnshire farm, "corn" was any cereal crop (which was very confusing for the American students who came to the local college). We grew wheat and barley; we grew "corn."

Lammas is a festival of the corn, but traditionally this referred to grain. Many thought—and still do—that the fields had spirits dwelling in them, and thus when the harvest is gathered, there is nowhere for those who live there to go. This belief gave rise to the making of corn dollies, to appease the corn spirits and give them somewhere to live once the grain had been gathered.

Corn dollies originated as something very simple so the spirit of the corn had a place to stay until the seeds were sown the following spring, at which time the dolly would be ploughed into the ground and the spirit returned to the growing field of grain. They have now grown into an artform, with different areas having different patterns. Some corn dollies are highly collectible, cherished as symbols of protection or given as wedding gifts to ensure the lives of the newlyweds are filled with prosperity and fertility.

Burns and John Barleycorn

The story of John Barleycorn has been around for centuries. Robert Burns's eighteenth century version seems to be the one that has become the most popular. Even more recently, folk songs about John Barleycorn have been recorded by Steeleye Span, Traffic, and more.

The tale tells us that John Barleycorn was killed by three kings, who ploughed him into a field, but he rose again the following spring. He grew tall and strong throughout the summer, then started to wither and fade with the coming of autumn. His enemies felled him once again, tying him to a cart, then they threw him into a pit, threshed him, ground his bones, and drank his blood. There's not much imagination needed to see that this is the story of the grain from planting to harvest, and from flour to ale.

Respecting the Corn

Here in the US, my Cherokee friends celebrate their Green Corn Ceremony around this time of year. Traditionally a four-day festival, now it tends to be held over a weekend because of other commitments or the need to travel to the gathering place. The practice of Going to Water (see the Samhain section) is an important part of the Green Corn Ceremony.

This was also a festival of dance, and the one I recall was the stomp dance, named for the way that the dancers' feet shuffled and stomped as they moved. Games were played, and on the second day the fast was broken with a huge feast of early-harvested produce. It was a place of forgiveness, and of restoring and strengthening friendships and family ties.

Honoring the Ways

Even though Lammas is not one of the more well-known yearly festivals there are still many ways that you can bring its traditions to your own celebrations and into your own home. You might want to make corn dollies or reenact your own version of the harvesting of John Barleycorn. Here at the Keep, we bake bread every year, adding herbs from the garden, always making enough to share. My husband has been known to use this as a time of starting his home brew so that we have ale for over Yule and Twelfth Night. I cannot stress enough that there is no right way and no wrong way; it's your intention that matters. Here's my recipe for Lammas bread. You'll notice that it includes both ale and flour, and that there are herbs from the garden in it. What better way to welcome in the harvest than to pay homage to John Barleycorn as well as what our own postage stamp of soil has given us?

12 ounces ale
1 tablespoon olive oil
2 tablespoons honey or maple syrup
1 teaspoon salt
2 ounces (¼ cup) old-fashioned oats

10 ounces (1¼ cups) strong bread flour
1 tablespoon fast-acting dried yeast
Pinch of rosemary
Pinch of sage
Pinch of thyme

Make sure all ingredients are at room temperature. Gently mix in the ale, oil, and honey first, then add the salt, oats, flour, and yeast. The dough should be soft and pliable but not sticky. Turn it onto a floured surface and knead it for several minutes. Put the dough back into a greased bowl to rise, covering it with a cloth and sitting it in a warm place. When it is double in size, knock it back and knead it again, this time adding the herbs.

Now is your chance to be artistic! Twist it, plait it, roll it into buns; it's up to you how you want the finished loaf to look. I usually divide the dough into three pieces, make larger circles out of the first two, then divide the remaining dough into two smaller circles and pop them on the top of the first ones, poking a hole from top to bottom to ensure they stick together. Cover and let rise again until double in size. Bake in a preheated oven at 375°F until golden brown and hollow sounding when tapped on the bottom. Cool at least half an hour before cutting—now *that's* torture!

References

Azarian, Mary. *The Tale of John Barleycorn, or From Barley to Beer: A Traditional English Ballad.* Boston MA: David R Godine, 2017.

Lambeth, Minnie. *Discovering Corn Dollies.* Aylesbury, UK: Shire Publications, 2008.

Sizemore, Donald. *Cherokee Dance: Ceremonial Dances & Dance Regalia.* Cherokee, NC: Cherokee Publications, 1999.

Traffic, "John Barleycorn (Must Die)," track 5 on *John Barleycorn Must Die*, Island Records, 1970.

Feasts and Treats
Sue Pesznecker

LANDING AT THE BEGINNING of August, Lammas is high summer, and the livin' is easy. The following recipes are perfect for a favorite summer tradition: the barbecue picnic. I've provided the ideas, you'll have to bring your own ants.

Angels on Horseback with Grilled Onions

I learned about Angels on Horseback when I went to Campfire Girls camp back in the sixties. To be honest, they've never tasted the same as they did at Camp Namanu, but they're still pretty darned tasty, and they remain a favorite summer treat. Cook them on a barbecue grill or light up the fire pit, hand everyone a roasting stick, and roast them over the campfire.

Prep time: 20 minutes
Cooking time: 60 minutes
Servings: varies

Onions
2–3 tablespoons vegetable oil
Yellow onions, 1 per person
½ teaspoon sugar
1–2 tablespoons butter

Prepare the grilled onions. Heat the vegetable oil in a large, broad-bottomed kettle over medium heat.

Peel the onions and slice in ½-inch-thick rings. Rinse* the rings under cool water and shake off excess water. Add the rings to the kettle.

Cook the onions, stirring often, until they begin to brown and cook down. As they do, they will caramelize. When they begin to look light brown, adding the sugar will speed the process along.

Your goal is for the onions to cook way down in size and volume, and to become a deep brown—this could take up to an hour. When you reach that point, add the butter to the onions, stir well, and take them off the heat. Let them sit, uncovered.

*Pro tip: Rinsing the rings removes some of the sulfur that's liberated when the rings are cut, making them cook "sweeter." They'll also be more digestible after this treatment.

Angels

Wooden toothpicks
Large, good quality hot dogs, 2 per person
Cheddar or cheddar-jack cheese stick, 2 per person
Bacon strips, 2 per person
Butter
Hot dog buns, 2 per person
Condiments: mustard, ketchup, mayonnaise, relish

Put a handful of wooden toothpicks to soak in a bowl of warm water.

Make a long slit in each hot dog and insert a cheese stick, squeezing it completely inside the hot dog. Starting at one end, wrap a strip of bacon around the dog, barber-pole style. Secure the bacon ends with the soaked toothpicks.

Roast the angels over coals or flame, turning until the bacon is done. While they cook, lightly butter the hot dog buns and toast over grill or flame until golden and crispy.

Place each finished angel dog in a toasted bun. Be sure to remove the toothpicks!

Offer grilled onions and condiments so each diner can dress their angels on horseback to order.

Better Potato Salad

The name comes from an ongoing joke in my family about whose potato salad is better and whose is best. All I know is that no summer picnic would feel right without potato salad. The one I favor is both simple and traditional.

Prep time: 45 minutes, including boiling the potatoes

Servings: 6–8

2½ pounds potatoes: russets or Yukon Golds
2–3 tablespoons apple cider vinegar
Salt
1–2 celery stalks, diced
½ of a sweet onion, diced
Hard-boiled eggs: 1 egg for each potato; 2 eggs for each big potato (and then I usually throw in 1 more egg!)
1 cup mayonnaise (to reduce the calories, you may substitute full-fat Greek yogurt for up to half of this)
1 tablespoon yellow or whole grain mustard
2 tablespoons parsley, chopped
½ teaspoon black pepper
Salt to taste
Paprika
Optional: celery seed, dill weed, chopped pickles, pickle juice, bacon bits

Peel the potatoes and cut into 1-inch chunks. Boil in a kettle of salted water until they are just tender, but don't overcook! You don't want the potatoes to start falling apart.

Drain the potatoes and immediately spread them out on a rimmed cookie sheet. This helps the hot potatoes dry and get rid of excess water. While still freshly hot, drizzle them with the vinegar and sprinkle with salt. Allow the potatoes to cool.

Once the potatoes are cool, add them to a large bowl. Layer on the celery, onion, chopped eggs, and any optional goodies.

Next, spread the mayo, mustard, parsley, and pepper over the surface, like frosting a cake. Using a rubber spatula, gently fold and combine the ingredients, the goal being to mix everything without breaking down the potatoes.

Taste the salad and add salt if needed.

Note: Because the salad contains mayonnaise, it's important to keep it in the fridge between uses and keep it cold when it's on the picnic table. Sitting the potato salad container in a larger bowl of ice is a good solution.

Ants on a Log

Ants are a traditional part of picnics, and this fun snack evokes eating outdoors, childhood, and summer fun. Making these is another fun kid project too.

Prep time: 15 minutes
Servings: varies

Celery stalks, washed and dried, ends trimmed
Peanut butter or other nut butter
Raisins, currants, or dried raisins (these are the "ants")

Cut the celery into 3–4-inch "logs." Fill each log with peanut butter and top with "ants."

Blueberry Buckle

This blueberry-packed, streusel-topped coffee cake is just plain scrumptious and a great way to celebrate fresh blueberries. I've made it for breakfast, brunch, afternoon snacking, and dessert. I wouldn't be at all surprised if I eventually make it for dinner!

Prep time: 30 minutes
Cooking time: 45–50 minutes
Servings: 8–10

2 cups fresh blueberries, washed and drained on a cotton towel
Flour and butter for preparing the baking pan

Wash and drain the blueberries; they'll be dry by the time you need them. Butter a 9-inch square pan and dust with flour. Preheat the oven to 350° F.

Streusel
½ cup sugar
⅓ cup flour
½ teaspoon cinnamon
¼ cup butter, softened

In a food processor or in a small bowl with a pastry blender, combine the streusel ingredients to make a coarse mixture. Set aside.

Cake
¾ cup sugar
¼ cup butter, softened
1 egg
½ cup milk
2 cups flour, sifted
2 teaspoons baking powder
½ teaspoon salt

Cream the sugar, butter, and egg for several minutes until light and fluffy. Stir in the milk. Then add the flour, baking powder, and salt, stirring just until mixed. Use a handheld rubber spatula to gently fold in the blueberries.

Pile the batter—which will be stiff—into the prepared pan, leveling the batter with a spoon. Spread the streusel evenly over the batter. Bake for 45–50 minutes, until a toothpick inserted in the center comes out clean and dry.

Summer Sangria

My summer sangria uses a plain or sparkling rosé with a mixture of berries and stone fruits. It will be a tasty and refreshing addition to your summer celebrations.

Prep time: 15 minutes
Inactive: overnight
Servings: 6–8

1 bottle (750 milliliters) rosé, either plain or sparkling
½ cup good quality brandy
¼ cup sugar
1 cup pomegranate or cranberry juice
Fruits: raspberries, blueberries, peaches, nectarines, plums, cherries
24 ounces seltzer, sparkling water, or ginger ale
Additional fruit for garnish

Combine the wine, brandy, sugar, and fruit juice in a large juice container or pitcher. (I like to use a ½-gallon mason jar.) Stir until mostly dissolved.

Wash and slice the stone fruits. Wash berries, and wash and pit cherries. Add a generous amount of fruit to the sangria mixture and place in the refrigerator to chill overnight.

Just before using, shake the sangria gently, then stir in the seltzer. Serve the sangria with fresh berries or citrus slices for garnish. Include some of the steeped fruit in each glass.

Crafty Crafts

Tess Whitehurst

THE WORD LAMMAS, an alternate name for Lughnasadh, comes from the Old English word *hlafmaesse*, which means "loaf mass." Even today, modern Pagans think of Lughnasadh as a time to celebrate bread, muffins, cereal, grains, the earth upon which grains grow, and the reliable daily sustenance that grain provides.

In *The Element Encyclopedia of Witchcraft*, Judika Illes devotes an entire chapter to the magical and sacred relationship between grain, the great goddess in the form of the grain or corn mother, and the agricultural relationship with the earth established by our ancestors. She writes, "The Earth sign Virgo is thus represented by a Virgin (originally meaning an independent woman) holding her child, which is simultaneously a human infant and a stalk of wheat. This is the basis of many mystery religions: the child is the mystery; the mother is the deity" (Illes 2005).

Lughnasadh is a time to give thanks to the earth for the first fruits and grains of the harvest season. In our modern culture where food is accessible year-round for so many of us, we can sometimes forget just how lucky we are—and how miraculous it is—that the earth provides us with healthful plant foods in such abundance. Lammas reminds us to consider everything that makes it possible for us to stock our kitchens and pantries with such a luxurious surplus: the water, sunlight, soil, oxygen, and pollinators, as well as the farmers, farm workers, drivers, and merchants that combine their labor and expertise to ensure our ongoing sustenance.

Golden Grain Wreath

This wreath has a beautiful natural look with a subtle hint of golden shimmer. If you're tired of the same old wheat wreath, this is a unique and attractive alternative. And it's very easy to make!

The circular shape symbolizes and magically promotes year-round abundance and everlasting sustenance.

(A quick caveat: be sure to hang this wreath indoors to prevent critters from compromising their health by nibbling on grain mixed with inedible craft supplies.)

Materials

A grapevine wreath
Glue (I used Elmer's)
A paintbrush (a cheap one for wall painting will do)
Rolled oats or a similar hot cereal (I used a multigrain hot cereal
   including rye, barley, oats, and wheat)
Fine gold glitter
Craft glue acrylic finishing spray (I used Mod Podge brand)
Hemp twine or another type of craft string to hang the wreath
Newspaper to line your workspace before you begin
   Cost: $10–$15
   Time spent: 10–15 minutes, plus time for glue and spray to dry

Dispense a generous dollop of glue onto a piece of cardboard or an old magazine. Dip the paintbrush into the glue and paint it liberally onto the front side of the wreath. Dispense additional glue as needed and repeat until the entire front of the wreath is coated in glue.

Next, sprinkle a thick layer of the grain onto the glue. Of course, only some of it will stick. Allow the rest to fall onto the newspaper

below. Then sprinkle the gold glitter on top, paying special attention to the tinier areas of exposed glue where the grain did not stick.

Allow this to dry for at least 4 hours or overnight. Lift it and shake it gently to allow any unglued grain and glitter to fall onto the newspaper. Then take it outside when there is no breeze and spray the front of the wreath with the finishing spray, following the directions on the can. Allow it to dry outside for at least an hour before moving it back inside.

Use the hemp twine or string to hang the wreath wherever you'd like to display it. You may like to hang it near your altar in your magical workspace. Or, to bless your food and remind you of the magic of the harvest and delicious abundance of the earth, you could hang it in your kitchen or dining area.

Barley Water: An Ancient Grain Beverage

Nourishing, mineral-rich barley water was a staple of ancient Greece. It was associated with the grain goddess Demeter and the Eleusinian Mysteries.

To this day, barley water is regularly enjoyed in many parts of the world. For example, it's a popular summer drink in Britain and India.

Particularly when prepared with mint, barley water is delicious, cooling, and refreshing. It's ideal for this time of year, and makes for a wonderful Lughnasadh libation, ritual beverage, or refreshment. Author Scott Cunningham recommended using it in love spells in *Cunningham's Encyclopedia of Magical Herbs* (Cunningham 1985).

Barley's association with magic and fertility is perhaps as ancient as agriculture itself. It's synonymous with both Demeter and her mother, the primordial earth goddess Gaia. Metaphysically, it protects from negativity, strengthens immunity, relieves pain, and intensifies romantic love.

Lemon is cleansing and is aligned with feminine energy and the moon.

Mint is, of course, a highly magical botanical that bolsters the energy field and purifies the mind, body, and spirit. It also attracts wealth and abundance.

Materials

1 cup pearl barley
2 lemons, scrubbed clean
1 bunch fresh mint
8 cups water
Organic honey, or another sweetener of your choice, to taste (perhaps start with 3 tablespoons)
Cost: $5–$10
Time spent: 1–1½ hours, plus time to cool

Before preparing the barley water, center yourself. Take some deep breaths and come into the present moment. Then call on the goddess Demeter. From your heart, thank her for generously offering her grain this harvest season and for continually blessing the earth with fertility. Ask that she bless all the barley water ingredients. Envision them being filled with golden white light and health-giving power.

Rinse the barley and place it in a large pot. Add the water and bring it to a boil. Cover and reduce heat to low. Simmer for 45 to 60 minutes, or until the barley is soft. While it's simmering, grate the lemon peels and juice the lemons. When you remove the pot from the heat, add the lemon zest (grated peels) and steep, covered, for 20 minutes. Drain. Combine with sweetener and transfer to a pitcher to cool. Add the lemon juice. To serve, crush a small handful of mint in a mortar and pestle, place it in a chalice or glass, and pour the water over the top. (Ice is optional.)

Before you discard the barley, take about ½ cup and go outside. Place it on the earth as a gratitude offering to Demeter. Consider all the grains that nourish you and your loved ones every day of the year, and feel thankful for the abundant nourishment Demeter endlessly provides.

References

Cunningham, Scott. *Cunningham's Encyclopedia of Magical Herbs.* St. Paul, MN: Llewellyn Publications, 1985.

Illes, Judika. *The Element Encyclopedia of Witchcraft: The Complete A-Z for the Entire Magical World.* London: HarperElement, 2005.

Spells

Michael Furie

BEING A FOREBEAR TO the late summer and early autumn fairs that we have today, Lughnasadh carries with it a rich history of hard work, networking, commerce, and the joyful games and well-earned after-party that follows such efforts. In modern times, not as many of us have a direct connection to the work of cattle raising or the grain harvest (though most benefit from such things), but we have each worked to maintain our lives and homes, and we can take this moment to pause and allow ourselves to celebrate this effort. We can also seek to ask for spiritual help in achieving and keeping abundance as we journey out of the light half of the year.

Cooling the Heat of the Sun

Since Lughnasadh is the first harvest celebration, some of the magic performed at this time has, in the past, been focused on protecting the crops so that they can be properly harvested over the next month or so. One aspect of this magical work has been to symbolically cool the heat of the sun so that its destructive power can be muted while keeping its positive energy intact. This distinction is similar to the relation of the Egyptian goddesses Sekhmet and Bastet. Sekhmet is viewed as the goddess of the destructive heat of the sun, and Bastet is seen as the sun's gentle warmth and creative power.

In regards to our personal magic, we can utilize this theme to help lessen the intensity of things we might deem harmful to us but are not able to quit such as tobacco, alcohol, junk food, or any other item that we feel may have a destructive influence over us. This magic is twofold: to reduce our craving for destructive habits and also to help cool the sun so that the farmers have an easier time harvesting the crops.

Materials

Cauldron or heat-proof bowl
1 gold or yellow votive candle
Cup or chalice of water
Pin

On the candle, carve the name of the destructive influence over you and place the candle in the cauldron. Light the candle and feel its heat rising, much like the heat of the late summer sun. Visualize the problem you are trying to remove and see yourself overcoming it—that it no longer has any harmful power over you. Pour the entire cup of water over the candle in the cauldron, extinguishing the flame, and say:

Harmful heat of summer sun and powerful burden I wish to release, both are extinguished now, their power does cease; of these troubles I am free, as I will so shall it be.

Pour the water outside and dispose of the candle.

The Grain Sacrifice

Most magic is focused on either gaining something or releasing something, but sometimes we need a magical way of simply saying thank you to the spiritual powers in our lives for the blessings we have already been given. Lughnasadh is an ideal time to give back in gratitude.

Materials

Bread or biscuit dough
1 knife
Offerings such as money, crystals, or small personal items
Trowel or shovel

The spell can use premade bread or biscuit dough if desired, but making homemade bread isn't that difficult.

Materials

1 tablespoon yeast
1 cup warm water
1 tablespoon sugar
2–3 cups flour
1 teaspoon salt

Mix the yeast, water, sugar, and ¼ cup of the flour together in a bowl and leave to "proof" for ten minutes. Then stir in the salt and enough flour to make a soft dough. Now, using your hands, knead the dough adding more flour as needed until it is smooth and elastic. Roll the dough into a ball, coat it with oil or cooking spray, and leave it covered in the bowl for an hour. Preheat the oven to 350° F. After an hour has passed, punch down the dough and shape it into a human figure. Then set it on a greased cookie sheet. Bake for 20 to 30 minutes, until golden brown. Remove from the oven and allow it to cool.

Once the bread has cooled, slice into the side of the bread man just enough so that you can place the offerings inside. Then put the bread man in a bag and take it outdoors. Find a suitable spot to dig a small hole and place the bread man in the hole with the words:

Gifts of the earth freely returned, to the great powers for how I've been blessed; my offerings added in thanks for concern, and gratitude for my joy and success.

Fill in the hole and walk away without looking back.

Sunscreen Protection Spell

With the coming of Lughnasadh, we also have the hottest part of the summer. Daylight hours still stretch past eight o' clock, which means that sunscreen is still a necessity. Aside from its intended benefit of protecting the skin from the harmful effects of prolonged sun exposure, a little magic can be added so that it will also serve as a protection from harm as well.

Materials
1 bottle of sunscreen
Cauldron or heat-proof dish
1 red candle
Rosemary oil

Anoint the red candle with the rosemary oil from the wick end to the bottom, visualize it being filled with red light in order to charge it for protection, and set it in the cauldron. Light the candle and hold the bottle of sunscreen above the flame, high enough to avoid a burn and say:

Shield of protection from sun's harsh rays, cover the skin to protect each day; empowered by magic to repel all harm, leaving the wearer safe and calm.

Extinguish the candle and remember to wear the sunscreen every day.

Butter and Grain Prosperity Spell

Butter has a history in magic of being a symbol of transformation and a potential offering to the Faery to gain their favor. And grains are almost all universally linked with protection and prosperity. It is the prosperity power that I will focus on here.

Materials
Butter
Whole grain bread (your preferred type)
Toaster

This is a very simple yet surprisingly powerful working. This food spell is about taking the magic within—essentially charging ourselves to be the magic we seek. Take one or two pieces of the whole grain bread and hold them while focusing on your desire for prosperity. Infuse this intention into the bread, then toast it. While the bread is toasting, charge the butter with the same energy by holding the dish of butter and infusing it with your intention. When the toast is ready, spread some butter on it, and before you take a bite, say:

I bring within, the earth's sweet grain, joined with butter for prosperity gained; to nourish my body and ensure success, with increased fortune I am blessed.

Eat the toast and visualize your entire body being charged by its magic.

Lammas Ritual

Mickie Mueller

I WANTED TO CRAFT a modern ritual that could be altered easily by a solitary witch, a family, a larger inclusive group like a coven or grove, or for a public group ritual at an event. This ritual focuses on building connections within a community and protecting and nurturing the people that we care for with the energies of the earth that sustains us.

Ritual for Community

You will need food pantry donations. If you're doing this ritual alone, include at least one package of quick bread mix and other items such as canned corn, seasonal berry jam, or local honey. If this is a group ritual, everyone should bring at least one item.

Materials

1 pillar candle colored gold, red, or white
1 small candle (tealight or small taper) for each participant in a
  color to match the pillar candle
Basket

You'll also need a small altar table in the center that can be decorated with symbols of Lammas/Lughnasadh that speak to you. The symbols may include sheaves of wheat, bread, apples, corn dollies, seasonal flowers, and a table covering of gold, red, or green. The basket to receive food pantry offerings can be on the ground next to the altar table.

The Ritual

If this is a group ritual, direct participants to stand a few feet apart in a circle around the altar table and set their food pantry offerings at their feet.

The parts may be spoken by a single person or shared among several participants as preferred or as necessary.

Awakening Magical Mindset

Soften your gaze, breathe in deeply through your nose, and exhale through your mouth three times. As you breathe in, visualize the golden light of the sun filling you with energy and lighting up each cell in your body; as you breathe out, send light out into the world through your heart.

(Pause and breathe with the group.)

The Wheel of the Year turns and brings us to Lammas (Lughnasadh) and the first harvest of the year. You might find that your mind, body, and spirit are becoming aligned with the influence of the season as you enjoy the energy of the sacred space created here. The celebration of this day is one of goodwill, harmony, and abundance. If you wish to nurture the feeling of fellowship and community in your heart today, you may find that you will receive the benefits of kinship with all humankind.

Circlecasting

One person should reach out their left hand and grasp the right hand of the person to their left. As they do, they will say, "Our hands are bound, the circle round," and that should continue around the circle until it is complete. The person who started states, "The circle now together cast, this sacred space we now hold fast." At this point everyone may drop their hands.

A solitary practitioner working this ritual alone may cast their circle in their usual way.

If your tradition uses directions for the elements, you may face those directions during the following elemental calls. These calls may also be reordered to fit your tradition. Each element should be visualized as aspects of ourselves rising up during each call.

Earth: *I call up the archetype of the earth elemental—the energy that aligns with abundance, stones, mountains, great trees, and plenty. We feel this energy in our bones, steady, solid, firm, and strong. The earth within us, we are one.*

Air: *I call up the archetype of the air elemental—the energy that aligns with wind, thought, song, music, expression, communication. We feel this energy in our lungs, breathing, filling, ever present. The air within us, we are one.*

Fire: *I call up the archetype of the fire elemental—the energy that aligns with bonfires, candlelight, the hearth, starlight, and raw willpower. We feel this energy in our nervous system, firing, sparking, transforming. The fire within us, we are one.*

Water: *I call upon the archetype of the water elemental—the energy that aligns with rivers, lakes, rainfall, the seas, and purification. We feel this energy running through our veins, flowing, saturating, cleansing. The water within us, we are one.*

Projective Aspect of Deity: *I call upon the archetype of the sun above our heads, the wild forests, the vigorous projective aspect of deity that lives within us all. Welcome to this sacred space the entity of life-giving sun that energizes everything into being and bestows fertility to all life on earth. Protector, mediator, explorer of possibilities, we are one.*

Receptive Aspect of Deity: *I call upon the archetype of the fields below our feet, the oceans, the giver of life, the receptive aspect of deity that lives within us all. Welcome to this sacred space the entity of the fertile growing soil that nurtures everything into being and feeds all life on earth. Gardener, caregiver, founder of societies, we are one.*

Statement of Purpose

We are one with the elements and all aspects of deity. We welcome them as they rise up from within ourselves and remind us that we are all part of humanity and the collective subconscious, and that we can make the decision to allow our similarities to create a bond. Communities of our ancestors once joined together at Lammastide to bring in the harvest as they celebrated their abundance in kinship. People interacted while competing at games and shows of skill, recognizing that everyone had common goals but also something unique to contribute. We can decide to open the divine within us and become part of a whole, something greater than the sum of our parts. Each member of a community is important, both similar and unique all at the same time. We can recognize our similarities and celebrate our differences while maintaining certainty of ourselves and our strengths. We can choose compassion for others while maintaining sovereignty over our own place in the world. May the magic of this Lammastide celebration strengthen this group and ripple out amongst the other communities that we are also members of, casting the energy of hope to the corners of the world.

We now bring the harvest in, each offering a small sacrifice while awakening fellowship, sparking community, and expressing gratitude for all that we have.

One by one in the order of the circlecasting, participants may bring their food pantry contributions to the altar. When each participant places their donation into the basket, the group leader proclaims: "A fitting sacrifice, the community shares the flame with gratitude," and offers the participant a small candle to light from the central pillar candle.

Once each participant has a lit candle and has returned to their place in the circle, the group leader states:

The abundant first harvest will bless many as we too are blessed. We have seen with our own eyes that the lighting of each flame does not take away from the source or any other flame; the fire of life is abundant. We all have flame to share. This is the true blessing of being part of a community.

We will now go around the circle as each of you states one thing that you have in common with everyone on Earth and one thing that makes you unique. Then you may extinguish your flame. Save your candle, light it later at home, and allow it to burn out and fill your home with the blessings of fellowship, gratitude, and empowerment.

Receptive Aspect of Deity: *Gratitude to the receptive aspect of deity that lives within us all, reintegrate within the pools of our subconscious. In honor and blessings.*

Projective Aspect of Deity: *Gratitude to the projective aspect of deity that lives within us all, reintegrate within the pools of our subconscious. In honor and blessings.*

Water: *Gratitude to the archetype of water that lives within us all, reintegrate within the pools of our subconscious. In honor and blessings.*

Fire: *Gratitude to the archetype of fire that lives within us all, reintegrate within the pools of our subconscious. In honor and blessings.*

Air: *Gratitude to the archetype of air that lives within us all, reintegrate within the pools of our subconscious. In honor and blessings.*

Earth: *Gratitude to the archetype of earth that lives within us all, reintegrate within the pools of our subconscious. In honor and blessings.*

All rejoin hands, swing them in and out, and join in the circle release: "Circle bound, circle unbound, circle of fellowship open but unbroken!"

All hands release on the last line and swing up into the circle. Follow this ritual with a feast, music, and merriment. The following day the food donations from the ritual should be dropped off at a local food pantry.

Happy Lammas!

Notes

Mabon

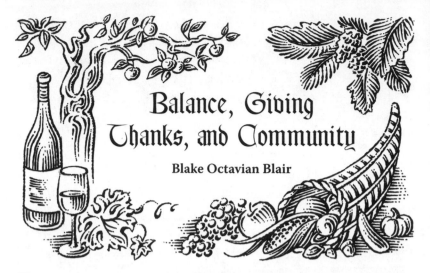

Balance, Giving Thanks, and Community

Blake Octavian Blair

THE AUTUMN EQUINOX HAS long been one of my favorite sabbats. For many of us, the weather is cooling, foliage is beginning to turn, beautiful, vibrant blue skies appear, and hot mulled apple cider abounds! The autumn equinox is a time of celebrating both the literal and metaphorical harvest. We celebrate the accomplishments we have made in the physical, emotional, and spiritual realms.

This sabbat has at times been referred to as the "Pagan Thanksgiving." While cliché, it is a pretty accurate conclusion to draw. While the American holiday of Thanksgiving is observed in the United States in November, it makes little sense as a harvest holiday to many of us in the timing of the Wheel of the Year. American Thanksgiving is also mired in the dubious history of colonialism. However, our beloved autumn equinox, aka Mabon, is a seasonally appropriate time for gathering in thanksgiving of the harvest, our communities, and our accomplishments.

The precedent of the autumn equinox being a time of feasting and giving of thanks and gratitude is cross-cultural. In Japan, the time of the autumn equinox is celebrated by many major Buddhist sects with a week of festivities called *Higan*. In Japanese culture, the cardinal direction west is believed to be the direction of the land of the afterlife, and because the sun sets due west on the equinox, they draw a special connection between the two at this time. Although many modern Pagan traditions don't fully turn their attention to the ancestors as a focus until Samhain, the association of the west and the realm of the dead is a shared one with many modern Neopagan traditions.

On the full moon that falls closest to the autumn equinox, the Chinese celebrate the Harvest Moon Festival. The tradition can be traced back to the Shang Dynasty, which lasted from 1600–1056 BCE! The Chinese people prepare for the occasion by hanging lanterns to decorate their homes and neighborhoods. Families and friends gather for feasting, celebration, and giving thanks. These celebrations are often held outdoors under the moonlight so as to observe the harvest moon during the festivities.

The German harvest celebration of *Erntedankfest* takes place after the autumn equinox proper, but still within the season, on the first Sunday in October. This scheduling move is largely connected to the Christianization of the celebration; however, many of its traditions and trappings reveal its nature as the harvest celebration it truly is. The people celebrate in ritual in the form of church services that honor the harvest of both produce and grains. During the church services, some of the bounty of the harvest is blessed and then distributed to those less fortunate. In fact, Pagan Pride celebrations in the United States actually share in a similar practice. Pagan Pride Day festivals are most often held near the autumn equinox and have a tradition of collecting canned goods for local food pantries in exchange for admission to the event in lieu of a monetary fee.

Hindu culture around this time of year celebrates the festival of *Navaratri*. This festival honors the warrior goddess Durga and the divine feminine. Although the details of methods of celebration and the different forms of the goddess celebrated during the festival can vary regionally, the nine-day festival almost universally includes many *pujas* (ritual to honor deity), feasts, and gatherings. The expression of our gratitude to divine entities is indeed an appropriate practice at this time of harvest.

Of course, this brings up a story of the divine feminine that many modern Pagans might be more familiar with in association with this time of year, the descent of Persephone into the underworld. Persephone is the daughter of Demeter, the Greek goddess of the land and fertility. Persephone famously eats the seeds of the pomegranate at the autumn equinox and is whisked away by Hades to the underworld. Of course, she takes with her the fertility and green of the land until her return at the vernal equinox. However, this sparks the celebration of our gratitude for what we have harvested, agriculturally and otherwise, up to this point of the onset of autumn and her descent. Many of us even express our gratefulness for the upcoming time of regenerative rest. For we know that even as the land goes quiet, its heart beats with life within the earth. At this point of balance in the Wheel of the Year, we express gratitude for both what came before this point and what shall come after it. Both have their blessings to offer.

In the United States, there isn't a traditional set observance or holiday in the dominant culture for the autumn equinox. However, celebration of the equinox is growing, both due to the increasing popularity of Pagan and nature spiritualties and people generally gaining an interest in living more in tune with and in observation of the seasons and cycles of nature. Also, as mentioned earlier, it seems a more natural time to gather to give thanks and share gratitude in community that isn't mired in the reminders of a messy colonial conquest.

One of my favorite ways to celebrate the agricultural harvest of the season is to indulge in all things apple. Apple picking is the quintessential New England autumnal rite of passage. Plus, my husband makes the best homemade apple pie on the planet, although I might be biased. I also think that we should pass a resolution making hot mulled spiced apple cider the official autumnal drink. One year we made a large batch of homemade apple butter with our bounty from a trip to a local orchard. One of the best parts of having so many apples is being able to make and share something to pass along to members of our communities, such as coworkers and grove, coven, or circle mates.

This brings me to one of my favorite parts about a harvest festival and sharing gratitude: community. It is hard to exist in isolation. We naturally want to belong to a community, especially at times of thanksgiving and celebration. Working as a contributing member of a community keeps us in balance. When we work toward common goals by supporting and lifting each other up, and playing upon each person's individual strengths for the betterment of the whole, we are striking a harmonious balance within the community. Certainly, in a large enough community, your weakness is someone else's strength and vice versa. Healthy communities are both balanced and a work in progress in this way.

At this time of balance, feasting, and thanksgiving, it is worth looking at a simple custom that appears cross-culturally, which any of us can partake in: the toast. Whether done casually among friends in a pub, at a family dinner, or in a formal ritual with your spiritual community, the act of raising a drinking glass and making an expression of gratitude to your health or someone or something you are grateful for is a simple and easy way to begin seeking balance and engaging with the spirit of the season.

Toasting Around the World

If you're looking for something more elegant, too, here are some international toasting phrases to consider for inclusion in your toasts:

United Kingdom: "Cheers!"
While not exactly exotic, this classic phrase merits inclusion! Its beginnings as a toasting phrase are actually quite recent, as it gained popularity in the early twentieth century. It essentially means an expression of gladness. Sometimes simple is best!

Scandinavia: "Skål!"

Skål essentially translates to "Cheers!" Although it may seem most at home in countries such as Denmark, Sweden, Norway, and Iceland, its popularity has spread beyond its region of origin. For anyone with devotions to the Norse pantheon, this is an excellent choice! Depending on the country, you can also expect to see a variety of spelling variations of the word.

Germany and Austria: "Prosit!"

The toast phrase "Prosit" essentially translates to "May it be beneficial to you!" and is a perfect toast in honor of those setting out upon new endeavors.

Ireland: "Sláinte!"

Let's be honest, we've all seen this one emblazoned on signs in our favorite Irish pubs. It simply translates to "health." Simple and covers many bases. So, the next time you're toasting over your meal of fish and chips, you can raise your glass and use the phrase with the confidence of knowing what it means!

Peru, Bolivia, and Argentina: "Salud!"

The Spanish term "salud," like many toasts, also translates to "health." Again, since health can encompass so many things, it is always a welcome and appropriate well wish.

If you do not already have a toasting tradition as part of your Mabon celebrations, perhaps consider starting one! You can make a long speech or keep it short and simple and tie up with an emotive and confident "Sláinte!" The point is not the intricacy of your toast performance but rather to exercise a simple way to express our gratitude at this special time of year and bring yourself into balance via the reciprocity and sharing with your community.

Another community-based tradition you can adopt from some of the world traditions mentioned earlier is to donate to local food banks and pantries. People often forget about this need outside of the few weeks surrounding mainstream American Thanksgiving and Christmas. However, hunger is a real problem in our communities year-round. On this sabbat in which we celebrate balance of day and night, realistically we are still striving toward the goal of balance among members of our greater communities. If you belong to a grove, coven, or other spiritual group you could adopt this as a group project. Perhaps you can collect the items at your sabbat ritual and include a very simple blessing of them before delivering them to the collection point.

It is helpful to view community as concentric circles, growing ever wider. It is quite easy to fall into a narrowly scoped view of community that—without the intention of doing so—creates an "us and them" mentality or an "othering." Some people may seem very different than us, but eventually—when we look at community as concentric circles—we reach a point where inevitably we share common ground. All of a sudden, despite our differences, we aren't so different after all.

Whether you have a simple feast with your family or a more formal ritual gathering with your circle, coven, or grove, I hope you'll have found inspiration in this short article to express your own gratitude and seek balance within your place in your circles of community. May you have a blessed autumn equinox. Cheers!

References

Etiquette Scholar. "International Toasts." https://www
.etiquettescholar.com/dining_etiquette/toasting_etiquette
/international_toasts.html.

Europe's Not Dead. "European Toasts." https://europeisnotdead
.com/european-toasts/.

Haynes, Kelsey. "Gobble Up These Seven Thanksgiving Traditions
Around the World." GoAbroad.com. 2016. https://www
.goabroad.com/articles/gobble-up-these-7-thanksgiving
-traditions-around-the-world.

History.com. "Fall Equinox." 2017. https://www.history.com/topics
/natural-disasters-and-environment/fall-equinox.

Illes, Judika. *Encyclopedia of Spirits: The Ultimate Guide to the
Magic of Fairies, Genies, Demons, Ghosts, Gods & Goddesses.*
New York: Harper One, 2009.

Cosmic Sway

Ivo Dominguez Jr.

THE AUTUMN EQUINOX IS on September 22 with Venus in Scorpio opposing Uranus in Taurus. Mars in Libra is trine to Saturn in Aquarius, and Mercury in Libra is square to Pluto in Capricorn. The Sun in Libra is closing in on a conjunction with Mars. The Full Moon in Pisces was on the twentieth and is waning in Aries. Jupiter in Aquarius, Saturn in Aquarius, Chiron in Aries, Neptune in Pisces, and Pluto in Capricorn are still retrograde, and the guidance from Lammas is still in effect. Uranus in Taurus is now retrograde as well. The three most influential planets in the chart are Mars, Saturn, and Neptune. The preponderance of air and/or cardinal planets amplify the Libra qualities of this Mabon.

With the coming of the autumn equinox, the efforts put into motion at the Spring Equinox are nearing their fruition or completion, and their value is now known. At Mabon, day and night are balanced, and the motion is inward rather than outward as it was in spring. Growth now is being redirected within to the maturation of thoughts and feelings and the ripening harvest. The air smells different, and the plants are showing the colors of late flowers, the fruit and grains are changing color, and in some places, leaves know that the green will give way. The colors of spring and autumn are banners for the charge of the change. Mabon is the sunset of the year, filled with beauty as the light begins to fade. The autumn equinox is like the exhalation after a deep breath: it can release tension and staleness from deep within.

In whatever rituals or spiritual practices you may engage in during this holiday, make sure to use references to the colors, the taste in the air, and other sensual elements of the season. Being consciously and fully present in the turning of the seasons is one of the best ways to observe this sabbat. Some of the keynotes for Mabon are repose, contemplation of accomplishment, and appreciation for the cycles of life. Include quiet and introspective time into your plans and practices for Mabon. This is one of the practical methods to work with the influence of having so many planets retrograde during the autumn equinox. They are all asking for reflection and an unhurried response to the state of the world around you.

Mars is trine to Saturn and drawing extra power from the Sun. This increases perseverance and lifts your aspirations. It helps to lessen the impact of disappointments and supports self-discipline in the face of distractions and too many options. In the context of Mabon, it can help in managing the resources that you have so that they can last for the long run. Mabon is also about organizing for the winter, literally and figuratively. The waning Moon in Aries adds impetus and satisfaction to your preparations. You may wish to collect and dry herbs for future use as a magical representation of the abundance set aside for a time of need. If you make oils, candles, incense blends, or craft magical objects you may wish to charge the energies of Mars trine Saturn.

Venus opposing Uranus craves excitement and the call of new and novel experiences. This aspect also helps to manifest fast moving and dramatic encounters. This type of energy is not immediately compatible with the pattern of Mabon or the Mars-Saturn aspects. In fact, unless you apply your will and due consideration to the situations that arise, it can lead to disruptions in your relationships, friendships, and so on. Rather than trying to manage this intense energy by brute willpower, find ways to redirect the energy to bring it into balance. Use this drive and desire for newness as fuel for your work rather than letting it take on the role of being your center and guiding principle.

Mercury is square to Pluto and beckons you to dig deeper, think more profoundly, see the interconnections between seemingly dissimilar things, and examine all the shades of gray of human nature. Since there is a trend this Mabon toward inner work, be careful that you balance what you explore so that the unwholesome does not exceed the wholesome. Let the ever-returning beauty of the season be your remedy. You may find yourself drawn into arguments or actions related to these deep matters. At this time the harder you push against others, the less forward progress you make. This time period is best used for collecting information and planning until the time is right for moving forward. If you push too soon, you'll only gather more resistance against you.

Overall the pattern of Libra is chief authority in what works or doesn't work at this sabbat. There is a prevalence of planets in air and the cardinal modality. The symbol for Libra is the scales, not a living being as is true for the other signs. This is a clue that the highest use of the qualities of this sign requires detachment, fairness, and equanimity. Libra is also associated with the setting Sun. The astrological symbol for Libra can be interpreted as the setting Sun on the line of the horizon. It also suggests that the glory of the sunset is best appreciated by thinking on all that has transpired since the sunrise with a quiet, just heart. Try to work the imagery and symbolism of the scales and the sunset into your observances of the holiday. Whenever you work with the natural flow of nature, success is more likely.

The Moon is waning in Aries and can give insight into how to move in harmony with this Mabon. Aries has the impulse to be directive, to get up and go, and move on to the next task or target. The waning side of the lunar cycle is about putting things in order, finishing up projects, and clearing away the old to make room for the new. This autumn equinox the waning Moon is gibbous, just past full, and that part of the cycle also emphasizes healing, caretaking, and the knack for setting things right. Tune into this Moon for the intuition to bring harmony and healing to this Mabon.

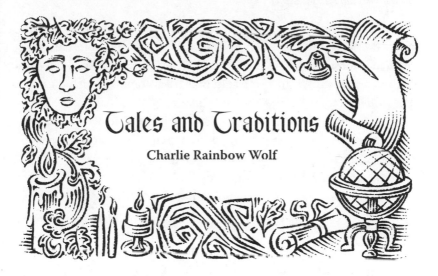

Tales and Traditions

Charlie Rainbow Wolf

THROUGHOUT THE WESTERN WORLD many cultures celebrate their first gathering of thanks starting with the autumnal equinox.

Harvest Festivals

It is a time for making the most of the last of the sunshine because light and dark are of the same length. There's a sense of urgency, trying to get everything finished before the first frost and potential snowfall.

Celebrating Autumn

My Cherokee friends celebrate their Ripe Corn Ceremony around this time. This is when their year is drawing to a close, and they are giving thanks for their harvest. Historically the focus was on the harvest of food for the winter, but today my friends give thanks for everything they have harvested: good friends, good food, secure jobs, safe homes, and more.

The celebrations center around a leafy tree. When I've attended such festivities, they were hosted at the tribal leader's home, where over time he had established a dance circle and a council house and more. The gathering involved the usual fasting followed by feasting and dancing. Dances often depicted the actions of gathering in the corn. Men danced separate from the ladies. We gathered into the council house while the men performed the green bough dance in the dance circle. This was a weekend gathering held toward the end of September, although I was told that traditionally it lasted for at least four days.

In England this is the time when the harvest festivals start in the schools and churches. The churches are decorated, and I've seen not just harvest items such as food and grain be displayed but also the work of artisans and master craftsmen, such as decorative loaves of bread, jars of homemade jam and local honey, garments woven or knitted from local sheep, wool being spun on wheels or colored from dyes made from local vegetation, and more. It is also a time when schoolchildren proudly display their first works of art from the school year, and choirs have special songs of thanksgiving to perform.

This was also a time when many bell ringers would travel to the local churches ringing the bells in thanksgiving for the bounty of the year. It was lovely to return to the farm after such an outing and see the fields ablaze with the controlled burning of the straw stubble as the sun set. There's not a set day for thanksgiving in the United Kingdom like there is in the US or Canada, which means that it is possible for people to travel from parish to parish and celebrate for many weekends. Bell-ringing tours, choir performances, and later summer folk festivals provide many opportunities to do just that! It's a very social time.

Honoring the Moon

In the east, the Chinese celebrate autumn's arrival with the Mooncake Festival, held at a time when the moon is at its fullest. This is an established custom which predates Christianity by several centuries, and the only celebration larger than this one in the Chinese calendar is the Chinese New Year. This autumn holiday is a time of visiting family and celebrating with them, making peace when there's been a falling out, and just generally gathering together in a good and harmonious way.

At this time, all the extended family gather together for a large feast. Regional foods are prepared throughout the day, and the meal takes place later in the afternoon or in the early evening. It is usually held at the elder's home, and very often there are three or four generations in attendance. It is a time of harvest, of giving thanks, and of prayers for the future.

During the festivities, incense is burned and gifts are offered to the moon. Often the prayers and requests made to the moon center around the usual topics of health, wealth, love, children, and good fortune.

Chinese lanterns—long thought to be a symbol of fertility—are lit and set free, and dances such as you might see during the New Year celebrations are performed.

The main food around this festival is the mooncake, from which the holiday got its name. These are light cakes baked and shared as gifts with loved ones. Traditionally it was the oldest member of the family who made the cakes, cut them, and shared them with others in a symbol of unity and harmony. This practice has evolved over time, and now everyone shares with everyone else, and mooncakes are commercially available. Other customary foods are lotus root and watermelon.

This is a time of courtship when the young women offer prayers and incense to the moon that they might find a suitable partner. Dances and gatherings for the purpose of dating and courtship are held. It is not uncommon for divination to take place during this festival, where young girls might be told how many children they can expect to have.

Honoring the Ways

Mabon is a good time for a Moon festival especially as the full moon falls so closely to the equinox this year. Add some of the Mooncake festivities to your ritual by including some divination or the sharing of a communal cake in the spirit of unity and friendship. There are recipes online for making Chinese mooncakes, but they are complicated and take quite some time to prepare. If you have a culinary group, making them might be an enjoyable challenge, but a larger, filled cake, or even a pie, made in the spirit of sharing and harmony will work just as well!

Something we've done in the past is take a large branch from a tree that we were felling and use it as our ritual tree. The women gathered in the kitchen to prepare the feast while the men gathered around the tree to discuss plans for future events. When it was time to leave, everyone took a piece of the branch home with them and returned with their pieces decorated as Yule logs for Midwinter.

There are many ways to mark the passing of Mabon. The main thing to remember is that its traditional themes are balance, thanksgiving, and harmony. When you include those themes in whatever festivities you have planned, you can be sure that you will not just have a great "harvest festival," you will make fond memories to carry you into future gatherings.

References

Johnston, Ronald John. *Bell-Ringing: The English Art of Change-Ringing*. New York: Viking, 1986.

Pennington, Daniel. *Itse Selu: Cherokee Harvest Festival*. Watertown, MA: Charlesbridge, 1994.

Tang, Sanmu. *Celebrating the Mid-Autumn Festival*. Shanghai Press, 2010.

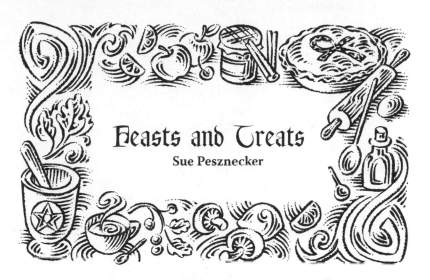

Feasts and Treats

Sue Pesznecker

MABON RINGS IN THE harvest and honors the bounty of the season. Pumpkins, squashes, and gourds are an important part of the fall harvest, and the pumpkin spice phenomenon has emerged as a pervasive and sometimes hilarious force. In that spirit, I offer a trio of pumpkin recipes for all occasions.

Pumpkin Spice Donuts

Breakfast? Snacks? Special treat? Dessert? You be the judge. These wonderful donuts are baked rather than fried, making them a tasty and not terribly sinful treat.

Prep time: 20 minutes
Cooking time: 20 minutes
Cooling time: 10 minutes
Servings: 6–8

You'll need a donut baking pan for these. Grease the pan lightly with butter, even if the pan is nonstick. If you don't have a donut pan, use muffin tins, but be aware your cooking time may be a bit longer.

Donuts

½ cup vegetable oil
3 large eggs
1¼ cups sugar
1½ cups canned pumpkin purée
1½ teaspoons pumpkin pie spice
1½ teaspoons salt
1½ teaspoons baking powder
1¾ cups flour

Cinnamon Sugar Mixture

¼ cup sugar
1 tablespoon cinnamon

Preheat the oven to 350° F.

Using a stand mixer or a whisk, combine the vegetable oil, eggs, sugar, pumpkin purée, pumpkin pie spice, salt, and baking powder, stirring or whisking until smooth. Add the flour, stirring just until smooth. (Don't overmix as this will toughen the donuts.)

Fill each crater in the donut pan about ¾ full. Bake the doughnuts for 15–18 minutes, until a toothpick inserted into a donut comes out clean.

Cool the donuts in their pans for five minutes, then gently loosen and remove them to a wire rack. Wait about 10 minutes—giving them a chance to cool a bit and firm up—and then shake them in a bag with the cinnamon sugar mixture.

These can be stored at room temp for several days, although I can't imagine they'll last that long.

Super Simple Pumpkin Pancakes with Cranberry Compote and Scrumptious Syrup

Every now and then I get "alittle" carried away with alliteration (#seewhatididthere). Sometimes a good pancake hits the spot, and if you have a favorite scratch recipe, by all means, use it. For those who want something a little quicker, I'm providing a shortcut recipe.

Want to make waffles instead? This recipe will work for that too, but add another tablespoon of vegetable oil or melted butter to the batter first.

Prep time: 25 minutes, including sitting time
Cooking time: quick!
Servings: 2 people, doubles or triples easily

Cranberry Compote

½ cup water
½ cup sugar
6 ounces fresh cranberries
¼ teaspoon ginger
1 tablespoon real maple syrup

Bring water and sugar to a boil in a small saucepan. Add the berries and simmer gently for about 10 minutes, until they pop and begin to break down. Remove from heat and scrape into a small bowl. Stir in the ginger and maple syrup.

Scrumptious Syrup

Stick of butter
2–3 cups brown sugar
½–⅓ can of evaporated milk
A dash of vanilla

In a small saucepan over low heat, melt the butter and brown sugar together. Slowly stir in the evaporated milk and add the vanilla. Pour into a small microwaveable pitcher and set aside.

Pancakes

¾ cup dry pancake mix
½ teaspoon baking powder
1 teaspoon pumpkin pie spice (or a mixture of cinnamon, nutmeg, cloves, and ginger)
¼ cup pureed pumpkin*
1 tablespoon butter, melted (unsalted is best)

½ cup water, add more as needed

Vegetable oil

*Sweet potato, acorn or kuri squash, or butternut squash will work too, although you won't get the same "pumpkin spice" cred going.

Combine the pancake mix, baking powder, and pumpkin pie spice in a medium bowl. Stir in the pumpkin, melted butter, and water, mixing slowly with a fork just until smooth (over-mixing makes pancakes tough and less fluffy). The batter should be on the thin side as it will thicken while it sits.

Allow batter to rest for about 15 minutes; this will help the baking powder activate, adding fluffiness.

While the batter rests, heat a pan over medium heat. Just before using, add about a tablespoon of oil and allow it to heat.

If the batter thickens too much while standing, add a bit of water and stir gently.

Pour batter onto the oiled pan. Turn the pancakes once, flipping when bubbles begin to break on the pancake's surface.

Serve the pancakes on warmed plates with the cranberry compote and special syrup.

Pumpkin Pie with Pumpkin Spice Whisky Whipped Cream

When I was a little girl, I loved to help make the pumpkin pie. Mom would let me stir everything together in a big bowl, and I loved watching the distinct, separate ingredients come together to form a beautiful, homogenous mass. It felt magical. Since then, I've tried a number of variations and have arrived at my own recipe, which is more or less a spin on the classic.

Prep time: 15 minutes (more if you make your own pie crust)
Cooking time: 45–60 minutes
Cooling time: 2–3 hours
Servings: 8–10

Pumpkin Pie

1 unbaked 9-inch pie shell, your own recipe or store-bought
2 large eggs
¾ cup granulated sugar
1–1½ teaspoons ground cinnamon*
½–1 teaspoon ground ginger
¼–½ teaspoon ground nutmeg
⅛–¼ teaspoon ground cloves
⅛–¼ teaspoon ground allspice (or use 2–3 teaspoons pumpkin pie
　　spice in place of the above spices)
½ teaspoon salt
15–16 ounces pumpkin purée**
12 ounces light cream (half and half) or canned evaporated milk
　　(not sweetened condensed milk!)***

Tip: Did you save any dough trimmings? Roll them out, cut into
　　cute shapes with a cookie cutter, and sprinkle with cinnamon
　　sugar. Bake on a cookie sheet at 375° F for about 5–7 minutes,
　　until they begin to brown. Cool these and arrange on top of your
　　pumpkin pie or serve alongside the pie. Or just eat them!

*Use the larger amounts of spices if you prefer a stronger, spicier
　　flavor.

**An equal amount of mashed sweet potato or red or golden squash
　　will work for this too, or any combination of them.

***For those who are dairy intolerant, lactose-free milk and almond
　　milk work fine with this. Coconut milk works, too, although it
　　will change the flavor somewhat.

Preheat oven to 425° F and set an oven rack to the middle
position.

Add the eggs to a large bowl and beat well with a whisk. Stir
in the sugar, spices, salt, and pumpkin purée, mixing until well
blended. Add the light cream (or evaporated milk) and stir until
completely blended and smooth.

Pour the pumpkin mixture into the pie shell. Bake for 15 minutes, then reduce the heat to 350° F and bake for another 40–50

minutes. When done, the pie contents should jiggle slightly, and a table knife inserted halfway between edge and center should come out clean.

Cool on a wire rack for at least 2–3 hours before cutting. If not eating immediately, store in the refrigerator, bringing to room temperature before serving.

Whipped Cream

1 cup heavy cream
½ teaspoon pumpkin pie spice
2 teaspoons whisky

Combine heavy cream, pumpkin pie spice, and whisky. Using a stand or handheld mixer, beat the cream until sturdy peaks form; this will take 2–3 minutes. (Don't overbeat or it will become grainy and buttery.)

Dollop the whipped mixture atop each pie slice and dust with additional pumpkin pie spice.

Crafty Crafts

Tess Whitehurst

AT THE FALL EQUINOX, we celebrate the sweetness of life and all the abundance and magic the earth provides. Not only is Mabon the central festival of the harvest season, it's also a time of balance and harmony, when the days and nights are of roughly equal length. And it's the time when the sun enters Libra—a sign aligned with beauty, balance, and Venus: the goddess of love.

It's no wonder, then, that the apple is omnipresent at Mabon. In addition to simply being in season at this time of year, the apple (like Mabon itself) holds the energy of sweetness, abundance, balance, harmony, and even—as a botanical sacred to Venus and Aphrodite—romantic love. Apples are sacred to many other deities as well, including Idun, Dionysus, Athena, Diana, and Zeus. And unicorns love apples! Fairies do too.

The apple is further associated with longevity, immunity, vibrant health, and the eternal nature of the soul. In *Cunningham's Encyclopedia of Magical Herbs*, Scott Cunningham writes, "The apple is a symbol of immortality. A branch of the apple which bore buds, flowers and fully-ripened fruit (sometimes known as the Silver Bough), was a kind of magical charm which enabled its possessor to enter into the land of the Gods, the Underworld, in Celtic mythology" (Cunningham 1985). Similarly, the moniker "Isle of Apples" is sometimes used to describe both the enchanted Avalon and Summerland, the idyllic, eternal dwelling place of the beloved dead in many magical traditions.

Indeed, the apple is a powerful symbol as the Wheel of the Year turns to fall and the seasonal "Underworld," also known as the dark half of the year.

You may also recall that the apple, cut horizontally, reveals a five-pointed star. It's true, each and every fruit secretly contains a perfectly formed pentagram, which indicates its correspondence with all five elements: earth, air, fire, water, and spirit. There's no doubt about it: the apple is a magical botanical indeed.

Gilded Apples

While these gilded apples contain no pentagrams, they do shimmer, which brings to mind the legendary "Silver Bough" (a sacred apple branch in the ancient Irish poem *The Voyage of Bran*). You'll find they make for beautiful altar items at this time of year. If you'd like, you can make a number of them and place them in a basket as a seasonal decoration or centerpiece. By adding a silvery or golden shimmer to the already-powerful symbolism of the apple, these gleaming apples remind us of wealth, luxury, and abundance. I also like them because they make plain old faux apples into unique and enchanting works of art. Not to mention they're super easy.

Materials

Faux apples (I used red, hollow, shiny, realistic-looking ones)

Metallic acrylic craft paint in one or more colors (I used light green, gold, and purple, but any metallic color will work)

A soft, high-quality paintbrush, about an inch or so wide (smaller paintbrushes will make the craft more labor intensive, and low-quality ones will create more visible brush strokes than you may prefer)

A notepad or something else to dispense your paint on

Newspaper to protect your table

Optional: fine metallic glitter and matte craft glue finishing spray (I used Mod Podge brand)

Cost: $10–$15

Time spent: 5–10 minutes per apple, plus dry time

Begin this simple project by shaking the metallic paint and dispensing a small amount onto your notepad or scratch paper. Hold a faux apple by its stem. Dip your paintbrush in the paint and simply brush the paint onto the apple's surface, starting at the base and working up toward the stem. Be aware that for most faux apple surfaces, the paint will not completely cover the color and will have somewhat-visible brush strokes. This is fine; as the title of this craft suggests, you are going for a lightly gilded look rather than total uniform coverage.

Continue painting until you've covered most of the apple. Lightly rest the apple on the newspaper, let go of the stem, and carefully paint the remaining area near the stem. Please note: if your apple isn't flat on the bottom and doesn't remain upright on its own, you may want to rest it on the top of a plastic or paper cup as you finish painting and while you're allowing it to dry.

Repeat with each additional apple. I found that varying the colors created a fun and whimsical look.

If you like, you can dust each apple with fine metallic glitter after you've finished painting, and then spray the apple with the finishing spray to help the glitter stick. Just be sure to use the spray outdoors when it's not windy and to let each apple dry very thoroughly before bringing it back inside.

Apple Pie Trail Mix

This is a delicious, nutritious, and magical treat to eat before or after your Mabon ritual, serve at any fall celebration, or give away as a beautiful equinox gift. When packed into a mason jar, the appearance of this trail mix is reminiscent of autumn leaves.

You'll find that the cinnamon brings out the sweetness in the fruit. If you like your apple pie á la mode, or if you just like your trail mix to include a bit of candy, add white chocolate chips or chunks for their sweet taste and creamy texture. (Seek out a non-dairy option if you want to make the recipe vegan and lactose free.)

Apples, as mentioned above, are closely aligned with Mabon and hold the energy of sweetness, sustenance, abundance, beauty, harmony, health, wealth, longevity, immortality, elemental harmony, and romantic love. Raisins are a lucky food, and golden raisins draw money and financial success. Walnuts are aligned with the planet Jupiter, which promotes expansion in every form, including expansion of prosperity, perspective, and good fortune. Pecans—perennial stars of the harvest season in North America—are also great for summoning wealth. And cinnamon, of course, is among the most famous botanicals for luxury and money.

Materials

1 cup dried apple pieces (I sliced dried apple rings into smaller pieces)
1 cup golden raisins
1 cup walnut pieces
1 cup pecan pieces
½ tablespoon cinnamon
⅛ teaspoon salt
32-ounce mason jar with lid
Optional: ½ cup or more vanilla or white chocolate chips or chunks
  Cost: $5–$10
  Time spent: 5–10 minutes

Place all ingredients in a large bowl. Stir with a wooden spoon in a clockwise direction to combine. While you stir, envision golden light spiraling and swirling through the spoon and into the mixture as you say:

Harvest season, sweetest light,
Time of equal day and night,
Golden orchards, vineyards bright,
Infuse with magic every bite.

Continue stirring until all ingredients are combined. Use a spoon to transfer the trail mix to the mason jar and close tightly.

Reference

Cunningham, Scott. *Cunningham's Encyclopedia of Magical Herbs.* St. Paul, MN: Llewellyn Publications, 1985.

Spells

Michael Furie

THE SECOND EQUINOX OF the year is another time of balance, though this time it is our turn to look ahead toward the coming dark half of the year. We can seize this moment to give thanks for what we have and also to ensure that our families and homes are properly cared for and prepared for the approaching cold weather and long nights. We can bless and protect all that we love and ward off and banish any threat of harm. Then we are free to offer gratitude to those forces which watch over us.

Food Blessing for a Happy Home

Since one of the aspects of Mabon is gratitude for the harvest, it has come to be termed the "witches' thanksgiving," and being that this day initiates the season of autumn when the air becomes crisp, the daylight hours shrink, and home life gains greater focus, a blessing over the Mabon meal is a wise idea. This blessing centers on ensuring a peaceful, happy home environment. After the meal has been prepared, make a plate for loved ones that have passed into Spirit before serving anyone else. After everyone has a plate of food, all should join hands and focus on the good feelings they have for one another while the eldest in the group (or other chosen member) casts this verbal spell with the words:

Gathered here in love and peace, I bless this food to nourish and heal; we all join in for harvest feast, keeping a happy home through every meal; to our ancestors I ask this favor, grant us joy and loving bond; of this food we shall savor, and offer a portion to those beyond.

After the meal bury the ancestor portion either outdoors or in a flower pot with thanks and reverence.

Harvesting a Local Stone

Though the beginning of autumn is "harvest time," a great many of us don't have any literal crops to sow. We can still partake of this same energy though by connecting to our local land. This spell utilizes a stone found in your local area to create a charm that will increase the connection to the spirit of place—the energy of your local environment—and this will increase the strength of your magic. This spell is best cast on a nature walk. It really does not matter whether one's home location is a city or out in the country as long as you are able to go outside and find a stone. It is about creating a bond between your local area and your magic, so do not travel too far or go in an area that makes you feel ill at ease.

Once you have found a stone that calls to you, hold it in your strong hand and try to feel its energy. The stone being directly of earth makes it strongly linked to the seasonal energy shifts. If you feel connected to the stone, bring it back to your home, and as you place it on your altar or in another special area, say:

An ally sought from the natural realm, to increase connection to this land; earthly treasure is now found, a bond created, awareness expand; for this gift I shall honor the spirit, I guard this stone and forever keep it.

When doing rituals of all types, keep the stone on your altar and honor it as an ally.

The Poisoned Apple Banishing Spell

Though it sounds scary, this spell is about using the most magical of fruits to banish things we no longer desire. Since this is now apple season and autumn is an excellent time to conduct spells to banish and release, we can tap into the greater energy to fuel our magic.

Materials

1 apple
1 small knife
Small pieces of paper and black ink pen
1 paper bag
1 black candle

By the light of a single black candle, write what you wish to banish on a piece of paper, using one paper for each item. Fold up the paper to cover what you have written—being sure to make each fold away from you—until you can't fold it anymore. Once you are finished, use the knife to make a small cut in the apple just big enough to press in the paper. If you have made more than one, make a new cut for each paper. Once you have finished, pick up the apple and mentally pour all of your negative emotions, grief, and/or guilt that you wish to banish into the apple. Envision that as you do so the apple turns brown as it becomes poisoned with this energy and say:

Magical fruit of Avalon, sacrificed to heal this heart; poisoned by such harsh emotion, to banish these wounds for a new start; I cast away what does not fulfill, restoring myself to my true will; through power of autumn and apple tree, this spell is cast, so mote it be.

Put the apple in the paper bag and take it to an outdoor location such as an empty field. Once there, take it out of the bag and throw it away from you as far as you can. Then leave without looking back.

Harvest Magic Charm Bag

This spell taps into the power of the autumn equinox to create a charm bag that keeps the home free from harm throughout the season. The dry ingredients used in the spell are each aligned with protection and also connected to the autumn season. The charm bag is designed to last through the autumn season and then should be discarded, buried in the earth or a flower pot with thanks around the Winter Solstice.

Materials
1 small cloth drawstring bag (orange or brown)
1 brown candle
1 part cornmeal
1 part barley
1 part buckwheat
1 nail
Hammer

Hold the brown candle and charge it by envisioning your home being surrounded by an impenetrable barrier that can only be crossed with your permission. Charge the cornmeal, barley, and buckwheat in this same fashion, one at a time. When you are ready, light the candle and place the cornmeal, barley, and buckwheat into the cloth bag. Tie the bag shut and hold it in your strong hand high over the candle. Charge it by visualizing that the bag is creating the protective barrier, and say:

Harvest gleanings make this charm, a powerful protection against all harm; above the door to hold at bay, malevolent forces cast away; let this power fully last, until the season of autumn has passed; through this spell, ensured safety, as I will so shall it be.

Extinguish the candle, then hammer the nail above the front door and hang the charm bag from it.

Mabon Ritual

Blake Octavian Blair

THE AUTUMN EQUINOX IS a time of fulfillment. It is a time of celebration when we harvest the fruits of our labor physically, spiritually, and metaphorically. Often referred to as the "Pagan Thanksgiving," this is a time for expressing our gratitude. In true magical style, one of the best ways to express our gratitude is with ritual!

Toasting Gratitude!

This simple ritual takes inspiration from the Norse sumble rituals and is presented in a way that resonates across traditions. The sumble-style ritual essentially consists of rounds of ceremonial drink toasts. Most commonly there are three rounds of toasts, a most magical number! Each toasting round has a different gratitude-related theme. The first round is generally comprised of toasts honoring one's deities, totems, and patron spirits. The second round consists of toasts generally made to one's ancestors or another figure that one personally looks up to or views as a hero. The third, and often final, formal round of toasts express a "boast" or sharing of an accomplishment.

The traditional and most commonly used drink in this ritual is mead. Beloved by Vikings, Druids, and other Pagan traditions alike, mead is a most fitting drink for a number of reasons. It is made from the harvested honey of the sacred bee. The bee and its hive community are a wonderful model and totem for the spirit of community and our gathering for such rituals, and mead thusly carries the current of that energy into our celebration.

The setup and supplies necessary for this ritual are rather simple, and you're also afforded a great deal of room for adaptation as needed. The ritual can be performed solitarily just as well as in a large group such as your grove or coven. You can easily perform all the roles yourself for a private rite or distribute the roles among those gathered for a joyous community celebration. However, for practicality's sake, I'd say this ritual works best for a couple dozen or fewer participants. If performing this ritual in a group, I do recommend having at least two drinking vessels that look distinctly different from each other, one with the alcoholic beverage and one with a nonalcoholic beverage. Because the toasting and the drink are the central part of the ritual it is vital to have a drink all can partake in. For a nonalcoholic libation, this ritual uses the seasonal and tasty chilled mulled apple cider, readily available this time of year.

Supplies:

Smudge of some kind
Fireproof vessel
Rattle, drum, chime, or other similar instrument
Mead*
Nonalcoholic beverage*
Two (or more) drinking horns, chalices, or other drinking vessels*
Candle with appropriate, safe holder
Matches or lighter
Corkscrew and/or other necessary bottle openers
*Have the two drinking vessels be visually distinct from each other
    to eliminate confusion as to which has the alcohol and which
    has the nonalcoholic option. For example, one chalice and one
    drinking horn.

Prior to beginning the ritual, have the drinks, drinking vessels, candle, and any other desired altar items gathered on an altar in the middle of the ritual space. Place the rattle or other instrument, the smudge supplies, and a lighter in an easily accessible basket near the altar.

Ritual

Gather all participants just outside the ritual space. Appoint persons to smudge and rattle (drum, chime, etc.) near each person as they enter the ritual space. Have the smudger and rattler form a gateway that each participant can pass through as they enter the ritual space. Always moving clockwise, have each person take their chosen place in the circle.

Once all participants have been purified and have taken their place in the circle, proceed to create sacred space as per your tradition. Various ways of doing this include circlecasting, calling the spirits of the directions, calling upon the spirits of the land and spirits of the ancestors, or some combination thereof. Once sacred space is established, the ritual leader steps into the center of the circle and addresses those gathered.

Ritual leader: *On this autumn equinox, we celebrate the harvest and our gratitude for its abundance. The bounty of the harvest takes many forms, on many levels in our lives...literal, metaphorical, spiritual, physical, individual, and communal.*

Light candle on altar.

Since ancient times, peoples have gathered around the central fire to share food, drink, ceremony, community, and their sacred thoughts and prayers. They are warmed by the fire and by each other. Today we will offer toasts of our gratitude in three rounds: the first to the divine; the second to our ancestors, teachers, and heroes; and the third to a milestone or goal we have personally accomplished.

If performing solitarily, open a libation bottle and fill a drinking vessel. If performing in a group, call a participant forward to hold a vessel as you open a bottle and fill the vessel with mead.

Ritual leader: *Today we offer two libations. The first, mead. As the old saying goes, "Ask the wild bee what the Druids knew!" Bees are a symbol and totem of celebration, community, and productivity. Lessons we can strive to learn from the bee!*

Pour mulled apple cider into the second vessel.

Ritual leader: *The second libation is of mulled apple cider. This is the season of the apple harvest. The apple is a spirit of wisdom, magic, and healing. Sacred fruit of Avalon! We shall now begin the first round of toasting! When it is your turn, raise the vessel and make a toast to a beloved deity, patron, helping spirit, or other form of the divine!*

Ritual leader makes the first toast, serving as an example, then passes the vessel to someone in the circle for it to begin to make its round. Each round, the ritual leader, as needed, will ensure each person has whichever drinking vessel aligns with their needs (mead or nonalcoholic cider). When every person has been able to make their first toast the ritual leader will proceed.

Ritual leader: *The second round of toasts will be made to our beloved ancestors of blood, spirit, or tradition. Beloved teachers, mentors, and heroes are included as well. May the toasts begin!*

Ritual leader again begins the round of toasting. The vessels are passed once again until each participant has made their toast, at which point the ritual leader proceeds.

Ritual leader: *Now, for a third and final round of toasting, we shall raise our vessels and toast to a personal accomplishment we have made or goal we have met! Additionally or alternatively you may make an oath to carry out a goal within a timeframe you declare here.*

Ritual leader begins the final toast round. When all have made their toasts, completing the round, the ritual leader proceeds.

Ritual leader: *May we now pour an offering onto the earth for the ancestors of this land, and the spirits of nature and place!*

Pour a small amount from a vessel onto the earth.

Ritual leader: *As the bees gather together in community, so we have gathered here today at this autumn equinox celebration. On this day of balance between light and dark, we too have found our own balance in expressing gratitude for our blessings and accomplishments and celebrating members of our community. We bring our individual strengths with us to combine into the greater force of community just as the bees join together to form the strength within the hive. For those of us that made oaths, the seeds of future growth were planted, just as the seeds of fallen apples begin the journey to future fruit harvests! May we be blessed with the Apple Spirit's wisdom and may our souls be healed by its mystical touch! May we all be filled with the balance brought by gratitude this equinox!*

Now you may close the ritual by releasing sacred space in accordance with the protocols of your tradition and releasing any entities you may have called upon.

In Conclusion

As some participants may have chosen to consume alcoholic beverages, please be a responsible host and remind your guests to refrain from driving until they feel safe to do so. I suggest actually discussing this with the gathered group prior to the start of the ritual and encouraging them to stay for a while after the ritual. The goal of this rite is not to consume large quantities of drink. Most participants take only a handful of sips the entire ritual. Nobody is required to consume alcohol, and nonalcoholic libations should always be provided for the ritual as well. Mead or an alcoholic drink is traditional but by no means a requirement. Ritual toasts are made effective by intent and not by the substance within the vessel. However, I suggest using the invitation for your guests to hang out and visit as a good reason for one of my favorite standard post-ritual activities among Pagans, the potluck feast!

This Mabon, may you be blessed with community and accomplishment just as the bees are blessed by the hive and their honey! So mote it be!

Notes

Notes

Notes

Notes

Notes